AFTER THE FALL

AFTER THE FALL

From the End of History to the Crisis of Democracy, How Politicians Broke Our World

IAN SHAPIRO

BASIC BOOKS
New York

Basic Books
Hachette Book Group
1290 Avenue of the Americas, New York, NY 10104
www.basicbooks.com

Printed in the United States of America

First Edition: May 2026

Published by Basic Books, an imprint of Hachette Book Group, Inc. The Basic Books name and logo is a registered trademark of the Hachette Book Group.

The Hachette Speakers Bureau provides a wide range of authors for speaking events. To find out more, go to www.hachettespeakersbureau.com or email HachetteSpeakers@hbgusa.com.

Basic Books publications may be purchased in bulk for business, educational, or promotional use. For more information, please contact your local bookseller or the Hachette Book Group Special Markets Department at special.markets@hbgusa.com.

The publisher is not responsible for websites (or their content) that are not owned by the publisher.

Print book interior design by Amy Quinn.

Library of Congress Cataloging-in-Publication Data has been applied for.

ISBNs: 9781541606265 (hardcover), 9781541606272 (ebook)

LSC-C

Printing 1, 2026

Contents

AFTER THE FALL

Introduction

The End of the End of History

The explosion of virulent politics across much of the democratic world since 2016 stands in stunning contrast to the widespread optimism that prevailed a quarter century earlier. Then, the Soviet Union was collapsing and the Cold War was ending. The stagflation of the 1970s and the industrial strife of the 1980s were in the rearview mirror. Economists were debating whether the fine-tuning expertise of central bankers had rendered business cycles obsolete. The trifecta of deregulation, privatization, and free trade—christened neoliberalism at home and the Washington Consensus abroad—reigned supreme. The United Nations had authorized a multinational force to expel Iraq from Kuwait, signaling the advent of a new global order. Democracy was on the march in Eastern Europe, Latin America, and much of Asia. Long-stalled peace negotiations in Northern Ireland and the Middle East were moving forward after decades of bloody gridlock. Amazingly, a peaceful transition was unfolding even in apartheid South Africa. Surviving communist regimes in China and Vietnam were adopting capitalism with the zeal of converts and angling for membership in the World Trade Organization and other international bodies. Russia would soon join the G7, turning it into the G8. Francis Fukuyama became a celebrity for declaring that the end of history had arrived.

All that euphoria had evaporated by 2016. By then, the worst financial crisis since the Depression had shattered American financial hegemony and the Washington Consensus. Emerging economies no longer felt constrained by the US model or its rules of economic engagement. China had rolled out its Belt and Road Initiative, exporting its Beijing Consensus by investing heavily in infrastructure across Africa, Asia, and Latin America. The new international order had been stillborn, battered by the Global War on Terror that had turned into quagmires in Afghanistan and Iraq. NATO's orchestration of Libya's collapse had added one more to the trail of failed states that the US was leaving in its wake—along with the remnants of any notion that it could serve as an honest broker to prevent predatory governments from slaughtering their own populations. Russia, whose lobbying—first to join NATO and then to limit its relentless eastward expansion—had repeatedly been brushed aside, had invaded Georgia in 2008 and then Ukraine in 2014, reviving Cold War patterns of interaction with the West. The Middle East peace process was dead. Benjamin Netanyahu's ultra-right-wing coalitions had won three successive Israeli elections and seemed set to control the government for the foreseeable future, expanding Israel's grip on the West Bank while Gaza seethed.

Not that Israel was special. Populist parties were on the rise everywhere, selling protectionist, anti-immigrant, and even nakedly authoritarian agendas that posed the first serious threat to liberal democracy since World War II. Debates about expanding an ever-closer European Union had been displaced by worries about whether it could survive, as the European Central Bank flailed at the downstream effects of the financial crisis, and Greece and Italy threatened to follow Britain out of the union. Any hope that Brexit and Donald Trump's election had been aberrational would be undone in the years that followed. For the first time in American history—other than in 1860, when the country had disintegrated into civil war—the peaceful transition of power would come seriously into question after the 2020 election. Mainstream parties fragmented and antisystem ones flourished in almost all the older democracies. Democracy began atrophying in newer democracies like Poland, Turkey, and Hungary. Netanyahu, back in power after a brief interregnum, was attacking Israel's legal institutions and would soon become embroiled in a horrific new war in Gaza. Books with titles like *How Democracies Die*, *The Road to Unfreedom*, *How Democracy Ends*, and *The Crisis of Democratic Capitalism* captured the pessimistic alarmism of the chattering classes. Developing countries were not immune, as slow growth and rampant corruption fed populist candidates in India, Brazil, and South Africa. No one was celebrating the BRICS anymore.[1]

How did we get from there to here? How could the widespread optimism that prevailed when the Berlin Wall came down give way so quickly to politics whose closest historical parallels are to the 1930s, when fascism and communism obliterated democracies and took the world beyond the brink of catastrophe? Was it inevitable, or did political and economic leaders make decisions that produced our reality, or at least made it much more likely? If the latter, what can we learn from studying those choices and the forgone opportunities, from attending to the paths not taken? Those questions motivate this book.

Perhaps 1989 was a naive fantasy. After all, history is littered with end-of-history prognosticators who wound up with egg on their faces. Hegel, various Marxists, modernization theorists, Daniel Bell, and many others who have trumpeted the arrival of ever-more rational and benevolent politics have been forced to backtrack by events. Why should this time be different? Maybe we are living through a dispiriting regression to the mean.

This book contends that 1989 wasn't a fantasy. To be sure, nothing in history is inevitable or even irreversible, but the Soviet empire's collapse presented rare opportunities. Rigid constraints that had shaped politics after World War II suddenly became fluid, offering unusual opportunities for creative change. There was a real chance to extend and deepen the rules-based international order that Franklin Roosevelt and Harry Truman had started building at the end of the Second World War but was frozen when the Iron Curtain came down. There were opportunities to refashion Cold War alliances into different security arrangements that would have reinforced this emerging order. There were also opportunities to rethink economic policies that excluded millions of voters from the benefits of capitalism's triumph in ways that eventually would come home to roost. Rather than seize the moment, Western leaders mismanaged relations with the former Soviet bloc, undermined the emerging global order with their war on terror and their bungled efforts at regime change in the Middle East, and doubled down on neoliberal economic orthodoxy even after the 2008 financial crisis had shattered its political legitimacy. Rather than entrench and build on the post–World War II order, they manufactured a world that is more like the disastrously unstable one that the victorious powers established after World War I.

The future that the paths not taken would have opened up is unknowable, but there are good reasons to think that different and vastly superior possibilities would have emerged instead of the world we find ourselves in today. And this is not twenty-twenty hindsight. Serious people inside and outside government made credible arguments that offered prospects for a better future. Those arguments were brushed off or ignored. Instead of taking advantage of opportunities to fashion a better world, short-sighted leaders on the left and the right squandered them. Today, tens of millions of people are paying the price. In excavating the forgotten arguments, my goal is to give readers a better grasp of why we are where we are and how best to think about the challenges and opportunities going forward.

Opportunities for creative change in the fundamentals of politics are rare and often fleeting. Much of the time, political leaders' freedom of action is tightly constrained. Prevailing institutions, constellations of interests, and entrenched ideologies limit what people will accept—and often what they can even conceive—as viable options. But occasionally these structures loosen up or even disintegrate, widening the scope for innovative change until new structures solidify. That is what happened when communist economies collapsed and the Cold War ended.

This quickly became obvious in the Soviet bloc countries. Almost overnight, people found that they could buy things that previously had been off-limits: apartments, financial assets, and shares in newly privatizing firms. Some officials overseeing privatization became instant millionaires, as did others who saw ways to cash in on the rapid changes. For the first time in their lives, many people could travel unhindered to the West, start businesses, and pursue new legal and professional careers. Consumer products from Levi's jeans to McDonald's burgers and Hollywood films proliferated alongside more down-market American fare, some of it—like the Desert Storm condoms that I saw on sale in Moscow's Arbat street market in March 1991—kitschily comical (Desert Shield might have made better sense). Black markets became redundant. The Gum department store on Red Square in Moscow, whose shelves had been empty in the terminal years of the old order, exemplified the change as it filled up with luxury goods—mostly from abroad. It would soon be flanked by the three-story underground Okhotny Ryad shopping mall opposite the Kremlin, which was packed with dozens of stores selling expensive jewelry and designer clothes. Western visitors—especially Americans—could be seen everywhere. For the first time in living memory, no one was afraid of the secret police.

New dynamics also emerged in the West. Some commentators expected that the political left—newly immune from charges that social democracy was a nefarious way station on the road to serfdom, as Friedrich Hayek had put it in his polemic against creeping big government—would be strengthened. They were soon proved wrong. The end of the Cold War accelerated the global integration of labor markets and the accompanying decline of trade unions that had been underway in most capitalist democracies for decades. Organized labor's declining industrial might was matched by diminished political clout, so that governments became more focused on—and responsive to—business interests. With capitalism now the only game in town, left-of-center parties junked the last vestiges of Keynesian thinking and began selling themselves to voters and lobbyists as more Catholic than the Pope: better stewards than center-right parties of fiscal austerity and neoliberal orthodoxy. Economic elites—especially financial elites—suddenly found themselves with more political power than they had wielded at any time since the nineteenth century, perhaps ever. How they would use that power was an open question.

The worldwide collapse of communism also raised new questions about how countries would pursue their geopolitical interests. Would NATO endure? If so, who would belong and what would it do? What were the alternatives for global security? How might they be pursued? Would a triumphant US reign supreme, or would other structures prevail—perhaps something more like the balance of powers the European countries established in Vienna after the Napoleonic Wars? Or something altogether new? How would Russia and the former Soviet republics fit into the emerging architecture, not to mention countries like China, Vietnam, and North Korea? Different leaders and analysts pushed for a great variety of arrangements in the years after 1989, including outright abolition of NATO, immediate admission of all former Soviet bloc countries, including Russia, to the alliance, and various agendas for its gradual expansion. There were spirited debates in the US and other Western governments about how to proceed. No one knew what the terrain would look like once the dust settled. Major powers changed their approaches multiple times, even before al-Qaeda's September 11, 2001, attacks on the US scrambled reality again.

Ideologies that had long been ossified by Cold War oppositions also became fluid, with possibilities that had been unthinkable before 1989 suddenly coming into play. Intellectuals who had for decades been gaming out different scenarios for transitions from capitalism to socialism found themselves contemplating the reverse, often in the company of strange bedfellows. By the early 1990s, people as different as the Polish former Marxist Adam Przeworski, the conservative Hungarian economist János Kornai, and the American technocrat Jeffrey Sachs were all extolling the virtues of shock therapy to get people through the transitional pain and socialized into the new reality as fast as possible.[2] Nor was it just intellectuals. In the spring of 1991—even before the USSR collapsed—Western visitors were shocked to encounter Soviet Politburo members openly declaring their system to be bankrupt and in urgent need of dismantling.[3] In South Africa, the Marxist African National Congress turned on a dime—one of Nelson

Mandela's first foreign trips after prison had been to Havana to proclaim Fidel Castro "a source of inspiration to all freedom-loving people."[4] Within months of taking office, the ANC had discarded sacrosanct shibboleths, was openly collaborating with white big businesses like the mining conglomerate Anglo American, and was adopting the standard neoliberal economic policy diet. In this they were mimicking Britain's New Labour, the American New Democrats, and many European Social Democratic parties. The last vestiges of the Eurocommunism of the 1970s and 1980s soon faded away.

Long-stable institutions were also changing. The World Trade Organization started admitting former communist countries soon after the Berlin Wall came down. The United Nations General Assembly began adopting new mandates and asserting itself in unprecedented ways. The idea that national sovereignty was sacrosanct, enshrined in the UN Charter since its inception, was giving way to the doctrine that governments can be held accountable for gross human rights violations—both by prosecuting perpetrators in the International Criminal Court and even by staging military interventions within sovereign countries when authorized by the Security Council. By formalizing these doctrines in 2005 with its World Summit Outcome Document, which declared that all governments have an enforceable responsibility to protect their populations from genocide, war crimes, ethnic cleansing, and crimes against humanity, the General Assembly was, for the first time, asserting itself as a kind of global legislative body.

Institutions, ideologies, and interests need not all loosen up together for far-reaching change to become possible. Richard Nixon's opening to China in 1972, which created hitherto unimaginable possibilities for American business, involved a dramatic reordering of interests without questioning Cold War ideologies or the existing structure of institutions. Indeed, Nixon and his national security advisor, Henry Kissinger, saw it as a shrewd strategic move against the Soviets. Lyndon Johnson's decision to get behind civil rights in 1964 and 1965 was a frontal assault on Southern white ideology, yet he did so within the prevailing framework of electoral institutions and economic interests. But when all three loosen up at once, as they did at the end of the Cold War, an unusually broad scope for change opens that will not likely persist for long.

And indeed, it has not. Today, resurgent protectionism among the world's biggest economies limits the possibilities for growth, trade, and travel. Trade wars, like shooting wars, are a lot harder to end than to start. In the democratic countries, large numbers of angry, anxious, alienated voters continue deserting establishment parties when they cannot transform them, making it hard to see where the political impetus to begin reversing these changes can come from. Much of the West is once again in a standoff with Russia and China over Ukraine and Taiwan, with many countries from the Global South lining up as they did during the Cold War. NATO's eastward expansion has buttressed those divisions, even as Donald Trump has thrown the alliance's future viability into question. Institutions like the UN and the WTO, which used to blunt many of these tensions, are floundering, though it remains unclear what—if anything—will replace them. Communist economic ideologies have not resurfaced, but the benign cosmopolitanism that had so widely been anticipated at the end of the Cold War is on life support if it has not been obliterated. Donald Trump's resuscitation of Charles Lindbergh's America First ideology from the 1940s has been matched by aggressive nationalism elsewhere, not to mention the resurgence of both Islamic fundamentalism and Islamophobia—all of which limit the possibilities for international cooperation.

The speed with which these exclusionary ideologies have erupted should alert us to the fact that they don't have to be with us indefinitely. Dialing them down will be hard, however, even if their political champions peddle remedies that amount to little more than bloodletting. It is unlikely to work unless mainstream politicians and economic leaders do what so many of them have failed to do for decades: get behind industrial and ameliorative policies that address the economic insecurities that lead so many voters to embrace exclusionary ideologies in the first place. Failing that, there will be more economic anxiety and political alienation. More Donald Trumps, Marine Le Pens, Vladimir Putins, and Viktor Orbáns.

Things are much more constrained today, but not hopeless. The new Cold War is not cast in stone, but political leaders will need to become alert to ways of escaping today's destructive dynamics—even if the opportunities to do so are unlikely to materialize until new leaders take the helm in the US, Russia, and China. The always fragile institutions that foster international cooperation have been dangerously weakened. Reviving them will require leaders who can relearn the tit-for-tat benefits of acting with restraint, lessons that were cavalierly tossed aside in the 1990s and 2000s. It will likely mean taking baby constructive steps before bigger ones become viable. NATO might conceivably evolve into a constructive force to limit aggression between—and in some circumstances even within—countries, but this will require rethinking its mission and governance in ways that the US and the other leading members of the alliance have not yet been willing to do. That, in turn, will require a better understanding of how the alliance came to be what it is and the missed opportunities along the way.

The prospects for interrupting the baleful dynamics that have swamped so much of our politics are daunting, but giving up is neither productive nor warranted. The early years after World War II must have seemed at least as dispiriting for people with democratic sensibilities who aspired to leave their children a better world than they had inherited. The Great Depression had ushered in extraordinary levels of unemployment and inequality, widespread insecurity, fascism, the Holocaust, and the most devastating war in history that by conservative estimates killed at least sixty million people and shattered the lives of countless millions more. Few, then, would have predicted the economic and political renaissance that subsequent decades would bring: unprecedented levels of wealth and economic growth whose benefits were widely shared; the Great Society in the US and stable democratic welfare states in many countries that had been devastated by the war; and international peace—at least when compared with the first half of the century. The superpowers managed to limit their continuing tensions to proxy conflicts in the developing world, avoid the Damoclean threat of nuclear catastrophe, and navigate a peaceful exit from the Cold War.

Except that "the decades" didn't "bring" these changes. It took sustained imagination and focused effort to design, fund, and implement the Marshall Plan in Europe and the economic revitalization of Japan; to create and then sustain the UN where previously the League of Nations had faltered and failed; and to negotiate arms reduction treaties and a phased disengagement from nuclear brinkmanship. Effective leadership was required, to be sure, but leaders also had to mobilize broad public support behind what they were doing. As Albert Hirschman once said, people need to be convinced that their government is creating a better world if they are to support establishment institutions.[5] The resulting positive feedback loops that sustained postwar Western democracies have atrophied. The challenge is to create new ones.

We should be encouraged that Western elites have begun learning the costs of their blinkered pursuit of self-interest. They are discovering that desperate people do desperate things, that people who aren't surfing the waves of new global supply chains and technologies can be mobilized by charlatans and demagogues to support trade wars, protectionism, and other political movements that many among the elites find alarming. The Business Roundtable has called for revising models of corporate governance that are based on maximizing shareholder return to the exclusion of other stakeholders, and business school curriculums are starting to follow suit. These shifting attitudes create openings for political leaders to garner business support for policies that will promote inclusive growth, support that will be vital in an era when private-sector unions have all but disappeared and the political power of organized labor is moribund. Just as mainstream parties once converged on economic policies whose benefits accrued to the very rich, undermining social democracy in Europe and the New Deal–Great Society consensus in the US, they must now converge on policies whose benefits are widely shared.

And it's vital to grasp that things can get worse. History never repeats itself exactly, but many of the economic, social, and political dynamics that fostered the horrific democratic breakdowns of the 1930s are disconcertingly familiar in today's world. That decade did not end well. In 1919, John Maynard Keynes predicted much of what subsequently transpired in *The Economic Consequences of the Peace*. Keynes turned out to be shouting at the wind, as parliaments fragmented and political elites—in thrall to retributive economic nationalisms—ignored the destabilizing consequences of structural economic change. This book is written to help reduce the likelihood of a comparably malignant future. First we must understand how we got here.

Chapter One

Waging a Global War on Terror

When President Joe Biden withdrew the last American forces from Afghanistan in August 2021, he was ending the longest and most expensive war in American history. Together with the $2 trillion cost of the Iraq War, the $2.3 trillion price tag of the intervention in Afghanistan amounted to just over half the $8 trillion that the US had spent on its war on terror since the original invasion two decades earlier. Some 2,300 American soldiers had died in Afghanistan, along with 1,100 allied troops, 500 journalists and humanitarian workers, and almost 4,000 US military contractors. The conflict had claimed 170,000 Afghan lives, 46,000 of them civilians. Comparable numbers for Iraq were 4,600 US military killed, as well as over 300 allied troops, 3,600 military contractors, 300 journalists and humanitarian workers, and 300,000 Iraqis, two-thirds of them civilians.[1]

Both wars were ignominious failures. The Iraq that the US left in 2011 was a failed state. The Islamic State, or ISIS, would soon control 40 percent of the country, spawning new terrorist nightmares for the West and hundreds of thousands of Iraqi and Syrian civilians. In Afghanistan, the Taliban chased American-backed President Ashraf Ghani out of the country and seized power before the US left. Within months, the regime was sheltering al-Qaeda leaders in violation of the US departure agreement. A year later, it reinstated bans on women in higher education, government jobs, most professions, gyms, and parks, and required them to wear all-encompassing burkas with face coverings in public. The UN would soon declare Afghanistan the most repressive country on earth for girls and women. Public floggings of accused adulterers resumed. The twenty-year war had accomplished virtually nothing.[2]

The staggering human and financial costs of these fiascos were the tip of the iceberg. To grasp what else the US and the world lost, we need to recall America's global standing between November 9, 1989, when crowds of Germans began dismantling the Berlin Wall, and March 20, 2003, when the George W. Bush administration began its war that would topple Saddam Hussein's regime in Iraq. This interregnum marked the high point of America's post–Cold War legitimacy and prestige, when anything seemed possible.

It was America's unipolar moment. The Washington Consensus was unrivaled. Democratic capitalism and American consumer goods proliferated across much of the former Soviet bloc and the developing world. The new Russian economy was limping along, heavily dependent on the West, and its nascent democracy was struggling. China was emerging as the premier Asian tiger, but its crackdown on peaceful protesters in Tiananmen Square had tarnished its global image. The country enjoyed head-turning growth rates, but they began from such a low base that by the turn of the millennium, China's economy was still less than half the size of Japan's and a fifth that of the US. China's per capita income was less than $1,000 at the turn of the millennium, about one thirty-sixth of the US number. No one saw China—yet—as a serious challenger.[3]

By themselves, the 9/11 attacks did nothing to undermine America's global standing. If anything, they enhanced it. The United Nations condemned them immediately, soon following up with resolutions requiring member states to criminalize support for terrorism. The Security Council did not explicitly authorize the US-led invasion of Afghanistan, but it quickly endorsed it. Governments and regional organizations all over the world declared support for the US. Despite sporadic street celebrations of the attacks in some Islamic countries, almost all Muslim religious leaders condemned them outright, as did the Palestinian Authority and the Egyptian, Syrian, Iranian, Pakistani, and Libyan governments. Muammar Gaddafi even offered to share intelligence with the US in the run-up to the invasion. Vladimir Putin was one of the first leaders to call President Bush, pledging full Russian cooperation. A "shocked" Chinese President Jiang Zemin declared his solidarity. *Le Monde* captured the moment, declaring, "Nous sommes tous Américains." It would be hard to identify another time when geopolitical support for the US was as widespread. It would be equally hard to identify another time when an American government squandered its moral and strategic capital as gratuitously or completely.[4]

Stopping the Bully Without Becoming One

George W. Bush's father had ushered in the era of unparalleled American prestige. It wasn't his management of the Western response to the imploding Soviet empire that was decisive. True, that involved perilous moments that someone less levelheaded might have handled more clumsily, but for the most part, he and other Western leaders were startled bystanders to the events that began snowballing across Eastern Europe in late 1989 and climaxed with the peaceful dissolution of the USSR two years later. Taking credit for them would have been like a rooster taking credit for the rising sun and, in any case, they missed important opportunities during and after those transitions, as we will see. It was in response to events that unfolded nineteen hundred miles from Moscow when Bush rose to the occasion and started etching vital new rules and norms into the architecture of post–Cold War international politics.

Saddam Hussein's invasion of Kuwait in August 1990 was the first time after the Cold War that one country attacked another. No NATO country was threatened, and there was no meaningful risk of the conflict escalating into a nuclear confrontation between the major powers, so the question was cleanly put: How would the international community now respond to gratuitous international aggression? Much was at stake. The invasion almost doubled the oil reserves Iraq controlled to a fifth of the world's supply. More alarming, it raised the specter that Hussein, facing virtual bankruptcy after Iraq's devastating but inconclusive war with Iran in the 1980s, would set his sights on neighboring Saudi Arabia next. Iraq, with more than 1,000,000 soldiers under arms, had rolled over Kuwait's 25,000 troops in two days. The Saudis, with fewer than 150,000 troops, seemed unlikely to fare much better. If Iraq also took control of Saudi Arabia's oil, Hussein would control close to half of the world's proven reserves. With the risks so high, there was little chance that the world would do nothing. But what? And how?[5]

Bush understood the stakes, but also the possibilities they presented. "We stand today at a unique and extraordinary moment," he declared to a joint session of Congress shortly after the invasion. The crisis created a "rare opportunity" to foster a "new world order" in which "the rule of law supplants the rule of the jungle" and nations ensure collectively that "the strong respect the rights of the weak." Bush further understood that for this new world order to have a fighting chance, he would need to act decisively but also with robust legal authorization and the widest international support that could be mustered. That would mean making a convincing case at home and abroad that nations would be better served by respecting the rules-based order he was seeking to establish than by acting with impunity whenever they could. As the world's most powerful country, the US would need to lead by example.[6]

Acting legally meant working closely with the UN throughout the crisis, seeking authority for his actions, and operating within the Security Council's mandates. The council quickly condemned the invasion, demanding Iraq's immediate and unconditional withdrawal. But Hussein defied SC 660 and five additional resolutions reiterating it, even though the council also authorized a trade embargo with a naval blockade to enforce it. It soon became obvious that Hussein would not leave Kuwait—which he had declared was Iraq's nineteenth province—without a credible threat of force, and even that might not be enough. Accordingly, at the end of November, the council adopted SC 678, which required Iraqi forces to leave by January 15, 1991, and authorized other countries to use "all necessary means" to expel them if they did not. This would be the legal authorization for war. The resolution requested all countries to provide "appropriate support" to intervening ones—who were merely asked to keep the Security Council "informed" of their actions. It took intense American lobbying to secure the adoption of this sweeping resolution, with only Cuba and Yemen opposing and China abstaining. If Bush wanted it to be precedent-setting, he would need to act carefully and with restraint.

It was also vital that his actions not be seen as a US or Western power grab. To that end, Bush assembled a forty-two-nation coalition of countries from all over the world. Importantly, he recruited many predominantly Muslim countries: Egypt, Oman, Qatar, Saudi Arabia, the United Arab Emirates, Syria, Turkey, Pakistan, and Morocco. Assembling the coalition required a heavy diplomatic lift from Bush and his secretary of state, James Baker. Holding it together would be an ongoing challenge that would require close adherence to the Security Council's mandate. It would also mean acting with dispatch. The longer the episode dragged on, the more likely countries would begin peeling off—especially if it began to look as if Saddam Hussein's defiance might succeed. Bush had to prevail quickly.

Bush had other reasons for ensuring a swift, decisive result. Ever since the Vietnam War, American political and military leaders had been loath to take on open-ended military conflicts, especially those that were not demonstrably essential to America's national security. The decade-long Vietnam disaster had killed more than 58,000 American soldiers, wounded 300,000, and cost $140 billion (about $1 trillion today), not to mention the humiliating blow it dealt to America's prestige abroad and the damaging rift in the social fabric at home. The war had also been a textbook case of mission creep. Lyndon Johnson first committed 3,500 combat troops in 1965 after military advisors proved insufficient to sustain the South Vietnamese regime, a number that kept rising to more than 540,000 four years later—all to no avail. The war was by then so unpopular that Johnson had to deny requests for even more troops from General William Westmoreland. He also had to abandon his reelection plans in 1968, even though he had won the presidency by one of the greatest landslides in American history four years earlier, enabling him to enact his Great Society programs. None of Johnson's successors wanted to risk suffering a comparable fate.[7]

Vietnam had prompted a major rethinking of America's approach to national security. First spelled out by Ronald Reagan's defense secretary Caspar Weinberger—though better known as the Powell Doctrine, for Colin Powell, who held senior positions in the Reagan, Clinton, and both Bush administrations—it required that the US become involved in wars only when stringent conditions are met. A vital national interest must be at stake. War must be a last resort after every other avenue for dealing with the threat has been exhausted. The US must prosecute the war "wholeheartedly, with a clear intention of winning," which in turn means being able to sustain congressional—and therefore public—support for the war's duration. To meet these conditions, an administration that goes to war must deploy overwhelming force to achieve clearly attainable objectives and have a viable exit strategy once they are achieved.[8]

Powell, who was George H. W. Bush's chairman of the Joint Chiefs of Staff when Iraq invaded Kuwait, acted accordingly. "Our strategy to go after this army," Powell said of the Iraqi army in Kuwait, "is very, very simple. First, we're going to cut it off, and then we're going to kill it." He doubled initial estimates of what would be required to an American commitment of 500,000 troops, which eventually became almost 700,000. This was supplemented by another 300,000 troops from other coalition partners, mainly Saudi Arabia, Egypt, Britain, Syria, France, Morocco, and Kuwait, by significant contributions from Oman, Pakistan, Canada, the UAE, Bangladesh, Qatar, and by lesser commitments from other coalition partners, including even 300 Afghan Mujahideen (jihadist) fighters. The vast ground assault through the Saudi desert began in late February after a devastating six-week bombing campaign had destroyed much of Iraq's air force, radar, and other defensive infrastructure. Iraqi forces fled almost immediately. The war ended in a ceasefire on February 28, a hundred hours after the invasion began, when all Iraqi forces had left Kuwait and Saddam

Hussein had abandoned his claim that it was part of Iraq. Battle plans seldom survive their implementation, but as General David Petraeus has noted, this one came remarkably close. It was a stunning success that vindicated the Powell Doctrine and restored much of the US military luster that had been so badly tarnished in Vietnam.[9]

The success owed a lot to meticulous preparation and planning, but also to Bush and Baker's diplomatic tenacity in holding the coalition together. A particular challenge had been to keep Israel out of the war, as its involvement would have threatened to escalate the conflict in ways the coalition could not have survived. Saddam Hussein tried to engineer that outcome by firing over forty Scud missiles at Haifa and Tel Aviv as soon as the conflict began. The US had deployed batteries of Patriot surface-to-air missiles to Israel to defend against that eventuality, but they were only partly effective. Two Israeli civilians were killed by direct Scud hits, and many more were injured. Few governments would suffer military attacks from another country without responding. Certainly not Israel, which had not done so before and hasn't since. Preventing Israel from becoming involved was a notable diplomatic feat.

Another vital decision Bush took was to resist the calls from neoconservatives inside and outside the administration to "finish the job"—go to Baghdad and topple the Iraqi regime. That would have exceeded SC 678, which was limited to expelling Iraqi forces from Kuwait. It would also have involved protracted urban conflict with significantly more than the 292 casualties that the coalition forces actually suffered. And it would have meant occupying Iraq, which few coalition members—and probably no Arab countries—would have supported. Indeed, many of them would have been infuriated because it would have left them vulnerable to charges that they had been duped into helping the US occupy an oil-rich Arab country in the heart of the Middle East. A US invasion of Iraq would have shattered the coalition. More important, it would have scuttled the chances of forming similar coalitions in the future as well as the possibility of securing comparable mandates from the Security Council.

And it would have meant junking the Powell Doctrine. Toppling the Iraqi regime might have been quick and easy, but installing a viable alternative was another matter. Questions abounded. Was it possible to install a government, and if so, what would its makeup be? How long would it take? When would the new regime be secure enough for American forces to leave? What would the cost be in American blood and treasure? Could those costs be sold to American voters? Bush's defense secretary Dick Cheney put it bluntly when fending off their critics:

> If you're going to go in and try to topple Saddam Hussein, you have to go to Baghdad. Once you've got Baghdad, it's not clear what you do with it. It's not clear what kind of government you would put in place of the one that's currently there now. Is it going to be a Shia regime, a Sunni regime or a Kurdish regime? Or one that tilts toward the Ba'athists, or one that tilts toward the Islamic fundamentalists? How much credibility is that government going to have if it's set up by the United States military when it's there? How long does the United States military have to stay to protect the people that sign on for that government, and what happens to it once we leave?[10]

Ironic as these words sound in view of Cheney's full-throated backing of regime change in Iraq twelve years later, they were not new. British Prime Minister H. H. Asquith expressed similar misgivings in 1915 when considering whether, if Britain beat the Turks in the Great War, they should take over Mesopotamia, as Iraq was then called. He demurred on the grounds that it would mean spending millions of pounds on basic infrastructure, sustaining "a large army white & coloured in an unfamiliar country, tackling every kind of tangled administrative question, worse than we ever had it in India, with a hornet's nest of Arab tribes, and even if that were set right having a perpetual menace to our flank in Kurdistan just like Afghanistan & the Pathan tribes who overshadow the Punjab."[11]

Little had changed by 1991. Iraq had never become a democracy. When government changed hands, it did so violently. Saddam Hussein's Ba'athists had most recently come to power in a coup in 1968 and held the country's centrifugal elements together with an iron fist. Sunni Muslims, who dominated the regime and its military, comprised less than a third of a population that was sharply divided along sectarian lines. History suggested that they would do whatever it took to hold on to power and to get it back if they lost it. Iraq's six million Kurds, some 15–20 percent of the population, had their own national aspirations. They lived in one of the most oil-rich parts of a country in which there were few other valuable resources. They also constituted part of the world's largest ethnic minority—the Kurds are spread across contiguous areas of Iraq, Iran, Syria, and Turkey—who lacked their own country but wanted one. Getting them voluntarily to subordinate their separatist ambitions to an Iraqi national state would have been a tall order. Cheney knew whereof he spoke in 1991.

In any case, Bush's larger agenda would have been thwarted by flouting the Security Council and destroying the coalition. The UN was innovating in responding to Saddam Hussein's gambit, so the way Bush used the power authorized in SC 678 was bound to become precedent-setting. Sticking to the resolution's terms and maintaining broad international support had the potential both to discourage comparable adventures and to become a template to manage them when deterrence failed. To be sure, the template would have to be followed in future conflicts to become entrenched into norms and expectations. But it would be a major start for a world in which there was no longer a high-stakes standoff between superpowers that had enabled and incentivized them to constrain the behavior of their allies and satellites. Otherwise, it would become open season for more powerful states to gobble up less powerful ones with impunity, with no realistic prospect of garnering Security Council support to stop them. Bush's military and diplomatic self-restraint—to stop the bully without becoming one—opened up the possibility of a better future.

This is not to defend everything Bush did in Iraq. His administration took significant criticism for failing to warn Hussein not to attack Kuwait before the invasion, and perhaps even encouraging him to think that it didn't oppose the invasion. Perhaps because the administration was preoccupied with intense negotiations with the Soviets over Germany's imminent reunification, it kept silent while hundreds of thousands of Iraqi troops began massing on Kuwait's border in July 1990. Whether this was just bandwidth overload or reflected more nefarious motives, as Ross Perot would contend in his 1992 election campaign, members of the Bush administration were asleep at the switch. Bush also took justified criticism for encouraging a Shiite uprising in southern Iraq and then failing to support it. Knowing that he had no plans to topple Saddam Hussein, this was, at a minimum, a tragic lapse of judgment that led to the avoidable slaughter of countless thousands of Iraqis when the inevitable crackdown came. But these failures should not obscure Bush's major achievement in charting a constructive new course for managing international aggression in the post–Cold War era. Had it become a template for the future, the world would be in a much better place than it is. His son's response to the September 11, 2001, attacks destroyed that possibility.[12]

Paths Not Taken in Afghanistan

Those attacks were shocking by any measure. Almost three thousand people were killed that day, more than in the attack on Pearl Harbor six decades earlier and orders of magnitude more than in any other terrorist attack in memory. Perpetrated by a terrorist group rather than a government, they were not strictly an act of war, but the sheer scale of attacks targeted on the nation's commercial, military, and political centers ensured that the Bush administration would treat them as aggression against the United States that demanded a military response. Eight years earlier, a Pakistani terrorist, Ramzi Yousef, had detonated over thirteen hundred pounds of urea nitrate explosives in the basement parking lot of the World Trade Center in New York City. Perhaps because there were only six fatalities—though over a thousand were injured—and Yousef's goal to collapse the towers failed, the attack was dealt with through the criminal justice system. He was caught in Islamabad, extradited to the US, tried and convicted in the Southern District of New York, and given two life sentences plus 240 years in prison. The 2001 attack masterminded by Yousef's uncle, Khalid Sheikh Mohammed, was bound to be seen, as the president declared to a joint session of Congress nine days later, as "an act of war against our country."[13]

But what kind of war would the US fight, and against which enemy? The al-Qaeda terrorist group was led by Osama bin Laden, a wealthy Saudi militant who had moved his base of operations to Afghanistan in 1996, when he was expelled from Sudan for sponsoring attacks on Arab leaders who cooperated with the United States. Al-Qaeda consisted mostly of Sunni Arab militants who were hostile to secular forces that they believed were corrupting Arab regimes across the Middle East, principally the monarchy in bin Laden's native Saudi Arabia, but also Egypt's military dictatorship, the secular Ba'athist regimes in Syria and Iraq, and the pro-Soviet regime in South Yemen. Many of al-Qaeda's members had been radicalized by fighting the Soviets in Afghanistan in the 1980s. As the USSR began pulling out in 1988, bin Laden organized them to fight for a fundamentalist regime in the coming Afghan civil war and to become a broader vanguard for jihadism. When Iraqi forces invaded Kuwait two years later, he proposed to the Saudi government that al-Qaeda lead the effort to expel them—a quixotic proposition for a few hundred fighters in the face of an invading army of 140,000 soldiers backed by 18,000 tanks. His estrangement from the Saudi regime accelerated after he was rebuffed in favor of their relying on the US, especially when American bases remained in Saudi Arabia and many other Arab countries after Iraq had been ousted from Kuwait. Bin Laden then became focused on toppling the Saudi government and, inspired by Hezbollah's precedent of inducing the Reagan administration to leave Lebanon after its terrorist attack killed 241 US soldiers there in 1983, forcing the Americans out of the Middle East.

Expelled from Saudi Arabia in 1991 because of his increasingly vitriolic denunciations of its leaders as corrupt American puppets, bin Laden relocated to Sudan, where he started training militants and conducting terrorist operations. In 1992, he ordered a car-bomb attack on a hotel in Aden, Yemen, that was used by US personnel on their way to distribute humanitarian aid in Somalia. The Bush administration stopped transiting through Yemen. That, plus Clinton's departure from Somalia after eighteen American soldiers were killed in a botched US operation there the following year, convinced bin Laden that the Hezbollah model from Lebanon worked. Like the Soviet Union, he concluded, the US was fundamentally weak. If forced to pay a price for interfering in Muslim countries, the Americans would pack up and leave, the corrupt Arab regimes they propped up would collapse, and fundamentalist regimes could replace them.

The US was "the head of the snake" that had to be cut off for the rest of his agenda to play out.[14]

And so bin Laden became more ambitious and outspoken. His relentless denunciations of the Saudi royal family led them to strip him of his citizenship in 1994. Al-Qaeda responded by exploding a car bomb in Riyadh the following year, killing five American soldiers. Al-Qaeda was also implicated in failed attempts to assassinate Egyptian President Hosni Mubarak on a trip to Ethiopia and US President Bill Clinton on a visit to Manila. Pressure from the Saudi, US, and Egyptian governments led the Sudanese government to force bin Laden to leave. He arrived in Afghanistan in May of 1996, just as the Taliban was becoming the dominant group in the civil war there. He divided his time between Jalalabad in eastern Afghanistan and the Tora Bora mountains on the Pakistani border, set up training camps, and sponsored increasingly bellicose assaults on US assets. Simultaneous truck-bomb attacks on the US embassies in Nairobi and Dar es Salaam in 1998 killed 220 people, 12 of whom were Americans. In late 1999, an Algerian al-Qaeda terrorist was caught trying to enter the US from Canada, foiling his plot to detonate a bomb at Los Angeles International Airport. This was the first al-Qaeda operation on the US mainland. The following August, seventeen American sailors died when al-Qaeda suicide bombers detonated a fishing boat loaded with explosives alongside the USS *Cole* while it was refueling in Aden.

By then, bin Laden and al-Qaeda had been on the CIA's radar for some time. In 1996, he had begun releasing press statements and giving interviews—including one on CNN—declaring that he was at war with the United States to get it to leave Saudi Arabia and the wider Middle East. But the growing alarm about al-Qaeda in intelligence circles did not travel up the chain of command in the Clinton administration. After the embassy bombings, Clinton did launch one round of cruise missiles on bin Laden's training camps in Khost, in eastern Afghanistan, killing seven al-Qaeda fighters and two dozen Afghan and Pakistani civilians. But there was no follow-up, and the camps were rebuilt in a few weeks. Senior officials vetoed several CIA plans to capture or assassinate bin Laden for fear of blowback if they failed, and of collateral civilian casualties that might antagonize friendly Middle Eastern governments. The administration did not judge bin Laden a serious enough threat to risk getting US military personnel killed, memories of dead American soldiers being dragged through the streets of Mogadishu, Somalia, being all too easy to conjure up. The US did not retaliate at all in response to the USS *Cole* attack, reinforcing bin Laden's faith in his strategy.[15]

If intelligence officials strained to get the Clinton White House to focus on al-Qaeda, they struggled even more with the incoming Republican administration. Bush, who had campaigned against embroiling the US internationally, focused his administration centrally on his domestic agenda of tax cuts, shrinking government, and deregulation. Speaking at the Pentagon the day before the September 11 attacks, his defense secretary, Donald Rumsfeld, likened his department to the sclerotic Soviet bureaucracy and announced plans to streamline it by outsourcing as much as possible and importing corporate management models.[16] Some members of the defense team—most prominently Rumsfeld's deputy Paul Wolfowitz, but also figures like National Security Council official Elliott Abrams, chair of the Defense Policy Board Richard Perle, and Undersecretary for Defense Policy Douglas Feith—favored a muscular US role abroad. These neoconservatives wanted to topple hostile authoritarian governments and replace them with what they believed would be US-friendly democratic ones. Wolfowitz was fixated on Iraq, which he believed—incorrectly—had been behind the 1993 World Trade Center bombing. But Bush did not subscribe to their agenda before the 9/11 attacks.

Intelligence officials repeatedly sounded the alarm during the summer and early fall of 2001 over increasingly credible reports that al-Qaeda was planning major attacks in the United States, but they failed to get anyone in the Bush White House to pay sustained attention. In April, Wolfowitz complained that even the one meeting they'd had about al-Qaeda was unnecessary. In May, Attorney General John Ashcroft refused to discuss FBI concerns about al-Qaeda. In July, CIA Director George Tenet and Counterterrorism Advisor Richard Clark briefed National Security Advisor Condoleezza Rice on threats of multiple simultaneous attacks being planned in the US that were predicted to be "spectacular." She took no action. In August, Bush himself was given a dedicated President's Daily Briefing entitled "Bin Laden Determined to Strike in the US," but like the others he did nothing. By then, national security journalist Peter Bergen, who had been studying al-Qaeda for two years, was sufficiently alarmed by publicly available information and bin Laden's video propaganda that he emailed *New York Times* columnist John Burns to say he thought it likely that "an al-Qaeda attack is in the works." Burns wrote up the story, but due to an editing dispute, it did not appear before the attacks took place.[17]

Blindsided by the attacks despite the steady stream of warnings, the Bush administration responded with a strategy best described as "Ready! Fire! Aim!" Al-Qaeda's responsibility for the attacks was quickly established and never seriously disputed, but that did not settle the matter of whom to respond to or how. Neoconservatives in the White House, who had mostly been on the fringes of the administration's policy due to the president's repeated rejection of foreign-regime-change agendas during his campaign, seized the moment. Rumsfeld, Rice, and Vice President Dick Cheney, not until then card-carrying neoconservatives, climbed aboard with the zeal of converts. At the first meeting of the National Security

Council on the day after the attacks, Rumsfeld and Wolfowitz started pushing hard for the US to attack Iraq. Three days later, Rumsfeld was arguing that waging a "war on terror"—the phrase Bush had first used in his address to the nation on the night of the attacks and that would soon become central to his revamped national security strategy—meant attacking not just Iraq but also Libya and Sudan.[18]

They would soon add other potential targets to their wish list, but Iraq was the priority—even obsession. When Bush asked what Saddam Hussein had to do with the attacks, Wolfowitz began postulating links between him and bin Laden that were quickly debunked by the CIA's counterterrorism chief, Cofer Black. That took Iraq off the table in the short run, but not for long. For years neoconservatives would assert that Iraq was somehow behind the attacks, claims they doubled down on once their other casus belli for invading Iraq—that Saddam Hussein was manufacturing weapons of mass destruction (WMDs)—evaporated. They kept insisting that he was a sponsor of al-Qaeda, even alleging meetings between one of the hijackers and an Iraqi agent in Prague shortly before the attacks, as well as asserting the existence of various other links—all of which would later be exposed as bogus. Bin Laden never stopped despising Saddam Hussein as a dangerous enemy whose regional ambitions had to be thwarted, denouncing him at different times in interviews as a hated atheist and a "socialist motherfucker." As Bergen points out, al-Qaeda in Iraq—which would eventually mutate into ISIS—emerged *in response to* the US invasion in 2003, not before it. There was no connection between Saddam Hussein's regime and bin Laden or the 9/11 attacks.[19]

If the US imperative was to go after bin Laden and al-Qaeda in Afghanistan, the two most pressing issues were how to do that and what to do about the Taliban regime in Kabul. The Bush administration fused the two groups from the start by giving Taliban leader Mullah Omar an ultimatum to "close immediately and permanently every terrorist training camp in Afghanistan, and hand over every terrorist, and every person in their support structure"—or "share in their fate." This assumed that the Taliban had the capacity to meet the ultimatum. It also assumed that it was wise, or even necessary, to destroy the Taliban regime in order to destroy al-Qaeda. Both assumptions were dubious. They were also loaded with implications for the future that the neoconservatives who took control of the Bush White House's national security policy after 9/11 never confronted.[20]

Bin Laden's relations with the Taliban had been fraught since his return to Afghanistan in 1996. At that time, the Taliban were the dominant force in much of the country but had not won the civil war. Even after they took control of Kabul in September, replacing Burhanuddin Rabbani's ethnic-Tajik-dominated government, the Taliban never achieved full control over the country. Members of the Rabbani government and militias loyal to him fled to Mazār-e-Sharīf in the north, where Rabbani and his former defense minister Ahmad Shah Masoud formed the Northern Alliance as a rump opposition to the Taliban government in Kabul. Taliban forces soon forced them out of Mazār-e-Sharīf as well, however, so that by the time of the 9/11 attacks they were confined to the Panjshīr Valley in the northeast as the only significant holdout to Taliban rule. Rabbani and his allies had been losing the civil war, even though the Taliban was unable to vanquish them completely. They were a thorn in the government's side, but they would not become a mortal threat to it until the US decided to ally with them to overthrow the Taliban regime.

Nor was the Taliban leader, Mullah Omar, fully secure inside the Islamist regime he was trying to consolidate. He and bin Laden had been kindred spirits dating back to the war against the Soviets, but they had since become aligned with competing Islamist strands that Omar was trying to hold together as he built a tenuous regime. Bin Laden had considerable cachet as a scion of one of Saudi Arabia's richest families who had sacrificed a comfortable future to the cause and had financed not only militant operations but also major development projects in Sudan. Antagonizing him would put Omar's legitimacy at risk. But bin Laden's presence in the country was costly to Omar because they had different agendas: Bin Laden wanted to use Afghanistan as a base from which to run international terrorist operations, but Omar was trying to build a viable regime and bin Laden's activities endangered his flimsy international legitimacy. The Saudi government that bin Laden regularly denounced was one of only three in the world that recognized the Taliban government. Bin Laden's presence in the country led to the imposition of UN sanctions in 1999. Omar responded to this predicament by repeatedly asking bin Laden to stop giving his vitriolic press interviews, to stop directing terrorist operations from Afghan soil, and, when bin Laden ignored those requests, to leave the country—which he also ignored.[21]

The Taliban government had no warning of the 9/11 attacks, which in any case violated what numerous ministers believed bin Laden had agreed to with Mullah Omar. Some in the government insisted that they condemn the attacks—which they did—and either kick bin Laden out or turn him over to a third country. Mullah Omar signaled his willingness to do the latter via Pakistan's intelligence chief, but the Bush administration rejected that option and brushed aside other efforts by the Pakistan CIA chief, Robert Grenier, to negotiate a way of extracting bin Laden that Mullah Omar could agree to while holding his regime together, rather than "hurtling toward war." Whether Omar had the political capital or even the police capability to turn bin Laden over is debatable. After all, bin Laden had, with impunity, repeatedly ignored Omar's requests, and even his demands, to change his behavior or leave the country. But all this did not mean the Taliban had to be toppled. And if the regime did have to go, the Bush administration did not have to do it in a way that was, if not with its eyes wide shut, almost guaranteed to be self-defeating.[22]

The least extravagant option would have been to ignore the government in Kabul and focus relentlessly on pursuing bin Laden and al-Qaeda. That is what Barack Obama's administration eventually did in Pakistan when the CIA learned that bin Laden was holed up in Abbottabad, knowing that, by then, the Zardari government in Islamabad would not have been likely to cooperate. In Afghanistan in 2001, the US could simply have declared that no Taliban interference in its hot pursuit of al-Qaeda would be tolerated. That strategy would have relied mainly on special operations forces and the CIA to go directly after bin Laden and his lieutenants, attack any Taliban forces that got in the way with devastating force, warn them that if they did it again, they would get hit again, and keep repeating these steps until they succeeded. Colin Powell's chief of staff, Colonel Lawrence Wilkerson, notes that a powerful case for this strategy was briefed up the chain of command but was vetoed by Vice President Cheney.[23]

Hunting down bin Laden and al-Qaeda with US forces would have taken more than the few dozen that were deployed. Estimates vary, but generals on the ground at the time believed it could be done with fewer than the three thousand personnel who were then available in the region and that the logistical challenges, while formidable, were surmountable. Successful hot pursuit of bin Laden by the US would also have required cooperation from Pakistan, but it was forthcoming in 2001 when the great majority of Muslim leaders were condemning the 9/11 attacks and the US still occupied much international moral high ground. Some members of Pakistani President Pervez Musharraf's government opposed his cooperative stance, but he overruled them and fired the religiously conservative head of his intelligence services as well as his cronies who were sympathetic to al-Qaeda. American relations with Pakistan would soon sour over the US decision to topple the Taliban and exclude them from a role in Afghanistan's future, a decision that fueled Pakistani fears that their regional archrival India would gain influence in the new Afghanistan.[24]

There were challenges to a hot pursuit policy in 2001, but they didn't come from Pakistan. They emanated, instead, from the Bush administration's fixation on a much more extravagant, even fantastical, strategy from the start: to destroy not just al-Qaeda but the Taliban regime as well, and to achieve both goals with a minimal commitment of US military force on the ground. As if that weren't enough, Bush would soon add the goal of creating a viable democracy in Afghanistan—even though he made no attempt to learn whether that was a plausible goal and, if so, what it would take.

Multiple considerations pushed the Bush administration to minimize US troop deployments to Afghanistan. Officials were skittish about repeating the recent Soviet experience: becoming an occupying army facing a relentless war of attrition in famously hostile mountainous terrain. They were leery of fostering a Vietnam syndrome at home, where mounting American casualties erode public support for a war before it can be won. Additionally, they worried about cost. Having just passed a massive tax cut in June that would reduce federal revenue by $1.2 trillion over the next decade and with additional tax cuts in the works, they were looking to slim down military spending—even though they were also determined to go to war to topple Saddam Hussein's regime in Iraq. That would obviously require major commitments of money and personnel, an additional source of pressure to minimize the American footprint in Afghanistan.

Squaring this circle meant relying on proxies, and the proxy at hand was Rabbani's Northern Alliance. Within days of the 9/11 attacks, CIA director George Tenet proposed embedding CIA military teams and Army special forces with the Northern Alliance, building up their materiel and other resources, and calling in air strikes to give them the upper hand in fighting both the Taliban and al-Qaeda. Bush quickly warmed to the idea, not least because the alternative proposed by the Joint Chiefs of Staff was to rely on bombing and cruise missiles—the strategy that had been conspicuously ineffective against al-Qaeda after the 1998 African embassy attacks. Grenier rapidly developed a battle plan involving five hundred CIA and special forces personnel, supplemented by some four thousand marines if necessary, but the bulk of the frontline fighting would be done by Northern Alliance and affiliated militias. Bush gave his regional commander, General Tommy Franks, the green light to proceed, overseen by Defense Secretary Rumsfeld.[25]

The Taliban collapsed much faster than American political and military leaders had anticipated. The offensive began on October 7 with a massive bombing campaign against al-Qaeda and the Taliban strongholds, followed by the first wave of ground forces twelve days later. On November 9, an Uzbek militia led by Abdul Rashid Dostum routed Taliban forces in Mazār-e-Sharīf in the north, followed within days by the collapses of Taloqan, Bamiyan, and Herat. Kabul and Jalalabad fell to the rebels on November 14, effectively ending the Taliban regime five weeks after the war had started. That day, the United Nations Security Council passed SC 1378, calling for a "central role" for the UN in establishing a transitional administration and inviting member states to send peacekeeping forces to promote stability and deliver humanitarian aid. The surviving Taliban forces fled to Kandahār, where they planned to regroup, but that city fell on December 5, after which the remaining Taliban forces fled to Pakistan or—like Mullah Omar—went underground.

The speed of the Taliban's collapse helped foster the illusion in the Bush White House that the Taliban could be disregarded in designing Afghanistan's future. The Taliban had never had a firm grip on power, but the new regime was bound to be equally challenged. A good rule of thumb to bear in mind when backing the losing side in a civil war is that it was probably losing for a reason. The Northern Alliance had thin support among Afghanistan's largest ethnic group, the Pashtuns, who live mostly in the south and east, and many of its leaders were associated with the corrupt Rabbani government that the Taliban had displaced in 1996. There had been few illusions about this in Washington before the 9/11 attacks. In 2000, Northern Alliance lobbyists seeking weapons and other support had been fobbed off as hopelessly unrealistic. Yet the roundtable negotiations held in Bonn to pick an interim government were dominated by Northern Alliance warlords, ensuring that they would control most of the ministries and be able to resume the atrocities and corruption many of them had engaged in when they had power in the 1990s.

More important, the Bonn process excluded the Taliban. Omar had signaled a willingness to surrender before the end of the war and afterward made multiple overtures to participate in a unity government. Cheney, Rumsfeld, and other senior administration officials repeatedly rejected overtures from Taliban figures and even vetoed those who wanted to talk to them, including the leader of Afghanistan's interim government and its first elected president, Hamid Karzai. They were convinced that the Taliban was a spent force that could be ignored.[26]

Karzai knew better. As the only Afghan leader who had been acceptable to the Bush administration, regional leaders, and the contending Northern Alliance warlords to run the interim government after the fall of the Taliban, Karzai was a unique figure. He was a charismatic politician and a skilled negotiator. He had substantial credibility as a Pashtun who had led an uprising against the Taliban in and around Kandahār in October 2001. His Popalzai heritage made him more acceptable to the Tajiks, Uzbeks, Hazara, and other northern tribes, but he was also able to draw on Pashtun support in the south and the east that enabled him to win a 55 percent majority in the 2004 presidential election in which some eight million Afghans voted. But unlike the Americans, he understood that the Taliban—whose leaders started reconstituting the movement underground and in Pakistan almost as soon as they were defeated—had substantial latent support in the south that they would mobilize against the Bonn process if they were excluded from it. But his arguments fell on deaf ears, not only in 2002 but also in 2003, when—unbeknownst to the US—Mullah Omar began reconstituting the Taliban as a military force that would soon explode into a new insurgency never to be vanquished. On May 1, 2003, Rumsfeld declared that "major combat" in Afghanistan was over. That turned out to be as accurate as President Bush's identical claim about Iraq on the same day, as he stepped out of a Lockheed S-3 Viking onto the USS *Abraham Lincoln* decked out in a fighter pilot's garb in front of a giant banner blaring, "MISSION ACCOMPLISHED."[27]

By then, the US was not just missing the Taliban's growing support in much of southern Afghanistan; it was also inadvertently abetting that support. Defeated former Taliban and Mujahideen leaders were often—or mistakenly—imprisoned for long periods or gratuitously attacked. Unsurprisingly, many of them eventually rejoined the insurgency. The US compounded this error with its disarmament program, fueling the country's collapse into chaos. Disarmament disabled the new government's rivals, but it also created a power vacuum in large parts of the country and alienated tens of thousands of former fighters who joined the insurgency—paving the way for the Taliban's takeover of much of the south in 2006 once it had regrouped.[28]

As the US ramped up military strikes and troop commitments in response to the growing insurgency, collateral civilian deaths inevitably mounted. Just as inevitably, Karzai became less cooperative with the US and more open to seeking an accommodation with the Taliban. He understood that he could not tie his legitimacy to the Americans, who were increasingly seen as an occupying force in much of the country, regardless of elections, the new constitution, or what was happening in Kabul. Karzai's relations with the Bush administration spiraled downward for the rest of Bush's term. The watershed occurred on the day before the 2008 US presidential election when an American airstrike hit a wedding party in Kandahār, killing dozens of civilians, the great majority of whom were women and children. By the time Barack Obama took office in January 2009, the fissure between Karzai and the US government was unbridgeable, even though he remained in office for the next six years while the US tried one fruitless strategy after another to pacify the country and quell the insurgency.[29]

The multiyear tragedy of errors that plagued the Bush administration's war with the Taliban from the start is laid out in devastating detail in Carter Malkasian's definitive history, *The American War in Afghanistan*. He shows that the administration never committed the forces needed to achieve its goal of destroying the Taliban, let alone of building an alternative regime that would have the wherewithal to do so on its own. It dislodged the Taliban but repeatedly underestimated the insurgency as it rebuilt itself into a national liberation movement by railing against the Karzai regime as the corrupt puppet of an occupying power. As the Taliban gained territory and support, the administration grudgingly increased military commitments that were being stretched thin by similar failures in Iraq at the same time. The dollar-short-and-day-late quality of the response in Afghanistan was an uncanny replay of Lyndon Johnson's policy of "graduated pressure" in Vietnam in the mid-1960s. He tried to prop up successive corrupt governments in Saigon and an undermotivated South Vietnamese military that never won the battle for legitimacy against Viet Cong insurgents who were fighting for the national reunification that had been promised in the Geneva Accords of 1954. The calamitous failure of graduated pressure had prompted the rethinking that resulted in the Powell Doctrine that Bush so cavalierly discarded after 9/11, condemning him to replicate the Soviet failures in Afghanistan—just as Johnson had replicated the French failures in Vietnam.[30] The best epitaph for this strategy became a common refrain among Taliban leaders in the 2000s: "The Americans have the watches, but we have the time."[31]

The astonishing mismatch between the Bush administration's ambitions in Afghanistan and the resources it was willing to deploy there also compromised what should have been its primary—if not exclusive—mission: to destroy al-Qaeda. The eighteen-day battle of Tora Bora in December of 2001 was bin Laden's last stand after his remaining fighters had fled there in late November. The US made negligible commitments on the ground, relying heavily on Northern Alliance–affiliated militias. They turned out to be unwilling or unable to corner bin Laden's fighters, forcing US commanders, who had only a few dozen American and British special forces troops at their disposal, to rely on local warlords instead. But the warlords' fighters, who insisted on going home every night because it was Ramadan, and some of whom also had mixed loyalties, engaged in stalling tactics, including phony surrender negotiations that enabled bin Laden and hundreds of al-Qaeda fighters to escape to Pakistan, where they soon became the nucleus of the insurgency. The CIA lead agent in Panjshir, Gary Bernstein, saw this happening in real time and made repeated requests to General Tommy Franks to send a battalion of eight hundred Army Rangers. His appeals were rejected, as were proposals by Brigadier General James Mattis to deploy Marines by helicopter from their base in Kandahār. This was the cost of subordinating the pursuit of al-Qaeda to replacing the Taliban, as Tommy Franks's number two, Lieutenant General Michael DeLong, later conceded to the Senate Foreign Relations Committee: "We didn't want to have US forces fighting before Karzai was in power. We wanted to create a stable country and that was more important than going after bin Laden at the time."[32]

We will never know whether the US could have caught or killed bin Laden at Tora Bora, but Malkasian is persuasive that it was the "last best chance." Even if bin Laden had evaded hot pursuit—there is some debate over how long he was at Tora Bora—few doubt that letting the hundred or so surviving al-Qaeda fighters escape through the Spīn Ghar mountains and begin reconstituting themselves in Pakistan was a costly mistake. It added to their mystique as the movement that had taken the battle to its most powerful enemy and survived to fight another day. More importantly, it meant that as the remnants of al-Qaeda began reorganizing themselves in Pakistan, they became tightly allied with the remnants of the Taliban that were doing the same thing. In effect, this created the strong alliance between the two that Bush had postulated before it existed. That development also made it all but impossible to begin negotiating with the Taliban once it became clear—as it had by 2006—that they were not going to be defeated on the battlefield by the US or the Karzai government with the resources the US was willing to deploy. The Bush administration ended up with the worst of all worlds. It failed to get bin Laden or destroy al-Qaeda, but having forced Mullah Omar and the Taliban from power, it was stuck with trying to build a viable Afghan regime. As Colin Powell would later say of the quagmire in Iraq, "If you break it, you own it."[33]

Iraq Redux

Achieving regime change in Iraq had been a cause célèbre among neoconservatives dating back to the early 1990s. Some of them saw it as unfinished business from 1991. They believed Saddam Hussein to be a continuing regional threat and that the containment regime, based on sanctions and no-fly zones to protect the Kurds in the north and the Shiites in the south, was costly, corrupt, and of dubious effectiveness. Some saw Hussein as an affront to American prestige, particularly after he tried to orchestrate former President Bush's assassination when he was visiting Kuwait in April 1993. Some were motivated by humanitarian concerns. Hussein was an abusive tyrant who had murdered opponents and maintained a power monopoly for his family and cronies. They hoped to replace the regime with a democracy that Ahmed Chalabi, a longtime London-based Shiite expatriate, had convinced them would be pro-American and would even make peace with Israel. Their efforts culminated in getting Congress to pass—and Bill Clinton to sign—the Iraq Liberation Act of 1998, which made it US policy to support efforts to remove Saddam Hussein's regime from power.[34]

The Iraq Liberation Act was limited to aiding opposition groups; it did not authorize the US to go to war or even to deploy clandestine military force to topple the regime. Clinton, who had signed the act while he was on the defensive in the wake of the scandal that had erupted over his extramarital affair with Monica Lewinsky, paid so little attention to it that eighteen months later its congressional champions were excoriating him for disbursing only $20,000 of the $97 million that had been authorized for assistance to Iraqi opposition groups.[35] Because President George W. Bush also showed no interest in revisiting the topics of Iraq or the neoconservative agenda before 9/11, the neoconservatives had to link them to the war on terror to get his attention—which they started doing on the day he announced it. Once the Taliban collapsed and they concluded that the war in Afghanistan had been won, they went to work on convincing Bush that toppling Iraq would be just as easy—and a logical next step in the war on terror.

They succeeded. But with their claims about Iraq's links to al-Qaeda failing to gain traction, they put all their chips on the alleged evidence—much of it traceable to Chalabi—that Saddam Hussein was manufacturing WMDs that could end up in the hands of terrorists. This became the casus belli, but the challenge then became that the UN's chief weapons inspector for Iraq, Hans Blix, had found nothing to substantiate those claims, despite having conducted seven hundred inspections across the country. Concerned that they would lose momentum unless they acted with alacrity, neoconservatives in the Bush administration sidelined the inspection process by convincing Secretary of State Colin Powell to lay his prestige on the line with a highly publicized UN presentation of satellite images that were alleged to show WMD development sites in Iraq. But Powell had been given misleading intelligence, validating Blix's subsequent judgment likening the US administration to witch-hunters. Beyond the damage to Powell's reputation—he would forever regret the "blot on my record"—the disingenuous excuse for the invasion would be the first of several blows to America's standing. These culminated in the Abu Ghraib scandal in April 2004, when dozens of graphic photographs went viral depicting American soldiers torturing and sexually abusing naked Iraqis in a prison that had notoriously been a site used by Saddam Hussein's thugs to torture their own victims. The scandal shredded the last remnants of US credibility across the Muslim world. It was a gift to the nascent insurgency against the American occupation of Iraq.[36]

By then, it was obvious that the US had massively underestimated the military task it had undertaken. As with its Afghanistan operation, which in March of 2003 the Bush administration still believed to have been a success, the planning in Iraq was for a short war and a light American footprint, with scant attention to what would replace the Iraqi regime following its destruction. Rumsfeld—who was matched only by Lyndon Johnson's defense secretary Robert McNamara during the Vietnam War in his penchant for cheerleading for US military escalation while backing a draconian agenda to slim down the Defense Department—insisted on reducing initial war plan estimates of three corps and 380,000 troops by two-thirds to a force of 130,000. Even the initial estimates were less than half of the 700,000-strong US force plus 300,000 coalition troops deployed for the vastly less ambitious goal of expelling Iraq from Kuwait twelve years earlier.[37]

As in Afghanistan, in Iraq Rumsfeld and Franks oversaw an invasion in which the scale of their ambition was matched only by the extent to which they underresourced it. Partly because they believed Chalabi's assertions that American forces would be welcomed as liberators, neoconservatives in the administration, like Wolfowitz, rejected as nonsense estimates such as the one by Army Chief of Staff General Eric Shinseki—based on his recent experience in Bosnia—that stabilizing post-Saddam Iraq would take several hundred thousand troops. As had been the case with the Taliban in Afghanistan, their overconfidence was fueled by the speed with which Saddam's regime collapsed, with hundreds of thousands of Iraqi soldiers abandoning the fight and heading home. This raised obvious questions about how the soldiers would survive and become integrated into the new Iraq, yet the US official in charge of administering the country, Paul Bremer, disbanded what was left of the Iraqi army, refused to pay their salaries, and implemented a draconian de-Ba'athification policy that involved firing over eighty-five thousand civil servants—effectively rendering the country ungovernable when tens of thousands of former security personnel were joining the nascent insurgency. At the same time, Rumsfeld was drawing down the US troop commitment by thirty thousand troops, all but guaranteeing that the insurgency would snowball into the full-blown civil war that engulfed much of the country in 2006.[38]

David Petraeus—who commanded the 101st Airborne Division during the invasion—supplies a devastating account of these own-goals in both planning and execution. Drawing on their analyses of the failures in Afghanistan and Iraq, he and his Marine counterpart, General Mattis, oversaw a far-reaching review of American counterinsurgency strategy, published in 2006 as the *Counterinsurgency Field Manual.* The central idea was that a successful counterinsurgency strategy requires two things: Deployment of enough military force to provide security for the civilian population who would otherwise back the insurgency, and then building the civilian infrastructure needed to sustain that security over time.[39]

The *Field Manual* authors estimated that the first of these required a minimum ratio of one security force member to every fifty civilians. In Iraq, that meant a security force of six hundred thousand. This was achieved during the surge of 2007–2008, which Petraeus led by returning the US forces that had been drawn down four years prior, undertaking an aggressive program of hiring private military contractors and rebuilding the Iraqi military and police. None of this could happen until Rumsfeld—for whom the strategy was anathema—was fired following the disastrous Republican performance in the 2006 midterm elections.

Building a viable civilian infrastructure never happened, so the security achieved during the surge rested on a house of cards.

The fragility of the new order became obvious within days of the final departure of US troops in December 2011. Iraqi Prime Minister Nuri al-Maliki immediately started prosecuting opponents, appointing incompetent cronies to the officer corps, suppressing dissent, and disposing of the Sunni minority—driving them toward the nascent ISIS movement that was developing in Syria out of former Iraqi al-Qaeda insurgents who had fled there after their final defeat in northern Iraq in 2010. The country soon descended once more into near civil war, stoked by ISIS insurgents from across the border who would begin their takeover of central and northern Iraq with the conquest of Fallujah in January of 2014. By then, the success that had been achieved by the surge was a distant memory.[40]

The Democracy Fantasy

Afghanistan and Iraq were not going to become viable democracies. Afghanistan is extremely poor. Its per capita GDP was less than $200 when the US invaded in 2001 and never rose above $700 during the entire twenty years of American occupation. The threshold for sustainable democracy is orders of magnitude higher: $10,000 per capita GDP in 2001 dollars (or $18,200 in 2025 dollars). Even India, the only very poor country in which democracy has ever endured, is not that poor. And Indian democracy was helped along by a diversified economy, a well-developed bureaucracy run by an educated civil service, and a Congress Party that enjoyed widespread legitimacy from leading the decades-long struggle for independence.[41]

Other factors that help sustain democracy include a functioning rule of law, a middle class, a developed civil society, and a prior history of democracy—none of which was present in either country.

Afghanistan had almost no functioning economy or infrastructure. It was a tribal society with a rudimentary education system. Its most lucrative export was poppies for the narcotics trade. Iraq wasn't as poor as Afghanistan (its per capita income was $800 in 2003, rising to about $6,000 when the US left in 2011), but it was an "oil curse" country: Most income and wealth and virtually all foreign exchange came from oil. Democracy fares poorly in these settings because those who control access to the oil economy will not likely give it up when they lose elections, and people who can grab power often will. It is hard—if not impossible—for a country to avoid this dynamic unless the economy is already well diversified before oil is discovered, as in Scotland and Norway.[42]

This is all common knowledge among political scientists, yet you can read every page of Malkasian's history of the US war in Afghanistan and all four volumes of Bob Woodward's blow-by-blow account of the decisions to invade both countries without encountering Bush or anyone in his administration asking whether the democracies they sought to create would be viable. Bush finally wondered about it in Iraq two years after the invasion, by which time the US had disbanded the Iraqi military and fired tens of thousands of civil servants, and insurgent attacks were running at more than a thousand a month. The person he asked was John Negroponte when he was considering appointing him ambassador to Iraq. Whether Negroponte had any better idea than Bush what a heavy lift it would be is unclear: He ducked the question.[43]

In any case, the US did nothing that might have improved democracy's chances in either country, such as investing heavily in creating diversified economies, overhauling the educational systems, and building the civilian infrastructure needed for a functioning modern state—let alone a democratic one. Six months after the US invaded Afghanistan, Bush made one pro forma reference to the need for a Marshall Plan for Afghanistan in a speech at the Virginia Military Institute.[44] However, neither he nor anyone in the administration ever followed up on it, and Rumsfeld insisted that commanders on the ground avoid engaging in nation-building. In both countries, they actively destroyed the existing institutional infrastructure, effectively rendering what would have been an enormously difficult undertaking impossible. Bush's public and private pronouncements took it for granted that democracy blossoms when repressive governments fall. This had been a common refrain among neoconservatives at the American Enterprise Institute and the Heritage Foundation in the 1980s and 1990s, but never supported by research. Bush might also have been influenced by the ease with which democracy had been established in Eastern Europe after 1989. But most of those countries had diversified economies, educated populations, and prewar histories of democracy, and they were soon integrated into the EU. He would have done better to look at the former Asiatic republics of the USSR.

And then there was the huge challenge of a victor installing democracy in a defeated country, the only successful examples of which are West Germany and Japan after World War II. But both had educated populations and prior histories of democracy, and the US made massive investments in rebuilding their shattered economies and institutions. The US also drew both countries into its Cold War alliances—signing the US-Japan security pact in 1951 and incorporating West Germany into NATO four years later. Crucially, it was widely accepted by both the West German and the Japanese populations that their own leaders had brought disaster on themselves with reckless military adventurism. As a result, the new regimes were not dogged by the legitimacy deficits that have prevailed in Afghanistan and Iraq, where it was easy for insurgents to mobilize support by lambasting the governments as American puppets. There was some awareness of this challenge in the Bush administration, but its short war/light footprint solution undermined the military mission from the start, all but guaranteeing failure.

The Costs of Failure

The aggressive internationalism that distinguished neoconservatives from isolationists and libertarians in the Republican party came into its own after September 11, 2001. With the Cold War constraints gone and the end-of-history complacency of the 1990s shattered by the terrorist attacks, the neoconservative message that America is the indispensable leader in a Manichean battle between good and evil found fertile ground with an administration led by a born-again Christian who was convinced that he was doing God's will by taking on the "axis of evil," as he labeled Iraq along with Iran and North Korea in his 2002 State of the Union Address. The neoconservatives in Bush's administration didn't all share his religious motivation, but they matched his crusading certitude and blithe indifference to anyone who questioned the viability of their goals. Drunk on the conviction that the US had the power to work its way in the world, they were sure that the world could be remade in America's image. As a senior advisor to Bush put it to journalist Ron Suskind, "We're an empire now, and when we act, we create our own reality. And while you're studying that reality . . . we'll act again, creating other new realities, which you can study too, and that's how things will sort out. We're history's actors and you, all of you, will be left to just study what we do." A measure of their self-confidence was that, when Israeli officials asked why the US was invading Iraq when Iran was the greater threat, the response was: Don't worry, Iran will be next.[45]

The neoconservative rewrite of US national security policy was a root-and-branch repudiation of the Powell Doctrine. First spelled out by Bush in a commencement speech at West Point in

June 2002 and codified three months later in his *National Security Strategy of the United States of America*, the Bush Doctrine was the most aggressive internationalist stance taken by any administration in American history. It asserted the right to unilateral US military action anywhere in the world, effectively superseding the Monroe Doctrine, which had restricted the US sphere of interest to its own hemisphere. This right trumped alliance commitments and would be unconstrained by the UN Security Council. Instead, it would be pursued by coalitions "of the willing," with Bush admonishing the world that "either you are with us or you are with the terrorists." Rather than a strategy of last resort again against imminent threats, war would now be waged preemptively against "emerging" ones. The preamble to the *National Security Strategy* went well beyond US national security, incorporating the neoconservative agenda to remake the world in America's image: "The United States will use this moment of opportunity to extend the benefits of freedom across the globe," it thundered. "We will actively work to bring the hope of democracy, development, free markets, and free trade to every corner of the world." The final nail in the coffin of the Powell Doctrine was that the Bush Doctrine envisaged a state of endless war. Instead of insisting on achievable goals and viable exit strategies, the war on terror would be "a global enterprise of uncertain duration."[46]

The Bush Doctrine was spectacularly unviable. Beyond the vast financial cost of the war on terror, the Afghanistan and Iraq gambits turned out to be massive displays of American weakness that dealt humiliating blows to the country's influence and prestige. By 2006, when US forces were flailing against virulent insurgencies in both countries, with no end in sight, any suggestion that "Iran will be next" had become laughable. That year also saw the demise of the neoconservative fantasy that toppling autocrats would lead to the blossoming of American-friendly democracies. Determined to demonstrate a positive regional spillover from replacing Saddam, the Bush administration pressured Palestinian Authority leader Mahmoud Abbas to hold elections for the Palestinian Legislative Council in the West Bank and Gaza. To the surprise of the White House, Hamas won. But Condoleezza Rice's shocked demand for an investigation into "why no one saw this coming" was a testament to the administration's ignorance. Abbas had postponed the Legislative Council elections scheduled for the previous summer because he knew from their recent local election what the likely outcome would be. After Abbas succumbed to American pressure, his representatives had even lobbied Dennis Ross, the well-connected former State Department official who ran a think tank in Jerusalem, behind the scenes to try to get Israel to block the elections. Once Hamas won, the Bush administration found itself in the embarrassing position not only of brushing aside Hamas's proposals to form a unity government with Abbas's Palestinian Liberation Organization, but also of seeking to forcibly remove the party that had just won the election that US officials had insisted should take place.[47]

The appalling harm the George W. Bush administration did to American prestige and influence pales by comparison with the damage it inflicted on the fledgling post–Cold War international order that his father had begun building in 1991. The younger Bush's panicked response to 9/11, when added to a toxic mix of ignorance and self-assurance that would be surpassed only by Donald Trump, made him an easy mark for the neoconservatives on the fringes of his administration who seized the moment to turbocharge their agenda. But they, too, mistook wishful thinking for reality about the limits of both American power and their own knowledge. Their actions call to mind the comment about John Foster Dulles often attributed to Winston Churchill, that he was a bull who carried around his own china shop. The cost was not just the damage wrought by their ignorant—and ultimately self-defeating—flailing. More consequential were the missed opportunities to reinforce and strengthen a global regime in which aggressors are confronted by nations acting collectively, and when possible through the UN Security Council in ways that enhance its authority. This would have required the world's most powerful country to act with disciplined self-restraint, to speak softly while carrying a big stick, as Teddy Roosevelt said in 1900. Instead, they yelled from the mountaintops, only to discover that their stick, while big enough to obliterate a fragile emerging global order, was too small to achieve their goals.[48]

Chapter Two

Reviving the Cold War

Russia's invasions of Ukraine in 2014 and 2022 revived debates about enlarging NATO that had begun with German reunification in October 1990 and continued as NATO incorporated the Baltic states and every former member of the Warsaw Pact except Russia by 2009. Advocates of enlargement saw Vladimir Putin's aggression as vindicating the wisdom of expanding NATO's umbrella. Russia would never have dared invade a NATO country, they maintained, since Article 5 of the North Atlantic Treaty declares an attack on one to be an attack on all and obliges the alliance to defend the targeted country with armed force if necessary. They noted that Article 5 has never been triggered in NATO's seven-decade-plus history. Critics of this view responded that the absence of evidence is not evidence of absence. Like the American diplomat and historian George Kennan, who had opposed creating NATO in the first place and disputed that it had deterred

Soviet aggression during the Cold War, they remained skeptical that NATO's expansion to fifteen new countries, six bordering on Russian territory, had deterred Russian aggression in the years since the Cold War. On the contrary, they contended that the prospect of extending membership to Georgia and Ukraine, which had been publicly discussed by NATO leaders since 2008, provoked Russia's incursion into Georgia that year and its two subsequent wars on Ukraine.[1]

The debate is not new. Founded at the start of the Cold War when US-Soviet relations were descending into mutual acrimony, NATO has always been a strange duck. In his farewell address from public life in 1796, George Washington had warned future generations "to steer clear of permanent alliances with any portion of the foreign world."[2] Americans heeded this admonition until 1949, when Harry Truman led a dozen countries to create an unprecedented alliance that required a twenty-year initial commitment and contained no mechanism for expulsion. A year earlier, Stalin's Berlin blockade and his backing for a communist coup in Czechoslovakia had crystalized American domestic support for the treaty, smoothing the path for easy Senate approval over the objections of isolationists like Ohio senator Robert Taft and in the face of trenchant opposition from Kennan. Today, with thirty-two members, NATO is the largest peacetime alliance in the world and the longest-lived multilateral one.

Kennan had standing. He was the hard-nosed realist who had come to prominence in 1946 when, as the American chargé d'affaires in Moscow, he had warned the State Department in an eight-thousand-word telegram—published anonymously in *Foreign Affairs* magazine the following year—that the Soviet leaders were implacable antagonists who would never abandon their ambitions to entrench and export their system. He opposed creating NATO, however, because he thought that it would escalate the inevitable tensions and militarize them. He also thought it unnecessary. The Soviet Union's dysfunctional economic system would hobble its global ambitions and eventually cause it to collapse under its own weight. All the US needed to do in the meantime was block efforts at expansion—his doctrine of containment—and build up prosperous, democratic countries in the West. Arguing with communist leaders was pointless. The battle that mattered was for the hearts and minds of the Russian people. The best way to win it was to build enviably flourishing political and economic systems in Western countries. As would be true half a century later, Kennan's arguments fell on deaf ears.[3]

Geopolitical Terrain at the End of the Cold War

After the Berlin Wall came down in late 1989, growing momentum for German reunification forced questions about NATO's future onto the agenda. Changing events on the ground recast debates about options, as politicians scrambled to keep up with accelerating public sentiment in both East and West Germany in support of unification. Supermajorities in their parliaments voted for it on September 20, 1990, and the German Democratic Republic went out of business two weeks later. Only months before, Soviet President Mikhail Gorbachev had been debating with West German Chancellor Helmut Kohl and the post–World War II occupation powers about whether they should accept reunification before NATO's future was settled. But momentum soon sidelined the debates, and the final agreement on Germany they all scrambled to sign said nothing about NATO's future outside Germany. It didn't even specify which NATO troops or weapons could be deployed in the former German Democratic Republic. These questions would be revisited multiple times in subsequent years.

Gorbachev's cooperation was needed because in 1990 the Soviets still had some 338,000 troops, 4,200 tanks, 1,300 aircraft, and

180 rocket systems stationed in the GDR—artifacts of the occupation agreement signed at the end of World War II. They also had nuclear weapons there and in several other Warsaw Pact countries (the pact would be disbanded the following year), as well as in Ukraine, Belarus, and Kazakhstan—all of which would soon become independent countries. Gorbachev's bargaining position was weak—his economy was imploding and his political world was disintegrating—but with some 35,000 nuclear warheads in his arsenal, it was vital for the US to secure Soviet cooperation. This was not a time for bluff-calling, let alone confrontation.[4]

And the Russians were cooperating. Both Gorbachev and then, after the USSR ceased to exist in December 1991, Russian President Boris Yeltsin were both remarkably forthcoming. Gorbachev signed the START I nuclear arms reduction treaty in March of 1991. Yeltsin moved quickly to implement its requirements and began energetically on START II, which sought to shrink both the US and Russian nuclear arsenals by 60 percent from their Cold War peaks. He went out of his way to brief US Secretary of State James Baker on how he would retain command and control authority during and after the transition, even at one point sharing details on Soviet nuclear launch protocols and how they would change. There are no more closely held nuclear military secrets.[5]

Yeltsin's openness and willingness to trust Baker in these ways reflected and enhanced the strongly pro-Western sentiment then prevailing in Russia, as did his repeated assurances to Baker and Kohl that he would move rapidly to replace the remnants of the Soviet system with democracy and a market-based economy. He removed Russian weapons and forces from all the former Warsaw Pact countries on schedule, never did or said anything to suggest that Russia might try to regain control of any of them, and signed a series of cooperative agreements with NATO for joint management of regional security threats. Even the decision to retain docking rights for the Soviet naval fleet in Sevastopol was sanctified by a twenty-year agreement with Ukraine, which led to the Treaty on Friendship, Cooperation, and Partnership, signed in Kyiv in May 1997.[6] As with his efforts to implement market reforms—the so-called shock therapy pushed by Western experts—Yeltsin tried to create irreversible facts on the ground as fast as possible.

This transformation was neither easy nor painless. In hindsight, it is doubtful that the broad consensus in the West on the merits of shock therapy was right. Countries like Poland that established market economies overnight did not perform better than those like the Czech Republic that reformed gradually. The two best-performing postcommunist economies in the world are China and Vietnam. Both introduced market relations gradually, Vietnam sector by sector starting with agriculture and foreign firms, and China by growing the private sector alongside the state sector. Russia took the other path. Yeltsin leaped enthusiastically onto the shock therapy bandwagon, with Western leaders and commentators cheering from the rafters. Arguably, he had little choice. The Soviet command economy was so widely discredited and collapsing so fast that perestroika (literally "restructuring") became less a cautious reform, as Gorbachev had envisaged, than the opening of floodgates.[7]

What was inarguable, and what no one disputed at the time, was that shock therapy would produce widespread pain for millions of Russians. Indeed, this was so widely understood that some shock therapy advocates maintained that it should be accomplished before moving on to political reform, lest economically strapped voters use their new democratic rights to throw sand in the wheels of reform or even reverse it. But that was not a real option either, because the Soviet political system was as widely discredited and disintegrating as fast as the command economy.

Many features of the new political order—including basics like national boundaries—were yet to be hammered out, but it was obvious even to the casual visitor that the highly mobilized former Soviet citizens in Russia, who had shown themselves capable of taking to Moscow's streets in the tens of thousands, would no longer accept authoritarian rule. This came as a surprise to many Western commentators who had not fully grasped that although the Soviet Union had a strong Communist Party, it had a weak state. Once the party lost credibility with the population and even the confidence of its own leaders, the Soviet state turned out to be a paper tiger. Those pushing market reform had no choice but to pursue it in a chaotic new democracy that would be a work in progress at best.[8]

Misreading the Stakes in the Soviet Transition

That much was obvious, but the first President Bush failed to show the farsighted creativity in dealing with the Soviet collapse that he had displayed when Saddam Hussein invaded Kuwait. Some commentators have faulted him for flatly rejecting all proposals—from Gorbachev, German Foreign Minister Hans-Dietrich Genscher, French President François Mitterrand, and even his own Secretary of State, James Baker—for NATO to consider leaving, or at least denuclearizing, West Germany as a condition for Moscow's agreeing to its unification with East Germany. "To hell with that!" was Bush's response.

Those critiques of Bush miss the mark. When the momentum for unification began accelerating in the summer of 1990, no one knew that the Soviet Union would collapse eighteen months later, making the end of the Cold War a serious possibility. Many in Western capitals worried that hard-liners might force Gorbachev to backtrack on perestroika or even remove him from power. His celebrity status in the West—he would be awarded the Nobel

Peace Prize in October—was not matched at home. His popularity was plummeting amid snowballing food and consumer shortages that led to panic buying, spiraling inflation and unemployment, proliferating black markets, huge protests, and even shots fired at him on the Revolution Day parade in November of that year.[9]

The backlash against Gorbachev showed up in Soviet negotiations with the West. Hard-liners like KGB head Vladimir Kryuchkov, Central Committee member Valentin Falin, and decorated military veteran Sergey Akhromeyev astonished their German and American counterparts by openly opposing concessions Gorbachev was offering. Western concerns about his grip on power would be vindicated by a coup attempt in August 1991 that might well have succeeded had Boris Yeltsin—whom the plotters also planned to arrest—not faced down the insurrection by climbing onto a tank to denounce it outside the Russian Parliament building. In the summer of 1990, it seemed likely that some other Eastern European countries would soon follow the GDR out of the Warsaw Pact but not that the pact itself would disintegrate, and all bets were off about the Soviet Union's future. Nor, given the Nazi past, was there much enthusiasm in European capitals for the idea of a unified Germany that might be untethered from the Western powers and tempted to develop its own nuclear weapons. No American president would then have contemplated significant changes in the NATO alliance, especially its role in Germany.

But things were very different a year and a half later. By then, there was no Soviet Union or Warsaw Pact, and no danger of either returning. The command economies were obviously defunct and rapidly disappearing. Boris Yeltsin was in control of the new Russia and moving rapidly and transparently to implement far-reaching economic and political reforms and reduce the nuclear threat. In the first half of 1992, he secured unified control of the former USSR's nuclear weapons while also decommissioning large parts of the arsenal and announcing that Russia would no longer target the United States. He could not have been more cooperative. Bush acknowledged as much when they met at Camp David in February and agreed to sign a joint statement declaring the Cold War to be over and that their two countries were no longer adversaries. Unlike his predecessor, Yeltsin understood that wholesale transformation of Russia's economic and political systems was vital not only to the country's future, but also to refashioning its relations with the West. And as with Gorbachev before him, it was obvious that Yeltsin would soon confront reactionary headwinds. He needed help delivering tangible benefits for the Russian people if he was going to implement lasting change.[10]

At this, Bush failed spectacularly. Indicative of his myopia was his decision to side with Treasury Secretary Nicholas Brady—against the advice of Baker and even some neoconservatives like Richard Perle and Charles Krauthammer—in refusing to forgive Soviet-era debt. At the time, the US government held only $2.8 billion of the $65 billion held by foreign creditors, the bulk being owed to other Paris Club governments and the London Club of private investors. However, Germany—which was heavily exposed—needed American help to ensure that Yeltsin would follow through on Gorbachev's commitment to remove Russian troops and military assets from the former GDR. It wouldn't have taken much arm-twisting to convince the other creditors, all of whom had strong interests in Yeltsin's success, to follow suit if the Bush administration had led by example. Even forgiving the US's $2.8 billion would have helped Yeltsin face down the antireform forces that began congealing as soon as hyperinflation exploded after he abolished price controls within days of the Soviet Union's demise. Yet the Bush administration didn't even try, even though other distressed countries were receiving major debt write-downs at the same time. Yeltsin was obliged not only to keep servicing the

Soviet debt, as the US Treasury Department was demanding, but even to assume responsibility for some tsarist-era debt that Lenin had repudiated in 1918—lest he jeopardize US grain shipments on which Russia was critically reliant that winter.[11]

Bush's shortsightedness became the pattern for the remainder of his administration and the Clinton one that followed. Their modus operandi was to eke out last-minute assistance when Yeltsin was facing one imminent catastrophe or another, but little more. Instead of this dollar-short-and-day-late approach, what was obviously needed, as none other than former US President Richard Nixon argued in a memo that was widely shared with journalists in March 1992, was massive, transformative help. Nixon invoked the American failure at Versailles after World War I and the visionary leadership Bush had just shown in Kuwait to argue that Bush had a historic opportunity to seize the moment and an obligation to do for Russia what the Marshall Plan had done for Europe after World War II.[12]

Nixon had no doubt that it was in Russia, not Eastern Europe, that "the final battle of the Cold War will be fought." Lauding Yeltsin as the country's most pro-Western leader ever and its first democratically elected one, he detailed the hard changes Yeltsin had embraced and that Gorbachev had refused to contemplate: risking his life to defend the democratic transition against a reactionary coup; agreeing to the departure of the Baltics and then the dissolution of the USSR; ending aid to other communist regimes, notably Cuba; exceeding the cuts in nuclear weapons that Bush had proposed; and supporting what everyone knew would be painful free-market reforms at home—including freeing up the price system, decollectivizing agriculture, and privatizing state assets. Nixon excoriated Bush for providing Yeltsin with little more than "pathetically inadequate" photo-ops, leftover food and medical supplies from the Gulf War, and a handful of Peace Corps volunteers—"generous action if the target of our aid were a small country like Upper Volta but mere tokenism if applied to Russia, a nation of almost 200 million people covering one seventh of the world's landmass." Instead, Bush should step up with food and medical aid to get Russia through the critical months until the economic reforms began working; take advantage of the unprecedented pro-American sentiment in Russia to send thousands of Western managers to help restructure the economy; pressure international financial institutions to provide tens of billions of dollars for currency stabilization; restructure Soviet-era debt and suspend debt servicing; open Western markets to Russian exports; and coordinate large-scale government and private-sector assistance as was done in Western Europe after World War II. Without immediate help on this scale, Nixon insisted, in a few months, backlash would set in against the market reforms and their Western advocates. Time was of the essence.

And the costs of missing the opportunity were hard to overstate. Arms reduction would founder, ending the peace dividend, and the opportunity to get beyond Cold War antagonisms would be lost. But if Yeltsin succeeded, Nixon argued—invoking the political science finding that democracies do not fight one another—future generations need not face the fear of armed conflict that had hovered throughout the Cold War. And a free-market Russia at peace with the West would create opportunities for billions of dollars in trade that would produce millions of jobs in the US, just as rebuilding the European economies had done after World War II. Nixon conceded that making this case would be challenging with a sluggish US economy in an election year, but he noted that Bush had displayed the requisite leadership skills in building support for the Gulf War two years earlier. Now was the time to do it again, when the costs of failure and the opportunities offered by success were immeasurably greater.

Nixon's invoking of the Marshall Plan was salutary. The Truman administration had encountered rough sledding to convince Congress to enact it in April 1948, when—like Bush in 1992—the president was facing an uphill battle for reelection, and then to keep funding it after the US economy went into recession at the end of the year. Yet Truman and his secretary of state, George Marshall, mounted a massive publicity campaign that overcame considerable skepticism on Capitol Hill, with the House eventually approving the Economic Cooperation Act by a vote of 329 to 74 and the Senate approving it 69 to 17. In this they were helped along by the strongly positive endorsement of the House Select Committee on Foreign Aid, on which Nixon—then a young navy veteran and freshman conservative Republican congressman—sat. They convinced lawmakers that the rapid deterioration of the European economies in 1946 and 1947 risked a repeat of the 1920s, when Europe had become engulfed by communist and fascist uprisings with catastrophic results over the next decade. The logic, as Marshall explained in a Harvard commencement speech in June 1947, was that the US should invest in restoring health to the European economies, "without which there can be no political stability and no assured peace." Nixon understood that the West faced a comparable challenge with Russia early in 1992—not of a return to communism, but of Yeltsin's being succeeded by an "aggressive Russian nationalist" who would threaten the emerging post–Cold War peace and the possibilities for prosperity that came with it. Truman had defied the electoral risks and won reelection in 1948. Bush rejected Nixon's clarion call but lost anyway in 1992.[13]

The Marshall Plan had been expensive. The US spent $13.3 billion on aid to Europe and another $2.2 billion on the economic reconstruction of Japan from 1948 to 1952, for a combined cost of $15.5 billion—about $200 billion in 2025 dollars. (Between 1991 and 2000, by contrast—when the US economy averaged 3.4

percent growth, there was no recession, and Clinton was paying off the Reagan and Bush deficits to take the budget into surplus for the first time since the 1960s—the US spent $6.2 billion on bilateral aid to Russia, or about $12 billion in 2025 dollars. That was 6 percent of the Marshall Plan commitment and 0.15 percent of the $8 trillion the US would go on to spend on the Global War on Terror, a drop in the bucket by any measure.) Bush had no intention of committing resources on anything like this scale, even though the Marshall Plan's vital role in fostering thriving, peaceful economies across Western Europe was widely acknowledged. It had won Marshall the Nobel Peace Prize in 1953 and is often cited by historians as one of the main reasons they rank Truman in the top echelon of American presidents.[14]

Marshall's logic was surely all the more pertinent when the vanquished adversary possessed forty-five thousand nuclear weapons, many located in Eastern Europe or spread across four Soviet republics on the brink of independence, and over which control was uncertain. The dangers were not just of inadvertent deployment or nuclear blackmail by any of the republics or by third parties that might gain access through them, but also of proliferation. Rumors abounded of former Soviet officials who were searching for opportunities to sell nuclear weapons or the ingredients to make them, whether to governments or nonstate actors. There was also the danger of renewed conflict among parts of the collapsing Soviet empire if hard-liners gained the upper hand again in Moscow.[15]

These considerations made the case for a massive US investment to ensure stability in the post-Soviet countries overwhelming. "In victory, magnanimity," Churchill had declared at the end of World War II. Despite his uncompromising insistence on unconditional surrender of the Nazi regime, he was a champion of the Marshall Plan, without which, he wrote, "Europe might well have foundered into ruin and misery in which the seeds of Communism might have grown at a deadly pace." Kennan, who helped draft the Marshall Plan, agreed. They had lived through the consequences of ignoring the plight of defeated adversaries three decades earlier and had no desire to do so again.[16]

It wasn't just Nixon urging Bush to make major commitments to Yeltsin's Russia in early 1992. Dennis Ross, director of Policy Planning at the State Department, also pushed for an extensive program, and there was considerable pressure from Capitol Hill to act boldly—including from conservative stalwarts like North Carolina Senator Jesse Helms, who promised support for an ambitious program. Bush could have drawn on such commitments to create momentum for action had he chosen to, but instead of deploying the leadership skill he had used to move a divided Congress to military action in the Middle East the previous year, he dragged his feet. It was not until Bill Clinton started attacking him on the campaign trail for doing so little that Bush finally announced $24 billion of multilateral support funded by the G7 nations, the International Monetary Fund (IMF), and the European Bank for Reconstruction and Development. The pledge raised expectations in Moscow, where reaction against reformist Prime Minister Yegor Gaidar's policies was solidifying—fueled by the dire economic conditions. But much of the package turned out to be smoke and mirrors, and some of the aid—including a vital $6 billion stabilization fund—never materialized. The US contribution turned out mostly to be grants to buy American food products. What did come arrived in dribs and drabs after Gaidar had already been replaced by Viktor Chernomyrdin, who curtailed much of the reform agenda.[17]

By the start of the Clinton administration, supporting economic transformation in Russia was becoming a much more formidable task. Shortages and inflation had emboldened Russian critics, who portrayed Yeltsin as a gullible purveyor of self-serving Western advice. The reformers had been sidelined, and Chernomyrdin was backpedaling, facilitating corrupt takeovers of former state assets by oligarchs, restoring subsidies to defunct industries, and otherwise compromising with hard-liners to prevent a full transition to a competitive market economy. The confrontations escalated into a constitutional crisis in 1993 when Yeltsin, after ordering the army to open fire on the parliament building, dissolved the Duma and called new elections. Right-wing populists led by the ultranationalist Vladimir Zhirinovsky won the most seats, and the resurgent communists—against whom Yeltsin would fight a rearguard action for the rest of his presidency—also made a strong showing. The only thing that could have changed the dynamic was a visibly successful economic transformation. Helmut Kohl, who also talked up the Marshall Plan analogy to the new US president, understood this, as did others, including the British ambassador to Moscow, Sir Roderick Braithwaite, who insisted that the most important task was to supply what was needed to foster a viable democracy in Russia.[18]

Some members of the incoming Clinton administration understood that major infusions of Western capital would be needed to stabilize the new Russian economy and jump-start economic reforms, notably Treasury officials Larry Summers and David Lipton. Clinton agreed initially, promising much greater commitments. But once it became clear that he would not invest the political capital needed to seek congressional support on the scale they thought was required, they turned their attention to multilateral institutions. Summers had some success in convincing the IMF to relax assistance conditions that Russia could not possibly meet, but, as happened during the Bush years, key components of promised assistance were delayed and vital stabilization funds never materialized. The bulk of Clinton's bilateral assistance to

Russia was given with an eye to shoring up Yeltsin at moments of crisis. Almost half of his largest commitment of $1.6 billion in 1994 was for food assistance, $700 million of which was credits to buy American food. These were notably larger commitments than Bush had made, but they did nothing to help Russia move toward a diversified market economy that might sustain democratic politics in the medium term.[19]

Doing more for Russia would have been a tough sell in American politics after 1994, when Yeltsin began a brutal military campaign in Chechnya and the Republicans took control of the US Congress. It would also have been harder to accomplish on the ground. Following a Communist Party surge in the 1995 legislative elections (it won more seats in the Duma than the next three largest parties combined), Yeltsin only avoided all but certain defeat in the 1996 presidential contest with massive infusions of cash from the oligarchs in return for fire-sale giveaways of state assets that increased his dependence on them and accelerated the country's move toward gangster capitalism.[20] It might have been too late to reverse these changes after the mid-1990s, but the Clinton administration could at least have stuck by a political equivalent of the Hippocratic oath and avoided doing harm. Its approach to NATO enlargement failed even at that.

Misreading the Security Stakes

In June 1997, Secretary of State Madeleine Albright was invited to speak at Harvard's graduation. By then, senior figures in the Clinton administration had convinced themselves that enlarging NATO into the former Soviet bloc countries was in America's interest. To build public support for such a plan, Albright hoped to ride the coattails of Marshall's famous Harvard speech half a century earlier. Declaring that the administration was "striving to fulfill" Marshall's vision, she extolled NATO as a defensive alliance while insisting that it "did not regard any state as its adversary, certainly not a democratic and reforming Russia." Yet she never addressed the question that emanated from Moscow: If not Russia, which adversary was the alliance defending against? Russian suspicions might have been contestable if the country could plausibly have aspired to join NATO, but by then Yeltsin's requests to do exactly that had been rebuffed too often for anyone in the Kremlin or the Duma to take the prospect seriously, regardless of what Albright, her deputy and Russia hand Strobe Talbott, or others said in public.[21]

From the start, Clinton had been confident that Yeltsin's need for Western financial support meant that Russian objections to NATO expansion could be bought off. As early as 1994, the most aggressive enlargement hawks, such as Talbott and Assistant Secretary of State Richard Holbrooke, were arguing that even compensation would be unnecessary. Russian leaders should instead be made to see NATO enlargement as an inevitable process that they were powerless to stop, a sentiment that was soon echoed by Jimmy Carter's former national security adviser Zbigniew Brzezinski, who insisted—without explaining why—that NATO expansion was an "incomparably higher" imperative than managing relations with Russia. Events would prove the predictions made by Holbrooke, Talbott, and Brzezinski partly right. Yeltsin's government was too weak and too dependent on the US to do anything except complain at each step and then back down. The administration's real challenge that Albright was trying to address at Harvard was skepticism at home.[22]

Invoking Marshall's Harvard speech to legitimate NATO enlargement fifty years later betrayed willful blindness to his motivation. His goal had been to avoid replicating the errors of Versailles when an economically decimated and militarily isolated Germany was left floundering while the victors rebuilt themselves and crafted the postwar order. It was as if Marshall had proposed eking out financial assistance to a defeated Germany in dribs and drabs after 1945 while hemming it in with a powerful military alliance. Marshall's purpose had been to supply Germans with the tools and incentives to forsake their historical proclivity for military adventurism by helping them prosper in an economy that was well integrated with the West and under a security umbrella that would buttress their territorial integrity. Taking the comparison seriously at the end of the Cold War would have meant concentrating first and centrally on Russia, as Nixon had said five years earlier, not least because of Russia's nuclear capabilities. The obvious priority was to ensure that anti-Western hostility would not be rekindled there as had happened in Germany during the 1930s. If NATO was going to expand to the east after the Cold War, the first country to be included should indeed have been the new Russia.

There was an inescapable tension between focusing on Russia as a dangerously vulnerable defeated adversary and the aspirations of the former Warsaw Pact countries to integrate themselves into the West by joining NATO. This tension was present from the start, but it became manifest when Vice President Albert Gore visited Moscow in December 1994 to reassure Yeltsin that the various pronouncements that had been made about NATO enlargement would not happen before the 1996 Russian elections. On his return, Gore met with Clinton and his defense team to clarify the priorities. The majority view in the room was that "right" was on the side of Eastern European countries that were keen to join NATO as soon as possible. Deferring expansion until later in the decade was declared to be "not feasible." This meant that the remaining diplomatic task was what Gore had realized was impossible: convincing the Russians that expansion was not directed against them. The only dissenting voice was Defense Secretary Bill

Perry, who believed this priority to be badly wrongheaded. Russia was the former adversary that could become one again. Doing what was needed to get START I and START II implemented and then to secure additional arms reductions should trump the desires of the Eastern Europeans. He almost resigned over the decision but ended up staying to try to slow NATO expansion.[23]

In her definitive history of NATO in the 1990s, *Not One Inch*, Mary Sarotte portrays this as a tragic choice between two compelling but incompatible national security imperatives. The Clinton administration developed a creative solution to the dilemma early on, the Partnership for Peace (PfP), a cooperative security organization made up of NATO countries and former Warsaw Pact members. The brainchild of Joint Chiefs Chairman John Shalikashvili, PfP was intended to show that the former Warsaw Pact countries could cooperate with NATO members to manage regional security crises—the most pressing being the deteriorating situation in the former Yugoslavia. Initially, it did so, yielding the gratifying precedent of NATO and Russian forces working together to defuse a regional conflict. Beyond this, PfP had the merit of temporizing on NATO enlargement. Countries would be told that constructive participation in PfP was a way station on the road to possible NATO membership, making it unnecessary to confront the impact enlargement might have on dealing with Russia as the principal nuclear adversary. The US could continue to work with an enthusiastically committed Yeltsin to retrieve remaining stray nukes, particularly from Ukraine, ratify and implement START I and START II (which would reduce both nuclear stockpiles by 60 percent), and get going on START III as well as on new limitations on chemical, biological, and even conventional armed forces. Yeltsin grasped the larger picture, welcoming PfP as "a stroke of genius" that would dissipate growing anger in Russia in response to the rumblings about NATO expansion.

As Clinton said, creating PfP would avoid drawing a new line across Europe further to the east.[24]

On Sarotte's account, Clinton undermined PfP's efficacy early on, however, by proceeding with NATO enlargement willy-nilly. The pressure came from multiple sources. There were trenchant enlargement advocates in the administration, notably Tony Lake, Richard Holbrooke, Strobe Talbott, and, eventually, Secretary of State Warren Christopher. They disliked PfP just because it deflected pressure for enlargement, so they sought to sideline it, if not scuttle it completely. Pressure also came from aspiring NATO members, especially Polish President Lech Wałęsa and Czech leader Václav Havel, who enjoyed standing in the West as heroic former dissidents. They were induced to join PfP only after getting back-channel assurances that they would be fast-tracked into the alliance. There were military contractors like Lockheed Martin and Raytheon who coveted lucrative contracts from new NATO members. There were staunch Republican advocates of NATO enlargement in Washington, who wrote the policy into the Contract with America, their manifesto for the 1994 midterms in which they won control of the House of Representatives for the first time since the 1950s. Their victory spooked Clinton, who was keenly aware that he might need Polish American and Czech American votes in districts he had won narrowly in 1992 for his reelection in 1996. So he got off the fence and backed the enlargement advocates in his administration by declaring that whether NATO would expand was no longer in question; it was a matter of when and how. This left PfP on life support as a temporizing device that would satisfy Russia.[25]

And then there were the Europeans. Helmut Kohl, who had warned early and often of the dangers of humiliating Yeltsin with aggressive NATO enlargement, nonetheless welcomed adding Central and Eastern European countries because it would take

Germany off the front line between NATO and Russia. One of his advisors put this bluntly, declaring that it would be better "to defend Germany in Poland than in Germany." Kohl also favored NATO expansion to take pressure off the European Union quickly to accept Eastern and Central European aspirants. Likewise with French President Mitterrand, who, like Kohl, had been an earlier advocate of either replacing NATO with a broader pan-European security organization or at least submerging it in a larger entity to avoid replicating Cold War dynamics. He saw value in opening Western institutions to former Soviet bloc countries, but like other EU leaders, he balked at the expensive agricultural subsidies and associated costs of admitting them to the union. They preferred NATO enlargement as the cheaper path to integration.[26]

Sarotte makes a compelling case that pursuing enlargement undermined PfP as an instrument to stave off the tension between the incompatible imperatives, to respond to Eastern Europeans who wanted to join NATO, and to manage security relations with Yeltsin's Russia. She is less convincing, however, that the first of these was a strategic imperative for the US at all. There were many inside and outside the administration in Washington who, like Bill Perry and his eventual successor as defense secretary, Ash Carter, doubted either that it was a strategic imperative at all or, if it was, that it was anywhere near as important as securing major arms reductions and managing security relations with the new Russia for the long run. Much of the time, proponents of NATO enlargement proceeded as if its desirability was self-evident and shifted the focus to other matters. They insisted that the Russians had no right to veto expansion, regardless of what Baker, Genscher, and others might have said to Gorbachev in 1990, and they noted that the Helsinki agreement signed by the Soviets in 1975 recognized the right of all countries to choose their own alliances.[27]

As arguments about the merits of enlargement, these were non sequiturs. It was obviously true that Soviet agreement to enlargement was required only for Germany, where the Soviets had jurisdiction as a post–World War II occupying power, and also that no agreement about Germany would bind other former Warsaw Pact countries in the future. But that implies nothing about what strategic purpose enlargement might serve for the US, if any. Likewise with affirming, as they repeatedly did, that every country was free to choose its own alliance partners. Agreeing that people are free to marry whomever they want doesn't mean you have to marry someone just because they want to marry you. Placating Wałęsa or Havel with a promise of NATO membership in return for their joining PfP might have made Clinton—who, as Sarotte says, always liked to "bring everyone along"—feel good.[28] But that was hardly a reason to do it, not least when it undermined a central purpose behind PfP. Neither Polish nor Czech participation was essential to PfP's success. Russian participation was. Most likely, the others would have joined anyway if the US had continued insisting that there was no other path to eventual NATO membership.

The Europeans turned out to be more clearheaded realists than anyone who prevailed in the Clinton administration. The Germans' preference for adding members to NATO to keep themselves off the front line was manifestly self-serving, and the decision to reject early admission of any former Soviet bloc states to the EU in favor of countries like Austria, Finland, and Sweden made it clear that the main European concern was existing members' interests regardless of what new aspirants might want. It was cheaper, for them, to integrate the Eastern Europeans into Europe by expanding NATO—particularly because the US would bear much of the cost. This began with the NATO Enlargement Facilitation Act in 1996, in which the US committed $60 million to help prepare Poland, the Czechs, and Hungary to join the alliance. Despite considerable debate about the eventual cost, it soon became clear that the only way to include them by 1999 at a price American lawmakers would stomach involved retaining Warsaw Pact armaments that could not easily be integrated into NATO systems. This further antagonized the Russians. Even so, the price tag for adding these countries would run to at least $30 billion over the first decade and a half, most of which would end up being shouldered by the US.[29]

What of running scared of swing-state American voters with Eastern European heritages and pro-enlargement hawks on Capitol Hill? Clinton's freedom to maneuver on that front was limited until November 1996, but once he was reelected, the domestic electoral constraint went away. That was before the administration's full-court press to win public support in the run-up to the July 1997 Madrid NATO Summit, where invitations to Poland, Hungary, and the Czech Republic would be issued. Moreover, many conservatives in Congress and the broader national security community came out in trenchant opposition once the enlargement plan became common knowledge, starting with George Kennan, who wrote in *The New York Times* in February 1997 that expansion would be "the most fateful error of American policy in the entire post–Cold War era." It would jeopardize arms reduction by restoring the Cold War dynamic to US-Russian relations; it would "inflame the nationalistic, anti-Western and militaristic tendencies in Russian opinion"; it would retard the progress of Russian democracy; and it would "impel Russian foreign policy in directions decidedly not to our liking."[30]

Kennan was not alone. Two-thirds of the right-of-center Council on Foreign Relations were polled as opposed to enlargement, as were dozens of then-current and former senators and public officials, who signed open letters of opposition. Some skeptics believed that Eastern and Central Europe should remain nuclear-free, or that enlargement would saddle the US with responsibility for the security of countries that might get into unpredictable conflicts—not least because some had border disputes with one another. Others believed that the better course was to get rid of NATO, turn European security over to the Europeans, and refocus America on its other global interests, notably in Asia. Others saw the enlargement agenda as an ill-considered effort for an obsolete alliance, led by cheerleaders like its secretary general, Javier Solana, to find a new mission that would give it a new lease on life. In a widely quoted op-ed, Brent Scowcroft, former national security advisor under George H. W. Bush, and Democrat Sam Nunn, former chair of the Senate Armed Services Committee, argued that taking on new members that did not meet NATO military criteria would weaken the alliance. Like Kennan, they warned that it would undermine normalization with Russia, scuttling arms control. "The central failure of Versailles," they recalled—echoing Nixon's warning to Bush—"lay in the fatal miscalculation of how to deal with a demoralized former adversary. That, above all, is the error we must not repeat."[31]

Clinton never engaged the concerns that enlargement would undermine arms reduction and provoke a nationalist response in Russia, except to dismiss them at one point as "silly." From 1994 onward, the administration sought to redirect debate about the merits of enlargement to topics that took the question as settled. Creating momentum to get started with expansion in 1999 exemplified this tactic. It focused on that date after Solana declared in 1997 that the fiftieth anniversary of NATO's founding was too good a PR opportunity to miss, and enlargement came to be seen as a way to deliver a political win for a beleaguered Clinton after the Monica Lewinsky scandal broke the following January. The reality that, even with substantial subsidies, no aspirant could meet NATO membership criteria by 1999 deflected attention to yet other questions: Which criteria could be waived? How many countries could be added? Everyone had their pet candidates. The French wanted Romania and Bulgaria. Albright, born in Prague, wanted the Czech Republic. The Polish Brzezinski threw spitballs at PfP from the sidelines and lobbied for Poland. Talbott was so insistent about adding the Baltics that this became known as the Talbott Principle in the White House—though no one explained what turned an intense desire into a principle. And once it became clear that the British drew the line at Poland, Hungary, and the Czech Republic, the conversation pointed to a new set of questions: How could the White House sell those particular three on Capitol Hill, to allies, and to others in the government who wanted different or additional countries? The need to keep everyone on board made it all but inevitable that the price for adding any initial group would be adding others later.[32]

When Clinton signed the formal admission of Poland, Hungary, and the Czech Republic to NATO on April 23, 1999, declaring that doing so erased the "arbitrary line" that had divided Europe until that day, he was being disingenuous or worse. If no more countries were added, it would simply be shifting the arbitrary line to the east, an event he had repeatedly declared he wanted to avoid. But by then, he had been vocal for months about his "robust open door" policy on future expansion. In case there was any lingering doubt, NATO publicly welcomed the interest of nine additional countries, including the three Baltics that were former Soviet republics, at its 1999 summit in Washington, DC. This made it clear that the line would keep moving toward Russia, and that it would even intrude into former Soviet territory.[33]

By the time of the Washington summit, it had also long been clear that there could be no question of Russia's joining either NATO or the EU. It was also clear that the US was unwilling to accept limits on the personnel that could be deployed in new member countries or on Article 5 guarantees for future NATO members, such as Norway's prohibition of nuclear weapons on its territory and of NATO troops except during wartime. In effect, the US was insisting on the right to do exactly what the Soviets had tried to do by installing nuclear weapons in Cuba in 1962. Poland does, after all, share a border with the Russian enclave of Kaliningrad Oblast. Perhaps aware of this disturbing parallel, even Lech Wałęsa—the most ardent of Russia skeptics and expansion advocates—had indicated in 1995 that he was open to Norwegian-style conditions on Poland's accession. Holbrooke and Christopher brushed this offer aside as a poison pill that might limit future NATO deployments. They wouldn't even accept maintaining existing ceilings on weapons, ensuring that as NATO expanded, Russia would face an ever-growing "defensive" military force moving inexorably toward its territory and increasingly close to major cities such as Moscow and, especially, St. Petersburg. The only concession they ever made was to declare at the signing of the NATO-Russia Founding Act in 1997 that they had no current plans to station NATO forces in the newly added countries.

Was there a plausible way for the Russians to see this start to enlargement in benign terms? NATO remains a military alliance geared to protecting its members from attack, but perhaps a case could have been made that since the Cold War was over by then, it was evolving into an international peacekeeping organization that would work with the UN Security Council to prevent international aggression. Any such claim became an impossibly tough sell in March 1999, however, when NATO bombed Kosovo without Security Council authorization, despite no NATO member—or any other country—having been attacked or threatened. NATO's goal was to protect the Kosovar Albanian population, who were suffering ethnic cleansing at the hands of the Serbian majority.

Unsurprisingly, these events took US-Russian relations to a new low amid opinion polls showing that 93 percent of Russians disapproved of the bombing. Yeltsin suspended participation in the Permanent Joint Russia-NATO Council, and the Duma refused to ratify START II, obliterating the last remnants of momentum on arms control. Reformers like Yegor Gaidar and former Foreign Minister Andrei Kozyrev who favored openness to the West had by then been marginalized by Prime Minister Yevgeny Primakov and other hard-liners. As the first round of expansion went forward, they could do nothing except lament from the sidelines at the possibilities that had been squandered.[34]

The Clinton administration was tactically adept at exploiting Russian weakness and devising ways to co-opt or marginalize objectors at home and abroad to enlarge NATO all the way to Russia's border. But it never answered the skeptics who wanted to know how and why growing NATO served America's strategic interests. Nor did it seriously consider the chickens that would come home to roost when future Russian leaders found themselves less dependent on the West, about whom Gorbachev had cautioned in 1990 when he found himself powerless to prevent NATO's initial move into East Germany: "You cannot humiliate a nation and believe that there will be no consequences." Oblivious to such considerations, the Clinton administration enlarged NATO in 1999 and set it on a path to keep growing, regardless of Russian objections, for one simple reason: They did it because they could.[35]

NATO and Putin

NATO's 1999 enlargement and its action in Kosovo dealt a fatal blow to the Clinton administration's relations with Yeltsin's Kremlin. Reeling from the economic collapse that had forced him to plead for an IMF bailout the previous year, Yeltsin remained embittered for the rest of his premiership. But his successor, Vladimir

Putin, began by charting a different and more constructive course. As prime minister, he had tried in 1999 to defuse tensions over Kosovo in conversations with Talbott and Clinton's national security advisor, Sandy Berger. He had distanced himself from Russian efforts to interfere there and downplayed hard-line Kremlin rhetoric as preelection skirmishing. In his first meeting with Bill Clinton, he said that—unlike the Kremlin hawks—he was open to preserving the Anti-Ballistic Missile Treaty of 1972 despite congressional Republican moves to authorize a US missile defense system. And unlike Yeltsin, Putin remained silent about the initial round of NATO enlargement. In February of 2000, while still acting president, he told NATO Secretary General George Robertson, "I want to resume relations with NATO. Step by step, but I want to do it."[36]

Putin's reversion to Cold War attitudes that began in the mid-2000s is all the more notable in view of how he started out. On ascending to the presidency in 2000, he quickly revived the defunct NATO-Russia cooperative process, created a streamlined NATO-Russia Council, launched collaboration on a host of issues from counterterrorism to proliferation to maritime search and rescue, and began lobbying for Russia to join the alliance. Within two weeks of the 9/11 attacks, he promised to share intelligence on al-Qaeda and the Taliban with the US, opened Russian airspace to the US, agreed to give military assistance to the Northern Alliance in Afghanistan, and, most remarkably of all, agreed to have American troops in central Asia—an unprecedented move that went over like a lead balloon with his own military establishment. Nor did he make much fuss, initially, at the first round of NATO enlargement that took place on his watch. Evidently, he was probing for the possibility of a reset.[37]

Putin's early interest in NATO was matched by lobbying for Russian economic integration with Europe. In the mid-1990s, when still a translator for St. Petersburg mayor Anatoly Sobchak, Putin had responded positively to Helmut Kohl's remark that he couldn't imagine Europe without Russia. Kohl was not alone. In 1992, British Prime Minister John Major had urged the EU to "widen its imagination" and admit Russia, a move he thought would "banish utterly" the threat of nuclear war. Ten years later, Italian Prime minister Silvio Berlusconi was still calling for Russia to join the EU in the wake of newly elected President Putin's declaration that "no matter where our people live, in the Far East or in the south, we are Europeans." Everything Putin did in those years implied that he saw Russian integration into NATO and Europe as feasible and desirable, from openly lobbying for inclusion into Western institutions to working to harmonize Russian and EU economic regulations. As Joe Biden, then chairman of the Senate Foreign Relations Committee, put it, "No Russian leader since Peter the Great has cast his lot as much with the West as Putin has."[38]

Two developments changed Putin's outlook. One was the second Bush administration's aggressive unilateralism in Iraq. It wasn't just anger at the toppling of a regime that had no connection to the 9/11 attacks, even though—as Putin warned Bush multiple times—that move was exceedingly unpopular in Russia. It provoked vitriolic anti-American demonstrations in major Russian cities and sparked backlash from Kremlin hard-liners who complained that Putin's cooperation had yielded few benefits. Russia had not been admitted to the World Trade Organization. US trade restrictions had not been lifted, and foreign direct investment in Russia was falling. Another source of Russian anger was that the country held billions of dollars of Iraqi debt and was close to sealing a $40 billion bilateral trade deal that was jeopardized when the US toppled the regime. George W. Bush, who had welcomed NATO expansion "eastward and southward, northward and onward" in June of 2001, was tone-deaf to Russian concerns.[39]

Like the Kosovo bombing four years earlier, the Iraq invasion lacked Security Council authorization. As such, it undermined the premise of Putin's overtures: that with the Cold War over, Russia could aspire to navigate successfully in a multilateral world regulated by international institutions. Bush's actions made clear that the New World Order his father had sought to establish twelve years earlier was defunct. Instead, the US would act as a global hegemon when and where it chose—even in defiance of close allies like France and Germany, which also opposed the Iraq invasion. Like Yeltsin before him, Putin was discovering that cooperation was largely a one-way street. Unsurprisingly, he recalibrated. As he had warned in the same 2000 interview in which he declared that Russians were Europeans and their path forward was democratic, "if they push us away, then we will be forced to find allies and reinforce ourselves. What else can we do?"[40]

In December 2004, Putin declared that the recent round of NATO enlargement—in which seven countries, including the Baltics, had been added—was a negative "factor" in Russia's relations with the West, though he was still conceding the "sovereign right" of former Soviet republics to decide whether they wanted to join NATO through the following May. He became steadily more negative after that, as the Bush administration and NATO leaders made increasingly positive statements about membership for Georgia and Ukraine. In Munich in February 2007, he condemned the Bush administration's unilateralism as an "almost uncontained hyper use of force in international relations" that flagrantly violated international law, and he denounced NATO enlargement as a "serious provocation that reduces the level of mutual trust."[41]

Putin was, by then, reflecting widespread Russian opinion. As US ambassador to Russia William Burns warned Secretary of State Condoleezza Rice in February 2008, "In more than two and a half years of conversations with key Russian players, from knuckle-draggers in the dark recesses of the Kremlin to Putin's sharpest liberal critics, I have yet to find anyone who views Ukraine in NATO as anything other than a direct challenge to Russian interests." Offering Ukraine a Membership Action Plan (MAP)—a to-do list for countries aspiring to join the alliance—would be seen as "throwing down the strategic gauntlet" that would put the NATO-Russia Council on life support, if not destroy it. Proceeding down that path with Georgia would likely lead Moscow to recognize the Abkhaz separatists there, creating a high risk of armed conflict between Russia and Georgia. Burns's warnings did not prevent President Bush from going out of his way to visit Kiev in April 2008 and declare that he strongly endorsed NATO membership for Ukraine and Georgia. That same month, NATO's leaders announced in Bucharest that those countries' MAP applications would be approved, and that the alliance would "now begin a period of intensive engagement with both countries at high political level" to address outstanding issues, and would report on progress to NATO members' foreign ministers by the end of the year.[42]

Burns's prediction about Georgia came true in August, when Russian troops invaded the country in support of separatist rebels in South Ossetia. Putin also began questioning Ukraine's independent status, given its patchwork construction in the Soviet era. He started referring to Ukraine as closely tied to Russia, if not inseparable from it, and even claimed that all former Soviet ethnicities, including Ukrainians, *were* Russians. After Russia annexed Crimea in 2014, he said the move had been necessary to preempt Ukraine's joining NATO, which would have compromised Russia's security interests in Sevastopol. "Who does NATO act against?" he demanded. "Why is it expanding towards our borders?" By 2022, the prospect of Ukraine entering NATO had become a "red line," because Russia "cannot feel safe, develop and exist while facing a permanent threat from the territory of today's Ukraine."[43]

The other major change was that by 2003, Putin was well on his way to getting Russia's economic house in order. He had replaced Russia's sclerotic tax system with a 13 percent flat tax, reduced and greatly simplified the corporate tax, and begun aggressive tax enforcement. These reforms created a predictable stream of revenue and, for the first time since its creation, a solvent Russian state. He also took advantage of the global boom in oil prices aggressively to repay Russia's staggering foreign debt. By 2003, Russia's ratio of debt to GDP had fallen from over 100 percent at the time of its default five years earlier to less than 40 percent, lower than that of many Western countries. He was even prepaying Russia's foreign creditors, so that the debt would be all but eliminated by 2008. By the time the global financial crisis hit, Putin's government would largely have tamed inflation, financed the government's budget out of current revenues, and saved $160 billion of surplus oil income in a stabilization fund that enabled Russia to avoid a major collapse.[44]

Putin was also on his way to reining in the oligarchs who had dominated Russian politics since they had bailed Yeltsin out of his troubles in 1996. As soon as he came to power, Putin moved quickly to get them off his back by forcing them to pay taxes and clipping their political wings. Within months, he had arrested one media magnate who was critical of his reforms, Vladimir Gusinsky, and intimidated a second, Boris Berezovsky, into fleeing the country. In early meetings with oligarchs, he made it clear that those who evaded taxation would lose their assets and possibly their freedom. By mid-2003, he was taking down Russia's wealthiest oligarch, Mikhail Khodorkovsky, for avoiding taxes, building an oil pipeline to China that Putin opposed, and mocking Putin in the media. Khodorkovsky's business partner was arrested for tax evasion in July, followed by Khodorkovsky himself in October—an unmistakable shot across the other oligarchs' bows.

Khodorkovsky would spend the next decade in prison. In short, by 2003, Putin was the confident leader of a resurgent economy who no longer depended on Western largesse. He had few reasons to cooperate with a US government that acted with scant regard for Russia's interests or concerns.[45] As during much of the Cold War, Washington and Moscow once again found themselves trapped in a destructive dynamic known by game theorists as a prisoners' dilemma.

Prisoners' dilemmas arise when two parties who share an interest in cooperating face incentives not to do so. An arms race is the classic illustration. Both sides would be secure if both chose a low-arms strategy, avoiding the race. But in deciding what to do, each side reasons that it is better off with a high-arms strategy. Each wins if its adversary picks a low-arms strategy, and each at least keeps up if its adversary picks a high-arms strategy. Opting for a low-arms strategy carries the risk of being played for a sucker if the adversary picks a high-arms strategy, the worst outcome of all. But because both sides reason in the same way, the arms race continues indefinitely. This is why game theorists say that mutual defection is the dominant strategy in a prisoner's dilemma. It loads the dice against a cooperative outcome.

One way out of this dynamic is for one country to become so powerful that all potential adversaries will knuckle under and accept its authority. When the US used nuclear weapons against Japan in 1945, the philosopher Bertrand Russell—who realized that the American nuclear monopoly would be temporary—set aside both his pacifism and his antipathy for all things American to declare that the US should immediately declare itself the world's government and develop the most powerful nuclear arsenal possible to back up its authority.[46] President Truman wisely ignored that advice, but in its early years, the George W. Bush administration verged on a version of it by believing that the US could create its own reality, which others would have to accept. But in Afghanistan and Iraq, the administration soon discovered that the power to destroy an adversary does not translate into the power to govern it or even to stop lethal groups within its territory from attacking you. Doing that would take more resources than any government can commit indefinitely. It would also involve doing things that key constituencies find abhorrent—as Israel discovered in its invasion of Gaza after the Hamas terrorist attacks on October 7, 2023. In reality, even great powers must negotiate with adversaries, and they often invest in norms and institutions to help manage their conflicts lest they become unsustainably overextended. The New World Order that George H. W. Bush had sought to create was an example. Having obliterated it, his son forced the US to act alone, while his aggressive unilateralism made negotiations with adversaries vastly more difficult.

If no one can force adversaries to cooperate, the only way out of a prisoners' dilemma is to build enough trust between the parties to make promises of mutual cooperation credible. Because talk is cheap, it will never be enough. The adversaries must refrain from exploiting cooperative moves by the other side to signal their commitment to cooperation. This can happen through ongoing interactions using a strategy called tit-for-tat: Start by cooperating, then mirror whatever your adversary does. Benign tit-for-tat is exceedingly hard to initiate when the danger to you is potentially catastrophic if your adversary reneges. This is why successful negotiations among nuclear powers are difficult and rare. Because the stakes are so high, neither will likely risk cooperating unless they believe they have no choice. One such opportunity presented itself between the US and the USSR—and later Russia—at the end of the Cold War. Russia's economy was so devastated and its successive governments so weak that the country was willing to risk cooperating with the West to rebuild itself. This created the unusual opportunity to replace a malevolent tit-for-tat dynamic with a benign one. The moment would not last.

After World War II, George Marshall understood the risks of taking advantage of a vanquished adversary. If the defeated Axis powers were forced to accept adverse outcomes in the war's immediate aftermath, once they were back on their feet they would retaliate. That had been the lesson of Versailles. He also understood that refraining from taking advantage would not be enough. It would be important to create a host of mutually beneficial relationships among former enemies, so that they would have powerful incentives not to defect once they were able to do so. This is why he wanted the US to invest in rebuilding their economies and integrating them into a system of cooperative trade. Winston Churchill, who drew the same lesson from Versailles, favored a postwar European union that would include France and Germany. The goal was to ensure that they gained major economic, social, and cultural benefits from cooperation with each other—benefits they would be loath to jeopardize by returning to armed conflict. These relationships help sustain the mutual expectation that neither side will revert to military escalation. Both sides know that the other has a lot to lose: free movement of people and trading relationships among countries, joint educational and scientific ventures, and regulatory cooperation over issues like public health and the environment.

The tragedy after the Cold War was that the Clinton administration and both Bush administrations failed to act on the lessons of Versailles that had motivated Marshall and Truman after World War II. Whether out of shortsightedness, hubris, or both, they missed how fleeting the opportunity was or what the costs would be of failing to seize the moment with the country that mattered most: the former deadly adversary with whom a cooperative relationship could be created by helping jump-start its transition from communism to capitalism and then deepening economic, social, and cultural ties in the 1990s and early 2000s. Instead, they became sidetracked into the easy agenda of enlarging NATO into Eastern and Central Europe without taking seriously the damage this did to the rare opening that had arisen with Russia.

Putin might have evolved into a malevolent authoritarian at home and an assertive nationalist abroad, regardless of American actions. But the evidence is strong that he wanted something more than mere accommodation until the US turned to unilateralism in 2003. He saw this unilateralism as indifferent, at best, to Russian concerns, and he saw NATO's relentless eastward expansion as a gratuitous threat. By the same token, Putin's early support for Ukraine and other former Warsaw Pact countries joining the EU was motivated by his expectation that the Russian economy would also become closely integrated with the EU, even if Russia did not formally join the union. Once he realized that Russian integration with Europe was a nonstarter, the prospect of an ever-more powerful EU became a threat—particularly after the EU admitted the Baltics and five other former Eastern European countries in 2004. Unsurprisingly, Putin began beefing up the Eurasian Economic Community that he had created four years earlier and inducing Ukraine and other former Soviet republics to join it instead of the EU. Putin's growing frustration at being sidelined infused his Munich speech in 2007, when he complained about Western efforts to "substitute NATO or the EU for the UN."[47]

The following year was a turning point. By 2008, the US was a less intimidating adversary than it had been when Putin first came to power. Washington's hand-picked regime in Afghanistan, led by President Karzai, was flailing at a resurgent Taliban, and America's Iraq gambit had become a humiliating quagmire. The gathering financial storm—with the investment bank Bear Stearns failing in March and Lehman Brothers in September—shattered America's prestige as the incontestable arbiter of global economic relations and custodian of the world's financial markets. America's geopolitical and economic disasters meant that Putin had fewer reasons to accept US unilateralism or to tolerate NATO's overtures toward a country like Ukraine, with its large expatriate Russian population and strategic importance as Russia's only point of access to the Black Sea. It is not surprising that Putin, politically secure and economically empowered at home, was unwilling to stand passively by when NATO went public at its Bucharest summit in April with the blunt declaration that Georgia and Ukraine would soon join the alliance. From his point of view, it was a gratuitous, hostile move that signaled no interest in cooperative tit-for-tat with Russia. He responded accordingly.[48]

The US and its allies continued supplying reasons for him to keep pushing back. Once Albania and Croatia were added during the Obama administration in 2009, Russians had lived through NATO enlargement at the hands of two Republican and two Democratic administrations. This bipartisan pattern of relentless eastward expansion would continue, with Trump presiding over the addition of Montenegro and North Macedonia and Biden of Finland and Sweden, so that by 2024, six NATO countries shared boundaries with Russia. The addition of Finland in 2023 added 1,335 kilometers to NATO's shared borders with Russia, almost doubling it to 2,550 kilometers. EU enlargement into Eastern Europe also continued after 2004, if at a reduced pace, with the addition of Bulgaria and Romania in 2007 and Croatia in 2013. In September of that year, Ukraine announced its intention to sign a free trade agreement with the EU, a step toward membership that the Russians opposed as incompatible with Ukraine's existing Treaty on Friendship, Cooperation, and Partnership with Russia.[49]

Returning to the presidency in 2012 after a four-year stint as prime minister, Putin quickly became more nationalistically assertive. A year earlier, he had rebuked President Dimitri Medvedev for abstaining from the UN Security Council resolution authorizing NATO's intervention in Libya. Now he started pushing hard to consolidate and expand the Eurasian Economic Union as a competitor with the EU, sidelining Russia's recent accession to the WTO that Medvedev had initiated in 2009. In December of 2013, he induced Ukrainian President Viktor Yanukovych to shelve the proposed EU deal in favor of a $15 billion bailout and natural gas price concessions from Moscow. But this was only after the EU's shambolic attempt to woo Ukraine backfired when it insisted on terms so draconian that no Ukrainian leader could have accepted them. Putin's more generous deal required Ukraine to join the Eurasian Union. With Ukrainians equally divided over whether to sign up to the EU free trade agreement or the Eurasian customs union, Yanukovych accepted Putin's offer. This precipitated an escalating crisis in Ukraine that ended in Yanukovych's ouster and subsequent flight to Moscow in February 2014.[50]

Putin's decision to seize Crimea two months later was, in part, a successful bid to boost his sagging popularity at home in the wake of falling oil prices and slowing Russian growth. But it also reflected a growing sense of geopolitical and economic isolation, as successive American administrations and European governments froze Russia out of the post–Cold War Western order, encroaching on the country's western frontier with security and economic institutions that excluded Russia. This isolation was underscored when the new provisional government in Ukraine bypassed constitutional procedures, declared that it would rescind Yanukovych's agreement with Russia, sign the European Association Agreement, and negotiate new financial packages with the IMF and the EU.[51]

We will never know whether Putin would have evolved differently had the Clinton and Bush administrations responded more constructively to his overtures in the early 2000s. What we do know is that they never seriously tried. Repeating the US pattern with Yeltsin, they froze Putin out of the post–Cold War order they were constructing and squandered rare opportunities to try to forge something better. At critical junctures, figures as different as Richard Nixon, Jesse Helms, George Kennan, Brent Scowcroft, Sam Nunn, and Bill Perry urged them to focus on the real prize: a fundamental reordering of relations with the country that posed the real strategic threat to the United States and the rest of the West. They sacrificed this possibility to pursue dubiously beneficial tactical gains by expanding NATO onto Russia's doorstep. They expected Putin to swallow a relentlessly encroaching military presence that no US administration would have tolerated in the Western hemisphere, let alone on its own borders.

Russia and the US might have ended up in a new Cold War anyway, but they might not have. The choices US administrations made foreclosed other possibilities, trapping relations in a downward-spiraling prisoner's dilemma from which escape now seems as difficult as it had been at the height of the Cold War. In the run-up to Putin's second invasion of Ukraine in 2022, the Biden administration dismissed his demand for a commitment that Ukraine would never join NATO as ridiculous whataboutism, insisting that NATO was purely a defensive alliance with an open-door policy. By then, Putin had indeed become a threat to the rules-based international order that the US claimed to guard, but he didn't start out that way, and it was not inevitable that he would evolve as he did. The NATO door never opened for Russia despite Putin's benign early conduct, and successive American administrations compounded his alienation with their own blatant disregard for the rules-based international order. The US invaded Iraq and toppled its regime in flagrant violation of international law five years before Putin went into Georgia, and it led an illicit NATO mission to topple Libya's government three years before he first set foot in Ukraine. This was scarcely the action of a defensive alliance, and it sabotaged Medvedev's effort to reset Russian-US relations during his interregnum at Moscow's helm, reinforcing Putin's hardening line when he returned to the presidency.[52]

And what has been gained? A central unexamined conceit behind NATO enlargement was that it would make its members more secure, and the more that were added, the more secure they would all become. This safety-in-numbers rationale was fallacious for at least three reasons. One, which goes all the way back to George Kennan's rationale for opposing the formation of NATO in 1949, was that it would provoke a militarized response on the other side commensurate with the perceived threat. Helmut Kohl's candid admission to Bill Clinton in 1993 that he favored adding Poland on the grounds that he would rather fight the Russians there than in Germany gave impetus to this dynamic, because others would obviously invoke the same logic. Successive US administrations tried to blunt the predictable Russian reaction by pushing the line that, unlike the original NATO, the post–Cold War alliance wasn't directed at any country in particular, but this was never believable and never believed. The result was bound to be escalating tension as the relentlessly expanding NATO encroached toward, and then into, the former USSR.

Second is the danger that expanding alliance commitments might dangerously escalate conflicts. That risk became evident as early as June 1999, following NATO's unilateral action in Kosovo. Russian forces responded to NATO's action by advancing on the airport in Kosovo's capital city, Pristina, to be part, they said, of a peacekeeping force in the wake of the bombing campaign. US General Wesley Clark, then NATO's supreme allied commander for Europe, ordered NATO Secretary General Javier Solana to block Russian access to the airport. Escalation was avoided only because the British commander of NATO's Kosovo Force, General

Michael Jackson, refused to order his forces to block the Russians, declaring, "I'm not going to do that. It's not worth starting World War III." After a two-week standoff, the field commander on the ground negotiated a de-escalation with the Russians. The Americans later complained that the field commander's refusal to act amounted to insubordination, but his British superiors backed him up with the result that, eventually, the matter was dropped. Cooler heads prevailed in this instance, but the episode underscored the escalatory risks of multiplying security guarantees.[53]

Third, an ever-expanding NATO was bound to become increasingly unwieldy as conflicting interests and agendas of the different member countries began evolving unpredictably in a multipolar world. Turkey's military involvement in Syria in 2019 raised the possibility that alliance members might find themselves either dragged into an action they did not support or in violation of their treaty obligations. By 2025, the prospect of Poland becoming involved in the Russia-Ukraine war on the Ukrainian side, or for that matter Hungary on the Russian side, could not be dismissed as unthinkable. What would that mean for the countries tied to them by Article 5 guarantees? This is to say nothing of a direct conflict between two alliance members, put on the table in late 2024 when President-elect Donald Trump declared an American interest in annexing Greenland from Denmark. During the original Cold War, most conflicts and potential conflicts were subsumed into the overarching standoff between the capitalist US and the communist USSR. Neither the emergence of the Non-Aligned Movement in 1961 nor Nixon's opening to China in 1972 had much impact on this dynamic, at least not where NATO and Europe were concerned. That is no longer true. Threats to international security today have nothing to do with capitalism versus communism. They are also less predictable, placing inevitable strains on a sprawling alliance, not least because many of NATO's actions—as the interventions in Kosovo and Libya revealed—are unrelated to its members' security.

This lack of a well-defined rationale means that it would be generously euphemistic to describe NATO today as a Rube Goldberg machine. Its purpose during the Cold War was clear: to contain if not deter the Soviet threat to the US and its allies, a threat that was underscored by episodes like the Soviet intervention in Hungary in 1956, the Berlin Crisis in 1961, and the events surrounding the Prague Spring in 1968. Starting with the Clinton administration's enunciation of criteria for joining the PfP in 1993, once the Soviet empire collapsed and the world's other major communist countries embraced capitalism, NATO leaders began declaring that its purpose was to protect and promote democracy. This was perhaps explicable once the anticommunist rationale had gone away, but it has never been true. Portugal was a founding NATO member in 1949, decades before its democratic transition. Greece remained in NATO during its period of dictatorship from 1967 to 1974, as did Turkey through successive coups that ejected elected governments from power. Nor is it true today, given the democratic backsliding in Turkey and Hungary—an awkward fact for an alliance that has no mechanism for expelling members from its ranks.

The Cold War conflict also provided a rationale for NATO's economic structure that has not worn well since the Soviet Union collapsed. During the Cold War, American leaders judged it to be in the country's interest to provide security guarantees to its allies to promote cohesion and limit nuclear proliferation that would threaten US hegemony had those allies chosen to go their own way. Dwight Eisenhower's hope to forestall France's creation of an independent nuclear arsenal in this way failed, but the NATO security umbrella was sufficient to prevent additional proliferation among its members (Britain's nuclear program was well underway before NATO was formed) and keep everyone on board.[54]

The Soviets maintained cohesion among Warsaw Pact countries in a similar way. The quid pro quo for the Americans was to bear the disproportionate cost of Europe's defense.[55] This practice continued with NATO enlargement, with the new members heavily underwritten by the US. But once the strategic rationale that motivated the Cold War had disappeared, it was only a matter of time before a US administration would come to power that would ask why they were underwriting security for dozens of European countries—a question to which there is no obviously compelling answer.

It was not inevitable that decades of bipartisan consensus on enlarging NATO would be replaced by an America First ideology that thumbed its nose at allies and adversaries alike. But by the time Donald Trump was elected in 2016, the opportunity to create a post–Cold War international order that would have been more genuinely rules-based had been so thoroughly squandered by the disastrous wars in Afghanistan and Iraq and by NATO's relentless eastward drive that a reckoning was long overdue. By then, George Washington's admonition to avoid permanent alliances seemed to contain notably more wisdom than the series of quicksilver rationalizations for NATO enlargement that had displaced one another since 1990. The world that successive post–Cold War leaders had bequeathed had not quite descended into a Hobbesian war of all against all. But it did resemble one conjured up by Lord Palmerston when he said of his country, "We have no eternal allies, and we have no perpetual enemies. Our interests are eternal and perpetual, and those interests it is our duty to follow."[56]

Chapter Three

The Demise of Humanitarian Intervention

NATO's Kosovo operation was the final blow to the Clinton administration's collapsing relations with Boris Yeltsin, but there was a silver lining: It put the subject of humanitarian intervention squarely on the international agenda. Five years earlier, in the most shocking display of organized barbarism at least since Mao Zedong's Cultural Revolution and the Khmer Rouge genocide, Rwanda's Hutu-led government had egged on soldiers and vigilantes to massacre over eight hundred thousand people, mostly members of the Tutsi minority. Harrowing press reports complete with graphic images of the ongoing slaughter prompted widespread demands for intervention. But the Clinton administration, still smarting from the images of dead American soldiers being dragged through the streets of Mogadishu, Somalia, six months earlier, balked. Procrastinating administration officials engaged in disingenuous hair-splitting over whether genocide was in fact underway, a failure for which Clinton would eventually apologize—but neither the US nor any other country intervened. *The Guardian* published widely reprinted images of UN peacekeepers standing by while armed Hutu militias charged by in search of victims, underscoring the world's abdication. "Never again!"—the endlessly repeated admonition from Buchenwald inmates liberated in 1945—rang hollow.[1]

The United Nations was created to prevent war between the major powers, but it was poorly suited to prevent governments from committing genocide or other major human rights abuses within their own borders. The UN grew from its original fifty-one members in 1945 to eventually include all the world's countries (except for the Vatican and Palestine, which have observer status), but it remains a treaty-based organization of sovereign states. Indeed, its charter supplies a more robust defense of the sanctity of nation-states than had previously existed in international law, prohibiting the threat or use of force against the territorial integrity or independence of any member. The only exceptions are for self-defense and with Security Council authorization. And the UN Charter is hard to change, requiring approval from two-thirds of its member states, including all permanent Security Council members. The UN did adopt the Convention on the Prevention and Punishment of Genocide in 1948, but the convention does not empower the UN to act as an organization. Instead, it imposes duties on member states to adopt relevant legislation and punish perpetrators. Governments that try to hold perpetrators accountable often confront formidable jurisdictional obstacles. The only way the UN as an organization can interfere in a country is with Security Council authorization—a high hurdle because any member can veto, as Russia certainly and China probably would have done had Clinton pursued that route in Kosovo in 1999.[2]

Yet Clinton left no doubt that he meant NATO's action in Kosovo to be precedent setting. "Never forget," he declared in a speech to the American forces who had conducted the operation, "if we can do this here, and if we can then say to the people of the world, whether you live in Africa, or Central Europe, or any other place, if somebody comes after innocent civilians and tries to kill them en masse because of their race, their ethnic background, or their religion, and it's within our power to stop it, we will stop it." Clinton could claim at least some moral high ground because, whatever the legal difficulties, NATO's seventy-six-day, high-altitude bombing campaign worked. True, five hundred civilians were killed by the bombing, but the Serb armies and paramilitaries had withdrawn, ending the bloodshed and ethnic cleansing. Considering the harsh criticism Clinton had endured for his inaction in Rwanda, it is not surprising that he saw the Kosovo outcome as warranting a victory lap.[3]

Western enthusiasm for NATO's Kosovo action was not matched in the Global South. India's government declared it to be "a flagrant violation of all international norms, against the provisions of the United Nations Charter, and seen as direct and unprovoked aggression." The Non-Aligned Movement and Organisation of African Unity both condemned it in terms echoed by South Africa's government when it declared that "unilateral intervention, no matter how noble the pretext, is not acceptable." The recently retired president of South Africa, Nelson Mandela, went further, arguing that it invited chaos into international relations and noting pointedly that the US "did not do this when the secretary-general of the UN was white."[4]

The Responsibility to Protect

Faced with the disjunction between the widespread celebration of the Kosovo intervention in much of the West and the widespread condemnation of it across much of the Global South, Western leaders sought to legitimate it. As UN Secretary General Kofi Annan put it in his 2000 Millennium Report, "If humanitarian intervention is, indeed, an unacceptable assault on sovereignty, how should we respond to a Rwanda, to a Srebrenica, to gross and systematic violation of human rights that offend every precept of our common humanity?" Annan went further in his Nobel Peace Prize acceptance speech the following year, insisting that "the sovereignty of States must no longer be used as a shield for gross violations of human rights." The question was: How can an organization that is constitutionally bound to respect national sovereignty also insist that it should be violated in the name of humanitarian intervention?[5]

An early attempt to square this circle came from an ad hoc commission appointed by Swedish Prime Minister Göran Persson in 1999. The commission, co-chaired by South African judge Richard Goldstone and Swedish politician Carl Tham, concluded that NATO's military intervention was "illegal but legitimate." Fleshing out this seeming oxymoron, they said that although the intervention was illegal because it lacked UN Security Council authorization, it was justified because "all diplomatic avenues had been exhausted and the intervention had the effect of liberating the majority population of Kosovo from a long period of oppression under Serbian rule."[6] This was not strictly true because Security Council authorization had not been sought, but in any case it amounted to a question-begging restatement of the problem. If unilateral intervention was warranted on behalf of the Kosovar Albanians, what of the Kurds in Turkey, Iraq, and Iran, the Rohingya in Myanmar, the Uighurs in China, or the Palestinians in the West Bank and Gaza? The list goes on. And who is entitled to intervene when there is no adjudicator? Anyone who decides to do so and has enough military heft to succeed? In 2008, Russia went into Georgia on behalf, they said, of the South Ossetians. Ditto when Iran began backing the Houthi in Yemen against the regime in Sanaa. That list goes on too.

If there was a principle behind the commission's "illegal but legitimate" slogan, it was something like: Sometimes it is better to ask for forgiveness than permission. But that was question begging too, because the Russians would have been just as likely to veto a request for absolution as they would have been to veto a request for permission—which is presumably why no such resolution was ever sought. More dangerously, going down this path has the potential to undermine the UN's raison d'être: to maintain international peace and security. That risk became evident in 2002 when the African Union responded to the commission's Kosovo report by asserting its right "to intervene in a Member State pursuant to a decision by the Assembly, in grave circumstances, namely war crimes, genocide and crimes against humanity." Tellingly, the AU made no mention of the Security Council, implicitly challenging the UN Charter, which reserves to the council a monopoly on the right to authorize the use of force in nondefensive situations. If NATO can flout this monopoly, the AU was in effect saying, so can the AU. But in that case, so could others. If the right to intervene is triggered when the intervening country, alliance, or organization deems it warranted, there is nothing left of the Security Council's unique role. Pursuing this approach courts the possibility of prolonging conflicts, especially in failed states and civil wars where different factions are backed by different outside players—as with Iran and Saudi Arabia in Yemen since 2014 and Turkey and Russia in Libya since 2020. The way to head off this parade of horribles was to find a way to institutionalize a mechanism to authorize humanitarian intervention.[7]

An early, and ultimately influential, attempt to do that came from another ad hoc commission, this one created at the behest of the Canadian government in September 2000. The International Commission on Intervention and State Sovereignty, co-chaired by Australian politician Gareth Evans and Algerian diplomat Mohamed Sahnoun, saw itself as responding to Kofi Annan's challenge to come up with criteria for humanitarian intervention that could be authorized and monitored by the Security Council. Though the commission was not a formal creation of the UN, seven of its twelve members had significant UN connections, and Sahnoun was a special advisor to Secretary General Annan. The commission's goal was to come up with principles that the UN would adopt and that would prompt the UN to create a mechanism to enforce them.

A year later, following an intensive series of roundtables held in major cities across the globe, the commission issued a report entitled *The Responsibility to Protect*, quickly immortalized as R2P. It imposed a responsibility on all governments to protect populations in their countries. The commission reasoned that its recommendations had the best chance of adoption if they were limited to the most egregious abuses: "Large scale loss of life, actual or apprehended, with genocidal intent or not," and "large scale 'ethnic cleansing,' actual or apprehended, whether carried out by killing, forced expulsion, acts of terror or rape." Military intervention to stop these abuses would be warranted regardless of whether they resulted from deliberate state action, neglect, inability to act, or in failed states. Intervention was warranted only as a last resort, however, and the force deployed should not exceed what was needed to secure the "defined human protection objective."[8]

The report had its desired effect. At its 2005 World Summit, the UN General Assembly unanimously adopted the R2P framework, restricting it to four types of mass atrocity: genocide, war crimes, ethnic cleansing, and crimes against humanity. The World Summit Outcome document declared that every government has a responsibility to protect its populations from those crimes. If a government fails to do so and other efforts at peaceful resolution fail, then the Security Council may authorize military intervention. The commitment, affirmed by the Security Council the following year, was hedged in by requirements that decisions to intervene be made on a case-by-case basis, that military action be a last resort, that the force deployed be proportionate, and that intervention be coordinated with relevant regional organizations.[9]

In view of R2P's subsequent fate, it is worth pausing to underscore what a remarkable development this was. It amounted to a fundamental revision of the UN Charter, unanimously adopted at a summit meeting attended by more than 170 heads of government. By adopting the Summit Outcome document, they were accepting that the General Assembly had taken on a role akin to a quasi-international legislature. Their decision imposed an enforceable responsibility on all governments to protect all people in their countries (not just citizens) from mass atrocities, and it created new powers for the Security Council to authorize military intervention if governments failed to live up to that responsibility. This represented a substantial evolution in the UN, transforming it into an organization that went well beyond the treaty that had created it—one that could impose new responsibilities on governments whether or not they recognized them. If it could be sensibly implemented, R2P had the potential to remake international law as it affected humanitarian intervention—giving it both legitimacy and teeth. This opportunity had not occurred before, and it would be unlikely to occur again if those charged with implementing it made a mess of it.

Initial developments were promising. In 2004, even before the Summit Outcome document was adopted, the Security Council referred to R2P when threatening Sudan with sanctions if it failed to disarm the Janjaweed militia in Darfur and hold perpetrators of major human rights violations there to account. In 2008, France cited R2P when calling for intervention in Kenya in the wake of major postelection violence that killed over a thousand people and displaced over six hundred thousand. A mediating team led by Kofi Annan resolved the conflict, but it was plausible that the prospect of intervention had helped, and the occasion became celebrated as the first case of R2P in action. In 2009, UN Secretary General Ban Ki-moon published a report spelling out strategies to prevent R2P violations and detailing a framework for UN intervention when that failed. He also floated the possibility of intervening in Cameroon when troops loyal to coup leader Dadis Camara began attacking opponents, a possibility that was short-circuited when Camara fled the country.[10] These early intimations of the UN's willingness to deploy R2P suggested that it had begun working its way into the fabric of international law, but it did not face a real test until 2011 in Libya.

R2P in Libya

In December 2010, a fruit vendor in Tunisia's regional capital, Sidi Bouzid, set himself on fire following a conflict with local authorities, sparking what would soon become known as the Arab Spring. Demonstrations erupted across the country, forcing Tunisia's longtime dictator, Ben Ali, to flee to Saudi Arabia and precipitating the regime's collapse. Protests spread like wildfire across the Middle East, from Algeria to Yemen, Jordan, Egypt, and Morocco. King Abdullah II of Jordan was forced to dismiss his government and initiate constitutional reforms. Algerian President Abdelaziz Bouteflika had to rescind his emergency powers. The Egyptian regime, widely regarded as one of the most stable in the region, began collapsing in February 2011 when President Hosni Mubarak resigned following weeks of mass protests centered in Cairo's Tahrir Square. In the next few weeks, protests spread to

Iraq, Bahrain, Oman, and Syria. The one part of the world that had been stubbornly immune to the waves of democratic reform that had swept away so many authoritarian systems since the 1980s finally seemed to be succumbing. Triumphalist expectations ran rife among Western commentators, summed up in Thomas Friedman's breathless declaration in *The New York Times*: "We're just at the start of something huge."[11]

Libya became embroiled in the turmoil early. In mid-February, protests broke out in Benghazi, quickly spreading to other major cities in a "day of revolt" that protestors hoped would replicate the outcomes in Tunisia and Egypt and enable them to topple the corrupt autocrat Muammar Gaddafi, who had been in power since the 1970s. But rather than accommodate the opposition or negotiate with its leaders, Gaddafi cracked down. His forces fired live ammunition at crowds, killing more than a dozen protestors. He even began releasing convicts from prison and paying them to attack demonstrators. Gaddafi's use of lethal force provoked a unanimous Security Council resolution imposing sanctions, including an arms embargo, and referring Gaddafi to the International Criminal Court.[12]

In some ways, Gaddafi's response was surprising. Since the early 2000s, he had been evolving into a less repressive autocrat and had taken significant steps to end his global pariah status. As early as 1996, the US State Department had noted a sharp reduction in Libyan sponsorship of terrorism. Three years later, Gaddafi agreed to extradite the Pan Am flight 103 hijackers for trial in The Hague and to compensate victims of that and other terrorist attacks in which Libya was implicated. He was one of the first Arab leaders to condemn the 9/11 attacks, lambasting the Taliban as "Godless promoters of political Islam." In 2002, he signed conventions to suppress financing for terrorism by marking plastic explosives for detection. The following year, he agreed to dismantle his nuclear weapons program. This led to the lifting of sanctions, after which he moved quickly to normalize relations with the Western countries. He increased oil exports to Europe and began consorting with French President Nicholas Sarkozy, Italian Prime Minister Silvio Berlusconi, and British Prime Minister Tony Blair, among others. He bought a share in Juventus, Italy's most successful football team, and sent his son to the London School of Economics. Gaddafi also became distinctly less repressive at home. All the major human rights abuses described in Amnesty International's 2010 report on Libya had taken place before the turn of the century. By that year, Gaddafi had morphed into a run-of-the-mill autocrat—not notably worse than others in the Middle East—who had greatly improved his relations with the West.[13]

Gaddafi's decision to fight the opposition in 2011 set Libya on a different course from the other Arab Spring countries. It wasn't so much that its prospects for democracy were dimmer. That mirage soon vanished in almost all of them, so that by April 2013, even Thomas Friedman was conceding that the term "Arab Spring" should be abandoned. Certainly, Libya, a classic oil-curse country with no democratic history or traditions, had never been a good prospect. That was obvious from the start, because the leaders of the so-called democratic opposition had long been senior figures in the Gaddafi regime, and none of them had ever displayed an interest in democracy. They included his former justice minister Abdul Jalil, his former ambassador to India Ali Aziz, and one of his top economic advisors, Mahmoud Jibril. Among the leaders of the "rebel" military council were Omar El-Hariri, an architect of the coup that brought Gaddafi to power in 1969, who had been imprisoned for participating in a failed coup to overthrow him six years later, and former Interior Ministry head General Abdul Fattah Younis. Both had long histories of repressing democratic movements. The February demonstrations gave them a pretext to try to seize power. When Gaddafi fought back, the country descended into civil war.[14]

Initially, the rebels made rapid gains. They seized the entire coastline from the oil-exporting port at Ras Lanuf to the Egyptian border. Then they took control of Misurata on the central coast, Zawiya and Zuwara just west of Tripoli, and major towns in the mountains to the southwest. By early March, they controlled at least half of Libya's populated areas and six of the nine largest cities. Many observers believed that Gaddafi's regime was collapsing. On March 5, the rebel forces in Benghazi, by then styling themselves Libya's National Transitional Council (NTC), declared themselves to be the country's sole representatives. Five days later, the French government recognized the NTC as the "legitimate representative" of the Libyan people. Italy would follow in April, the UK in May, and the US in June.[15]

But the epitaphs on the Gaddafi regime turned out to be premature. The early rebel successes had depended mainly on surprise, and the insurgency soon faltered in the face of a major counteroffensive by Gaddafi's forces. It took less than two weeks for him to regain control of almost all populated areas west of the rebel stronghold in Benghazi. When the rebels were on the verge of total defeat there, they began trumpeting claims—later revealed as somewhere between wildly exaggerated and flat-out false—of the actual and imminent slaughter of unarmed civilians in Benghazi by Gaddafi's forces. Western governments affirmed these claims, as did the media, almost without exception. This triggered calls across the region to impose no-fly zones against the Libyan air force and the adoption of SC 1973 by the Security Council, authorizing foreign intervention "to protect civilians and civilian populated areas under threat of attack."[16]

Political scientist Alan Kuperman points out that the justification for intervention in Libya was based on reports that exaggerated the death toll by a factor of ten. Claims that Gaddafi was targeting civilians came from less than credible sources: principally an opposition that was hoping to get external support in a civil war that it was losing. In fact, there was no indiscriminate targeting of civilians, and—also contrary to contemporaneous claims by rebel groups—Gaddafi's forces did not engage in reprisals in cities as they retook them. Even in Misrata, a city of 400,000 where the fighting was most intense, a total of 257 were killed and 949 wounded on all sides of the conflict, of whom 22 were women and 8 were children. The story in Tripoli was comparable. Of the 200 corpses seen in the city's morgue by Human Rights Watch, all were adults and only two were women—hardly evidence of indiscriminate civilian slaughter. Some of the exaggerated press accounts of killing during the uprising can be traced to a French physician in Benghazi who extrapolated from a tiny sample in one hospital to claim that more than 2,000 deaths had occurred there by February 21, when in reality Human Rights Watch could identify only 233 deaths in the entire country by that date. But for the most part, the deceptive claims and numbers were taken largely on trust from rebel sources when there were good reasons to be skeptical of them.[17]

The West's rush to judgment is best understood in light of what happened subsequently. SC 1973, adopted on March 17, was the first time the Security Council had invoked R2P to authorize external intervention in a country, so it was a major precedent in the making. The resolution restricted intervening forces to enforcing no-fly zones and doing what was needed to protect endangered civilians. In conformity with the proportionality requirements of the 2005 Summit Outcome document, it prohibited the introduction of foreign ground troops. It created an exception to the arms embargo that had been imposed three weeks earlier to limit Gaddafi's ability to resupply his forces, but only for the purpose of protecting civilians. It said nothing about regime change, or even about taking sides in the civil war. Instead, it demanded a ceasefire. These limitations were vital not only to avoiding a veto on the Security Council (Russia and China abstained, along with Brazil, India, and Germany), but also to securing support from the African Union and the Arab League. This conformed with the Summit Outcome document's call for cooperation with relevant regional organizations. The limitations were in any case vital for the legitimacy of an intervention that would be enforced by NATO in a conflict that had nothing to do with the national security of its members.

It rapidly became obvious that the intervening powers were committed to the different agenda of toppling the Gaddafi regime. The day the resolution passed was the same day France recognized the NTC as the legitimate government of Libya. US, French, and British forces immediately imposed a naval blockade and began attacking Gaddafi's forces with Tomahawk missiles and bombing sorties across the country. Gaddafi's air force was destroyed in the first three days without the loss of a single Western aircraft, effectively completing the no-fly-zone part of the mission. At that point, in talks brokered by retired US Navy Rear Admiral Charles Kubic, Gaddafi's government proposed a plan calling for a ceasefire in which they would stop combat operations, withdraw from major cities, assume a defensive posture, and perhaps even negotiate a transitional government that would involve Gaddafi stepping down. The Obama administration unilaterally ended the negotiations, instead ramping up attacks on Gaddafi's forces with the clear intention of toppling him. The African Union denounced this operation two days after it began and tried to negotiate a ceasefire between Gaddafi and the NTC. The next day, the Arab League's secretary general, Amr Moussa, condemned the wide scope of the bombing campaign as going well beyond SC 1973's authority to enforce a no-fly zone to protect civilians, contending that if anything, it would increase civilian fatalities.[18]

These complaints fell on deaf ears. The following week, asked by a reporter how long British forces would remain involved, the Royal Air Force's Air Vice-Marshal Greg Bagwell replied, "You'll have to ask Colonel Gaddafi how long he wants to go on for but we're here for the long term." For the next eight months, NATO flew thousands of bombing sorties against Gaddafi's forces and supplied the rebels with weapons, training, logistical support, and supplies. Obama repeatedly denied that his agenda was regime change, but the evidence is overwhelming that NATO forces intended that result from the start, in flagrant disregard of the express limitations imposed by SC 1973. Obama himself had demanded that Gaddafi leave office two weeks before SC 1973 was adopted. When Gaddafi accepted the African Union's April cease-fire proposal, Obama supported the rebels' refusal to discuss any truce that did not require regime change. The same happened the following month when Gaddafi proposed a deal that included paying compensation to victims and negotiating a new constitution.[19]

By insisting on regime change, Obama was reflecting what was becoming bipartisan opinion on Capitol Hill. As Senators Joseph Lieberman and Marco Rubio put it with unusual candor in *The Wall Street Journal* in June 2011, regardless of the wisdom of the original intervention, NATO countries now faced an overwhelming imperative to get rid of Gaddafi because he would exact revenge against them if he remained in power. NATO acted accordingly, refusing to end its operation until Gaddafi was killed in October in his native Sirte—provoking Secretary of State Hillary Clinton's smug comment "We came, we saw, he died." There was never any doubt that NATO's goal was to enable the rebels to topple Gaddafi. They achieved it at the cost of prolonging the war by eight months and increasing the death toll by seven to ten times. That did not stop

Western commentators from celebrating the operation as a success and declaring it a triumph for R2P.[20]

It soon became obvious that it was neither. The Western powers made minimal investments to help rebuild the country. Unsurprisingly, the NTC never became a functioning government or even succeeded in disarming hostile militias once NATO withdrew. The secular moderate coalition government elected in July of 2012 quickly fell apart in acrimonious regional rivalries. The central government was unable to reestablish anything remotely resembling the monopoly of coercive force that is essential to a functioning national state, let alone the pro-American one that Senators John McCain and Marco Rubio, among others, had confidently predicted. The result was continuing militia battles over control of the major cities, airports, and government buildings, and new footholds for jihadist militias in Libya and its neighbors. By late 2014, ISIS had moved into Libya, seizing control of Derna near the Egyptian border. Both Obama and Hillary Clinton gloss over the debacle in their memoirs, begging the question why they, the French, and the British were so determined to topple Gaddafi in the first place. For Obama, who had opposed the Iraq invasion and was trying to extricate the US from the Middle East to pivot to Asia, it was a case of one step backward followed by another two.[21]

Much of the momentum to topple Gaddafi came from Europeans with major oil investments in Libya. They acted on the early predictions that his regime was finished to protect their interests in what they believed would be the new Libyan order. The NTC's Ali Aziz had close links to the oil multinationals dating back to his time in Gaddafi's government when British Petroleum had committed to spending more than $1 billion in Libyan oil exploration. The Italian company Eni was producing over a quarter million barrels of oil daily and operated a 310-kilometer pipeline between Libya and Sicily that was shut down by the civil war. Britain's Shell and the French multinational Total had also made commitments to invest in Libyan oil when the civil war broke out, which they were keen to pursue. The rebels promised favorable treatment once the dust settled, even if they and the Sarkozy government denied reports in the French media that the NTC had promised them 35 percent of future crude oil "in exchange for the total and permanent support for our council." The rebels also made it clear that Russia, China, and Brazil, who had abstained from SC 1973 and equivocated about regime change, would fare less well.[22]

Having backed what was turning out to be the wrong horse, the Europeans found themselves in a bind. Gaddafi had suspended diplomatic relations with France as soon as Sarkozy recognized the NTC. He was not going to be any more favorably inclined to the other countries that had jumped on the bandwagon when it looked as though he was finished. Rather than have to deal with a victorious Gaddafi who believed he had been burned by his erstwhile allies, they decided to get behind the NTC and help it topple him—which is what they did. Claims that they were protecting civilians were not remotely credible once that threat disappeared after the first few days of the bombing campaign. In fact, the insurgents, not Gaddafi's forces, were perpetrating the bulk of the violence. Yet in April, Britain, France, and the US declared that they would not end the war until Gaddafi left office. This wasn't mission creep. It was a mission leap. Unsurprisingly, Russia and China expressed outrage at the subterfuge, a charge that would later be validated in a report commissioned by Britain's House of Commons.[23]

Sarkozy was pivotal in pressing the other Western powers to support military action. Apart from his concerns about French oil interests, he seems to have been trying to bolster his low popularity at home, respond to criticism for having sat on the sidelines when events in Tunisia erupted, and distance himself from Gaddafi when the latter appeared to be losing the war and had become unpopular with other Middle Eastern leaders. Sarkozy's long association with the dictator, which reportedly included Gaddafi illegally funding his 2007 presidential campaign (for which Sarkozy would eventually be convicted and sentenced to five years in prison), had become an embarrassment he sought to shed. He was also strongly influenced by the sometime public intellectual Bernard-Henri Lévy. Lévy had a comic history of gullibility, coupled with enthusiasm for deploying Western military force to "liberate" Muslim peoples, so it is unsurprising that he convinced himself that Libya's opposition forces would be harbingers of democracy. But it is remarkable that he not only insinuated himself into the NTC's leadership ranks but also brokered the meetings between them and Sarkozy in early March, which led to Sarkozy's decision to recognize the NTC—bypassing the French minister of foreign affairs, Alain Juppé, in the process.[24]

Even more remarkably, Lévy brokered a meeting between Libyan opposition leader Mahmoud Jibril and Hillary Clinton on March 14 during her visit to Paris for the G8. Jibril reportedly won Clinton over because he seemed "impressive and reasonable" and he "said all the right things about how a future Libya would be governed." This conversation led her to overcome her skepticism and support those in the administration who were pushing for armed intervention in Libya. This meant ignoring the Germans, who opposed intervention in what they saw clearly was an ongoing civil war. Foreign Minister Guido Westerwelle worried that intervention would escalate the conflict, with unpredictable consequences for European interests in the region. The Italians, who had signed a Treaty of Friendship with Gaddafi in 2008, cementing their status as Libya's largest trading partner, were also equivocal. Foreign Minister Franco Frattini, who worried about reports of a Muslim Brotherhood presence among the insurgents, was reluctant to act on uncorroborated reports of the use of violence against civilians in support of an unfathomable alternative. Frattini climbed aboard only when it became clear that the momentum for regime change was unstoppable.[25]

As with Europe's leaders, the Obama administration was divided. Special Assistant for Human Rights Samantha Power, who was a strong R2P advocate, pushed hard for US military intervention, as did UN Ambassador Susan Rice and Deputy National Security Advisor Ben Rhodes, but the senior figures in Obama's military and national security teams were all opposed. Most vocal were Defense Secretary Robert Gates and Chairman of the Joint Chiefs Mike Mullen, but Vice President Joe Biden, White House Chief of Staff Bill Daley, National Security Advisors John Brennan and Tom Donilon, and Deputy National Security Adviser Denis McDonough were all opposed to military action. Gates, who told aides that he would likely have resigned over Libya had his retirement not been imminent, was surprised that Obama—who had campaigned against the Iraq invasion—would go looking for a new war in the Middle East while the US was struggling so badly in the other two. Gates was even skeptical of the no-fly zone proposal, partly because there was no evidence that Gaddafi was using his air force against the rebels and partly because enforcing it would be an act of war that might provoke escalation and make Americans targets in the region. Once Obama had decided on intervention and Gates found himself defending administration policy, he had no answers for the obvious questions from journalists and senators. Why was toppling Gaddafi in America's interest? Might it not empower terrorists rather than usher in a democratic regime? Wasn't this committing the US to another open-ended conflict? Wouldn't it involve costly nation-building? If not, what was the endgame?[26]

Whether Obama said he was "leading from behind" in Libya or it was a description by one of his staffers, he was uncharacteristically passive. Gates, to whom Obama said that it was a 51–49 decision, doubted that he would have gone forward without Clinton's advocacy. Obama was determined to turn the intervention into a NATO operation as quickly as possible to diffuse responsibility onto Sarkozy and the other European leaders who were so keen to intervene, even though there is no NATO operation in which the US is not centrally implicated. Obama subsequently conceded in an interview that "failing to plan for the day after" in Libya was probably the biggest mistake of his presidency, while continuing nonetheless to insist that intervening had been "the right thing to do." But that begs the question of what that planning could plausibly have entailed.[27]

The United States had learned the hard way in Afghanistan and Iraq that creating failed states is a lot easier than transforming them into viable ones. David Petraeus established in Iraq that fledgling governments facing insurgencies will be able to defeat them only if the civilians among whom the insurgents operate can be confident of their security from reprisal. This insight led to his major revision of US counterinsurgency doctrine, detailed in the 2006 *Counterinsurgency Field Manual*, built around the idea that it is vital not only to drive insurgents out of the areas they occupy but also to build enduring security for populations that would otherwise be vulnerable to their return. Because the government cannot provide that security on its own, the responsibility falls to the outside players on which the government depends to supply the wherewithal: substantial military capability and investments in building up and training domestic security forces. By the time of the Libyan intervention, experience in Iraq and Afghanistan had made clear that successful counterinsurgency requires vastly larger and longer troop commitments than American presidents are willing to contemplate. In this case, the ratio of one security force member for every fifty civilians called for in the *Field Manual* would have meant providing a force of 126,000 security personnel.[28]

Even if American presidents were willing to make commitments of this order, success is not guaranteed. Among others, Karl Eikenberry, a former US military chief and later an ambassador in Afghanistan, has pointed out that governments that rely on foreign forces and resources to defeat insurgents might never succeed. They are stuck with the Hobson's choice that was Hamid Karzai's undoing: They cannot win without external support, but the population might never trust in security that depends on external support. After all, the security that was achieved by the US surge that General Petraeus led in Iraq's Anbar Province in 2007 collapsed when the US withdrew four years later. Ditto for the surge in Afghanistan's Helmand and Kandahār Provinces in 2009–2010. The Taliban forces were never completely driven out, and they seized both provinces as soon as the US left a decade later. Setting aside both the improbable proposition that underwriting the rebels could have brought democracy to Libya and the inevitable legitimacy deficit any NATO-backed government would have faced, the US and its allies would still have confronted enormous challenges in creating a viable state there.[29]

At the very least, it would have taken massive investments not only in the military and security services, but also in Libya's devastated economy. But Obama had phased out of Iraq and put a strict time limit on the military surge in Afghanistan because he did not believe American voters had any appetite to continue funding expensive foreign ventures that were not vital to US national security. His refusal to countenance US ground troops in Libya and his eagerness to shift the military costs to the Europeans reflected that understanding. US financial aid to Libya had never been substantial, and—aside from releasing $25 million in frozen funds to the rebels a month after the civil war erupted—Obama never showed any interest in investing in the country. His administration gave between $70 million and $80 million a year until 2014, after which aid to Libya fell substantially. Despite modest increases in the early years of the first Trump administration, neither Obama nor Biden—whose opposition to the Libya operation as vice president centered on the lack of a credible plan for the aftermath—was willing to give significant aid to Libya, a country that no US administration has deemed vital to America's interests. Of the $600 billion spent on US foreign aid between 2013 and 2022, $787 million—or 0.13 percent—went to Libya. Any suggestion that Obama could have sold a substantial peace-building endeavor in Libya to Congress or American voters would be disingenuous, a fantasy, or both.[30]

Apart from those with R2P motivations, enthusiasm for the Libya mission was helped along by the belief, which had fast become orthodox in some circles, that the Arab Spring revolutions would sideline al-Qaeda. The empirical basis for this conviction remains puzzlingly elusive, not least because jihadist leaders saw the Arab Spring revolutions, and especially the prospect of Gaddafi's fall, as an opportunity to expand their influence in Libya and the region. Bin Laden, who had predicted that when Gaddafi fell he could open a beachhead into North Africa that would turn Libya into "the Somalia of the Mediterranean," welcomed the uprising. As he said in the journal that he dictated to his daughter shortly before his death, "This chaos and the absence of leadership in the revolutions is the best environment to spread al-Qaeda's thoughts and ideas." Gaddafi had been at the forefront of the fight against al-Qaeda for a decade, both in Libya and the region, and al-Qaeda militants were quick to sign up, along with other fundamentalist clerics, with the "rebels" fighting him. They were all happy to play along with the fiction of a popular uprising for their own purposes. This turned out to be a good bet for them, as they have thrived in the failed state that Libya has become.[31]

Obama's passive obtuseness in the face of these realities was a surprising lapse of judgment from a president who was usually clear-eyed and assertive. He had no trouble standing up to the defense establishment and the generals when they wanted to extend and expand American commitments in Iraq and Afghanistan.[32] Yet here they were arguing vehemently against the operation in Libya that he supported. He should at least have demanded serious fact-checking of the extravagant claims about imminent civilian slaughter and pushed the advocates of toppling Gaddafi to supply credible arguments about the desirability of what would come next. His capitulation to the European—and especially Sarkozy's—agenda to create unstoppable momentum for regime change calls to mind a comparable event fifty-five years earlier, when France, Britain, and Israel attacked Egypt after its president, Gamal Abdel Nasser, had nationalized the Suez Canal. President Eisenhower, who did not agree to the operation in advance and judged it reckless and unjustified, led the worldwide condemnation of the attack at the UN General Assembly and brought substantial diplomatic and economic pressure on the belligerents to abandon the venture—which they grudgingly did. That was the kind of American leadership that was sorely needed but notably missing in Libya in 2011.

The full costs of the Libyan intervention in lives, dollars, discredited NATO leadership, and regional fallout will not be known for decades, but there is no doubt that they have been enormous. A decade and a half after Gaddafi's fall, the so-called Government of National Unity in Tripoli controlled about a third of the northern (populated) part of the country with the backing of loosely allied militias. A competing Tobruk-based government in the east controlled the remaining two-thirds, backed by a militia loyal to the self-appointed Field Marshall Khalifa Haftar. Libya had joined Iraq and Afghanistan as one more failed state in the Middle East for which the West bore substantial responsibility. We cannot know what Libya would look like today had Gaddafi's regime not been toppled in 2011, but we do know that the US, France, and Britain engaged in a reckless gambit, despite strong opposition from sober voices within American and NATO leadership, with predictably damaging results. Some of the most ardent cheerleaders for the intervention would eventually be forced to admit this.[33]

Libya's Legacy

The legacy across the region was disastrous. Radical Islamists, long suppressed by Gaddafi, refused to disarm after the war and prospered as they had anticipated they would. Ironically, in view of French and American enthusiasm for toppling Gaddafi, these radicals mounted successful attacks on the French embassy in Tripoli and the US embassy in Benghazi, killing the US ambassador and three other embassy staff. Even more ironically, Hillary Clinton was relentlessly—and unfairly—attacked during her 2016 presidential campaign over lax security at the embassy, while the much more consequential failure in Libya, where she had played a pivotal role in persuading Obama, was hiding in plain sight.[34]

The most damaging regional by-product of Gaddafi's fall was in Mali, hitherto one of West Africa's few stable democracies. Malian ethnic Tuareg fighters in Gaddafi's security forces fled home with their weapons and launched a rebellion, triggering a military coup. The Tuareg rebellion was then hijacked by local Ansar Dine Islamists. They quickly gained control of large swaths of northern Mali, imposed Sharia law, and displaced hundreds of thousands of people, generating a humanitarian catastrophe. France intervened, sending four thousand troops when the rebels were advancing on the capital city, Bamako. Paris planned for a brief operation, after which UN peacekeepers from Chad and elsewhere were supposed to take over. But the peacekeepers failed to materialize, and although the French drove the rebels deep into the mountains on the Algerian border, they were not defeated before France pulled out most of its troops. The result has been a grinding conflict punctuated by a series of failed peace agreements between the government and the rebels, who continue pressing for an Islamic state in the north of the country.[35]

Nor was the regional fallout limited to Mali. A 2013 UN Security Council report documented extensive weapons flows from the remnants of Gaddafi's arsenals to Islamist rebels across North Africa. Fifteen thousand man-portable surface-to-air missiles, capable of shooting down civilian airliners, were never recovered. Some fell into the hands of al-Qaeda's North African affiliates, some went to Boko Haram in Niger and Northern Nigeria, and some ended up with Hamas in Gaza. Even more soberingly, political scientists Alan Kuperman and Marc Lynch have both identified evidence of fallout in Syria, where the so-called moral hazard of intervention kicked in. Comparatively peaceful protesters against Bashar al-Assad's regime saw the NATO intervention in Libya turn the tide against Gaddafi and then turned to violence themselves, anticipating that the predictable crackdown from Assad would bring NATO into Syria as well.[36]

Whether or not these commentators are right about the cause of Assad's escalation, NATO's action in Libya left Obama and other Western leaders toothless to do much about it. China and Russia, whose abstentions had facilitated the adoption of SC 1973, quickly condemned the Libya regime change agenda as unauthorized. Having been played for suckers there, they remained intransigent in resisting the imposition of significant costs on Syria despite the regime's escalating human rights abuses. In August 2011, Obama started insisting publicly that "Assad must go." He and British Prime Minister David Cameron then warned that Assad would cross a red line if he deployed chemical weapons, only to be humiliated when Assad called their bluff and it became clear that neither could muster the domestic political support needed to respond. Ironically, it was Putin who seized the diplomatic high ground by negotiating the decommissioning of Syria's chemical weapons, ensuring Russia's reemergence as an influential player in the Middle East.[37]

The Libyan debacle highlighted challenges to institutionalizing R2P that had not been evident after the relatively straightforward Kosovo operation. By the time of NATO's intervention there in 1999, the former Yugoslavia was already a failed state that had been in a condition of more or less continuous civil war for the better part of a decade. The evidence of ongoing ethnic cleansing and other major human rights abuses had been widely documented. The US and the other NATO powers had no significant interests in Kosovo, giving them plausible claims to having clean hands. The intervention took place before the 2003 Iraq invasion that so sullied America's international image. It helped, too, that the goal in Kosovo was to protect a Muslim population. This muted the—nonetheless significant—criticism that the operation provoked in the Muslim world and the Global South. Moreover, the operation was brief and evidently successful, fostering what would turn out to be unwarranted confidence in the effectiveness of "surgical" uses of air power. And the conflict ended in an agreement that led Yugoslav forces to withdraw from Kosovo. As foreign interventions go, it had a happy ending.

In Libya, by contrast, the intervention took place at the start of the conflict, when its trajectory and likely outcome were still unclear. The claims and counterclaims about human rights atrocities were debatable and debated, and anyway they became moot after the first few days of the operation. The intervening powers had manifest interests at stake in Libya, belying any pretense of disinterest. The intervention took place after a decade of stalemated NATO presence in Afghanistan and the Iraq invasion, both of which had taken their toll on Western—and especially American—credibility. Whatever might have been left of that credibility was shattered in Libya once it became obvious that the agenda had been regime change from the start. The final nail in the coffin was Western leaders' brushing aside of multiple overtures to negotiate a settlement—from Gaddafi and from regional third parties alike—rubbishing any pretense that they were acting as agents of the Security Council, whose arms embargo they were violating in any case. On top of all that, the intervention was a spectacular failure that eliminated any hope of gaining legitimacy from a felicitous outcome.

Beyond the damage in Libya and across the region, the operation's destructive consequences for the fledgling doctrine of R2P would be hard to overstate. Embedding the "illegal but legitimate" impulse behind R2P in international practice was always going to be a heavy lift considering the strong UN presumptions against interference and the domestic political constraints that operate on leaders in international politics. Getting the UN to adopt the World Summit Outcome document had been a major achievement by its proponents, but it was obviously a precarious one that depended heavily on judicious deployment of force by intervening powers if it was to gain any meaningful prospect of achieving traction as an enforceable norm. The challenge is built into the doctrine by the discretion that it confers on the Security Council and enforcing countries. R2P empowers the council to authorize intervention when governments fail to protect their populations from genocide, crimes against humanity, war crimes, or ethnic cleansing, but it does not *oblige* the council to authorize intervention.

Nor does it oblige members to enforce an R2P resolution once the Security Council adopts it. Entrenching R2P into international law and practice would have required countries that can exploit this discretion for national benefit to resist the temptation, which they signally failed to do in Libya.

There would have been no chance of weaving something like R2P into the fabric of international law during the Cold War, underscoring how much the NATO powers squandered when they abused it so cavalierly in Libya. Despite misgivings, Russia and China had agreed not to veto SC 1973, even though the resolution contained no oversight provisions, simply requesting that the intervening powers keep the council informed of their activities. For R2P to have had a fighting chance, the intervening powers would have needed to exemplify the sagacious restraint George H. W. Bush showed in resisting the pressure to topple Saddam Hussein in 1991. Whereas his son trashed that possibility twelve years later, it was Obama, Sarkozy, and Cameron whose actions ensured that R2P would be stillborn. They blew a rare opportunity to nurture and strengthen unprecedented limits on what barbarous governments can do with impunity. Instead, they indulged mercenary interests by co-opting the fledgling doctrine and abusing it for their own purposes. This undermined their credibility as plausible agents of R2P enforcement, ceding the moral high ground to adversaries and critics. Had they shown the requisite restraint in Libya, better options might have been available in Syria—not to mention in subsequent conflicts in Myanmar, Ukraine, Israel, Gaza, and elsewhere.[38]

Chapter Four

Obama's Missteps

The shock of Donald Trump's election in 2016 and the relentless dramas in his first administration took the spotlight off Obama, but history will not treat major parts of his domestic agenda any more kindly than it will his foreign policy. The financial crisis that erupted in the final months of Obama's first presidential campaign created major challenges for the incoming administration, but it also gave him more leverage than any president in more than seven decades had enjoyed. It gave him the chance to abandon the neoliberal orthodoxy that Democrats had been embracing since the Carter administration, the legitimacy of which was collapsing along with the financial markets. Like FDR in 1932, he could have made protecting Main Street the condition for saving Wall Street. Also like FDR, he could have started reorienting the economy toward more inclusive growth, reversing decades of wage stagnation and insecurity that were fueling widespread discontent among Democratic voters. This could have become a template for other center-left parties to reject the neoliberal model in favor of policies that might have restored their atrophying electoral bases. Yet as he did in the international sphere, Obama continued the American practice of ignoring those harmed by his policies who were not in a position to stop him. Also as happened in the international sphere, the bill would come due once they found that they could retaliate.

Obama did have one major domestic success. The Affordable Care Act—informally known as Obamacare—was a signal accomplishment that should not be gainsaid. It delivered the only meaningful extension of health insurance coverage since the adoption of Medicare and Medicaid in 1965, despite numerous failed efforts over the intervening decades. Obamacare would, however, have been notably more secure but for major missteps that left it vulnerable to future attacks. Central among these were Obama's response to the 2008 financial crisis and his complicit role in entrenching the highly regressive 2001 Bush tax cuts that were due to expire in 2010. Obama's choices reinforced the stagnation of working- and middle-class incomes and accelerated inequalities that had been growing since the 1970s, cementing the Democrats' image as handmaidens of coastal financial elites—an image that would cost them dearly in the 2016 elections and even more dramatically in 2024.

At first sight, Obama's approach was surprising. After all, he took office in January of 2009 with the wind at his back. His approval rating stood at 70 percent. After less than four years in national politics, he had soundly defeated Vietnam War hero and three-term Senator John McCain, winning the popular vote by more than seven percentage points and the Electoral College by a decisive 365 to 173—the best performance by a Democrat since Lyndon Johnson's landslide in 1964. Democrats had more than doubled their House majority to seventy-nine and picked up eight Senate seats. Counting the two independents who caucused with them and Arlen Specter, who switched parties in April, they had a filibuster-proof supermajority until they lost the deceased Ted Kennedy's Massachusetts seat in a special election the following January. The new president had decisive control of a unified government.

Republicans, on the other hand, were about as far back on their heels as anyone in Washington could remember. George W. Bush had left office with a 22 percent approval rating, the lowest on record. He had presided over two disastrously inconclusive wars and the worst economic meltdown since the Great Depression, which was widely blamed on his aggressive deregulatory agenda and inept economic team. He had squandered the budget surplus inherited from Bill Clinton on the wars, on regressive tax cuts that would cost the Treasury $1.2 trillion over a decade, and on hundreds of billions in giveaways to Big Pharma for Medicare prescription drugs. By any measure, Bush left office as the most discredited president since Richard Nixon had been forced to resign because of the Watergate scandal in 1974.[1]

Remarkably, Bush had managed to enact his ambitious domestic agenda despite having been dealt a much weaker political hand in 2000 than Obama would eight years later. Republicans lost seats in both chambers, leaving them with a slim nine-seat House majority and an evenly divided Senate. Bush himself lost the popular vote and squeaked to an Electoral College win only with a dubious assist from the five conservative Supreme Court justices, scarcely a mandate for anything at all. Yet he led aggressively from the start, with a sweeping deregulatory agenda and massive tax cuts that were enacted in record time—less than five months into his presidency and before the rallying effect that would strengthen him following the terrorist attacks on September 11, 2001.

Despite Obama's much stronger position and incomparably greater rhetorical skills, he made little use of his political capital. On taking office, he sidelined his economic advisors from the campaign—former Federal Reserve Chairman Paul Volcker, Chicago economist Austan Goolsbee, and Chairman and CEO of UBS Group Robert Wolf, all of whom advocated extensive restructuring of financial markets—in favor of former Treasury Secretary Larry Summers, former president of the New York Federal Reserve Tim Geithner, and former chair of the House Democratic Caucus Rahm Emanuel. In 2006, Summers had famously sought to bury Nixon's dictum "We are all Keynesians now" with the epitaph "We are all Friedmanites now." He and Geithner were widely associated with the deregulatory agenda that had led up to the financial crisis—culminating in the 1999 repeal of the last vestiges of the Glass-Steagall Act, which had separated commercial from investment banking. Throughout Obama's first term, they worked with Emanuel to clip the wings of his reform agenda and push for policies that were much closer to what might have come out of the Clinton administration, in which they had all served. The result was that Obama's response to the financial crisis and his signature domestic achievements—Obamacare and regulatory reform—were notably less extensive than they could otherwise have been.[2]

The Perils of Triangulation

Obama's accommodationist stance exemplified the "triangulation" Bill Clinton had pioneered in the 1990s. The idea—brainchild of former Republican strategist and Clinton friend Dick Morris—was to adopt enough from the Republican playbook to erode centrist support, secure in the knowledge that a disgruntled Democratic base would have nowhere to go. Triangulation seemed especially attractive after the collapse of communism. Once capitalism was the only game in town, Clinton and his New Democrats believed that they didn't need to worry about being outflanked on their left. For them, the political challenge was to convince voters that they were more responsible technocrats than the Republicans, better able to run the government and manage the economy through the vicissitudes of the business cycle. Triangulation marked Clinton's approach to welfare and criminal justice reform, trade policy, deficits, and much else besides—stealing Republican thunder in order, he hoped, to reestablish the dominance Democrats had enjoyed in Washington for much of the post–World War II era but had ceded with the advent of supply-side economics in the 1980s.

It didn't work out that way. Early on, it became clear that triangulation might be a good tactic, but in today's America it is bad strategy. Once the Republicans understood what the Democrats were doing, they responded by shifting the goalposts: adopting what previously had been fringe right-wing policies and then dragging the Democrats toward them. Bush's tax cuts were a case in point, a culmination of the "starve the beast" approach to shrinking government that dated back to Proposition 13 in California in 1978, which had placed a 1 percent maximum on the property taxes that funded major parts of the state and local budgets. Bill Clinton had leapt aboard this bandwagon when running for his second term. "The era of big government is over," he declared in his 1996 State of the Union Address while advocating draconian welfare reforms that the Republican Congress would enact later that year.[3]

By the time Bush took office five years later, Republican candidates were routinely signing pledges never to raise taxes under threat of sanction from Americans for Tax Reform, led by antitax activist Grover Norquist. A measure of how far the goalposts had moved was the reform of the estate tax, paid only by the wealthiest 2 percent of Americans, and half of which was paid by the wealthiest half of 1 percent. As recently as 1994, Newt Gingrich had proposed only modest increases to the exemption when designing his Contract with America. Bush's 2001 act phased out the tax by 2010, with the Democrats supplying fifty-eight House votes and twelve in the Senate.[4]

In theory this shouldn't happen. Triangulation by one party in a two-party system should force the other toward the political middle for fear of alienating mainstream voters. That would be true in a well-functioning two-party system, but the United States doesn't have a well-functioning two-party system. Primaries with low turnouts and caucuses dominated by activists on the party fringes pull the parties apart, a dynamic that has become more potent in recent decades due to the steady increase in the number of safe seats—seats that are not competitive in the general election, making the primary the only election that matters. There are more safe seats now partly because of migration, especially urbanization; partly because of the overrepresentation of rural areas and gerrymandering; and partly as a by-product of majority-minority districts, which tend to be safe Democratic seats surrounded by safe Republican seats—which is why the Reagan Justice Department got behind the move to increase majority-minority districts in the 1980s. The cumulative effect of these developments has been a steady increase in the number of safe seats, to the point where fewer than 10 percent of House seats are competitive between the parties. General elections have become decreasingly relevant as a result.

In this world, party leaders find it hard to manage their caucuses to enact policies that benefit most voters. This has been less of an issue for Democrats, whose left flank has been on the defensive in recent decades due to the apparent failure of Keynesian demand management to deal with the stagflation of the 1970s and the discrediting of planned economies after 1989. As a result, many in the progressive wing of the party have gone along with triangulation despite their antipathy for it. They complain when their priorities like free college tuition and Medicare for All are watered down by party leaders, but enough of them have gone along enough of the time for the party to hold together. The right wing of the Republican Party has, by contrast, been more ruthless and effective in flexing its muscles and demanding a hard-right social agenda and supply-side economic policies that orthodox Republicans used to dismiss as voodoo economics. This has fueled the Republicans' frontal assault on the New Deal and Great Society orthodoxies that both parties had largely accepted for the middle third of the twentieth century. And because more Republican House members are in safe seats than Democrats, they have been a more potent disruptive force in their party than their Democratic counterparts have been in theirs.[5]

This disruptiveness has become a standard feature of intraparty Republican politics since Newt Gingrich's 1990 attack on George H. W. Bush for backtracking on his pledge not to raise taxes two years earlier, widely believed to have contributed to his defeat by Bill Clinton in 1992. House Republicans routinely buck their leaderships with impunity. John Boehner, Paul Ryan, and Kevin McCarthy all found leading the House Republicans so challenging that they either quit in frustration or were forced out, and Mike Johnson only held on with a lifeline from Democrats in the final months of the 118th Congress. By contrast, Nancy Pelosi remained at the Democratic helm as either Minority Leader or Speaker continuously from 2003 to 2023, when she retired on her own terms—reflecting the Democrats' greater cohesiveness.

Practically the only policy that unites Republicans is tax cuts. Even on a high-valence issue like repealing the Affordable Care Act, which they voted to do seventy-one times when they were the opposition party, once in power they could not muster the support to enact it. Senate Republicans rejected the single bill that squeaked through the House, and there was no other bill they could agree on. Centrist Republicans vetoed bills that were acceptable to the far right and vice versa. After Republicans won back the House with a slim majority in the 2022 midterms, it became impossible for McCarthy or Johnson to unite them behind any policy agenda at all, limiting them to investigations, impeachment efforts, and battles over their own leadership. The second Trump administration confirmed the pattern. Despite the return of unified Republican control of Congress and the White House in 2025, extending and increasing Trump's 2017 tax cuts became the nonnegotiable centerpiece of his legislative agenda. Tax cuts were the quid pro quo to get conflicting Republican factions to acquiesce to his Medicaid cuts, the addition of trillions to the national debt, and spending billions on border enforcement.

Obama got an early taste of this world three weeks into his presidency. Candidate Obama had endorsed the Republican Treasury Secretary Hank Paulson's emergency stabilization proposal in October 2008, giving political cover to the 172 House Democrats and 40 Democratic Senators who gave the Bush administration $700 billion in Troubled Asset Relief Program (TARP) bailout funds for the banks. Yet not a single House Republican voted for Obama's stimulus plan in February 2009, and only 3 Republican Senators did. This set the pattern for the intransigence Obama would encounter on Capitol Hill from the moment he entered the White House. It was fueled by the Tea Party movement that emerged shortly after his election and immediately began pressuring House and Senate Republicans to fight every aspect of his agenda.

It was no surprise that Republicans played hardball with Obama. It had worked for them since the mid-1990s, even when they were in the minority, not just to block Democratic initiatives but to exploit Democrats' triangulation to shift the ideological terrain of American politics to the right. What was surprising was that Obama engaged in preemptive capitulation from the start, and then seemed surprised that his efforts at cooperation were not reciprocated. This began with his $787 billion stimulus bill. Two weeks before his inauguration, President-elect Obama met with congressional leaders, promising cooperation and asking for input. Republican leaders responded by declaring they would not support anything that would add to the deficit—even though the country was in a major recession and they had lost credibility as deficit hawks after driving it up during the Bush years. Minority Whip Eric Cantor's proposal consisted of five different tax cuts and nothing else. Senate Republican leader Mitch McConnell added that maybe they should make the states refund federal Medicaid subsidies, without explaining how this could possibly work in a collapsed economy.[6]

Yet Obama welcomed these Republican ideas as meriting serious consideration. He was so accommodating that the Republicans left the meeting worrying that his cooperative stance might put them at a political disadvantage, a reasonable concern for a party whose tried and true strategy was to adopt extreme positions and then pillory Democrats as unreasonable if they failed to compromise. Cantor responded accordingly, whipping his members to ensure that not a single House Republican would vote for the stimulus bill, even though it contained $288 billion in tax cuts and other pro-business provisions that Republicans typically support. Obama, Summers, and Emanuel—who had predicted that a substantial number of House Republicans would support the bill—were all shocked. It was as if they had learned nothing from the Clinton years.[7]

Republican intransigence continued throughout the Obama administration, shrouded in accusations that he was an extreme-left, polarizing figure. It was an exercise in anticipatory projection that would later be perfected by Donald Trump: Accuse the other side of whatever transgression you yourself are about to commit. In March of 2010, the Affordable Care Act garnered one House Republican vote and none in the Senate. Four months later, the Dodd-Frank financial reform bill managed three Republican votes in each chamber. In November, after the Republicans regained control of the House—though not the Senate—in the midterms, they took their intransigence into overdrive. McConnell summed up their approach in a *National Journal* interview declaring that his "number one priority is making sure president Obama is a one-term president." In this he echoed soon-to-be Speaker John Boehner's comment on Obama's legislative agenda: "We're going to do everything—and I mean everything we can do—to kill it, stop it, slow it down, whatever we can."[8]

And they did. They began a campaign of chipping away at Obamacare and refusing to fund it, stonewalling his appointments, and refusing to collaborate on any legislative initiatives. As a result, the administration had no significant legislative successes for the remaining six years of Obama's presidency. This was unsurprising because, unlike the British system, in which the governing party has full control of legislative and executive institutions and thus usually governs unilaterally, the American system forces cooperation among the branches. In addition to all legislation having to pass both chambers of Congress, the party controlling the House wields leverage because revenue bills must originate there, and the Senate's filibuster rules empower minorities to block most legislation. Moreover, the House Speaker and the Senate Majority Leader are powerful gatekeepers. It is exceedingly difficult to circumvent their authority to decide which legislation gets to the floor for a vote.[9]

In this world, if one party flatly refuses to compromise except on its own terms, the other party must capitulate if it wants to do anything at all. By 2012, the vast majority of House and Senate Republicans had signed Norquist's antitax pledge, committing them to refuse to vote for any tax increases. Most of them were vocally committed to blocking the Obama administration at every turn. The threat of primary challenges, often funded by antitax groups, had enforced this discipline since 1990—the last time Republicans had voted to raise taxes. The advent of the Tea Party solidified and expanded this discipline into the wall of defiance that would culminate in McConnell's refusal to consider any Obama nominee for the Supreme Court when Antonin Scalia died nine months before the 2016 election—even though he would ram through Donald Trump's nominee Amy Coney Barrett when Ruth Bader Ginsburg died six weeks before the 2020 election.[10]

Squandering Political Capital

The mystery was not that the Republicans played hardball. They had been doing so since the early 1990s and reaping big dividends. The mystery was Obama's ceding so much terrain from the start, not just to congressional leaders but also in his dealings with Wall Street. He signaled this two months into his presidency in a meeting with CEOs of the thirteen largest banks, who were facing intense public backlash over their exorbitant compensation packages after their institutions received gargantuan Federal Reserve liquidity injections and Treasury bailouts. Their claims that limiting executive compensation would impede competition for top talent were by then laughably shopworn, coming as they did from leaders who had failed so spectacularly that only trillions of dollars in government and central bank support prevented their companies from crashing the global economy.

Obama began by taking a tough stance, warning the CEOs that "my administration is the only thing between you and the pitchforks." But he soon made clear that he was just pleading for voluntary self-restraint, not demanding any changes in return for shielding them from congressional and public rage. By the end of the meeting, it was clear to all—to the surprise of many in the room—that business would proceed as usual. As one of the CEOs told journalist Ron Suskind, "Lots of drama, but at day's end, nothing much changed." As Suskind recounts, they had expected to be held to account at this moment of great vulnerability, but the fact that Obama huffed, puffed, and backed down signaled that they could ignore him with impunity. They discounted his complaints and demands thereafter, confident that with Geithner at the Treasury and Bush appointee Ben Bernanke at the Fed—whom Obama would reappoint in August, as Clinton had done with Reagan appointee Alan Greenspan in 1996—their interests would be well protected.[11]

They were right. Geithner sabotaged every attempt to prevent public funds from being used not only to pay $165 million in bonuses to American International Group executives, whose company had received over $180 billion in federal funds, but also to meet AIG's obligations on credit default swaps to Goldman Sachs and other banks—whose identities they sought to conceal for fear of public backlash. Geithner also successfully opposed restructuring the banks, despite proposals to do that from Summers, FDIC chair Sheila Bair, and Council of Economic Advisors chair Christina Romer. He then slow-walked Obama's insistence that at least an example be made of Citigroup, the most egregious offender—which had received more than $476 billion in government funds and guarantees, and had a decades-long history of reckless behavior—by taking them into bankruptcy. Obama eventually gave up, leaving all the banks that had been bailed out through

TARP unaccountable. Some later paid fines that were manageable for them. In 2016, for example, Goldman agreed to a $5 billion settlement for misleading clients about the quality of securitized mortgages it had sold them. But no one was charged with securities fraud, fueling the perception that everyone got off scot-free.[12]

Emanuel and Geithner took more ambitious reforms off the table, maintaining that they couldn't press Congress to support anything more after TARP and the stimulus. This was ironic in Emanuel's case, since he is famous for the dictum that you should never let a crisis go to waste. It was as if they were allergic to the prospect of taking the fight to the Republicans by deploying the president to rally public opinion—as Bush, in a much weaker position, had done to create momentum for his tax cuts when the shoe was on the other foot. In the battles over the Dodd-Frank bill, which sought to reregulate the banks, Geithner tried hard to prevent the inclusion of the Volcker Rule, which prohibits investment banks from trading on their own accounts—a measure the banks strongly opposed. After he failed, he worked to limit its effectiveness during the rule-writing process. He was also quick to compromise with Republicans and financial industry critics on the design of the Consumer Financial Protection Bureau championed by Senator Elizabeth Warren to curtail predatory lending. And in a textbook case of preemptive capitulation that was the hallmark of the administration's triangulation, he refused to support Warren's candidacy to lead the CFPB when Republican senators signaled that they opposed her confirmation. Princeton economist and former Federal Reserve vice chairman Alan Blinder likened the hamstrung bureau that was eventually created to a Rube Goldberg machine.[13]

Central to the Democrats' triangulation had been the tactic of broadcasting that they were more serious deficit hawks than the Republicans. At the start of his administration, Obama agreed with Democratic Senator Kent Conrad of North Dakota that they must reduce the deficit and debt, even volunteering that he was willing to be a one-term president over the issue. Conrad was the first to propose the idea Republicans would later adopt: He and a group of like-minded senators would not agree to raise the debt ceiling without a mechanism (he favored a commission) to reduce the debt. Obama did aggressively begin cutting the deficit once the worst of the financial crisis had passed, so that by early 2013 the administration was boasting of a $2.5 trillion reduction—the steepest decline in discretionary spending as a percentage of GDP since the Eisenhower administration.[14]

Yet by then, Republicans had a long-established record of denouncing deficits and debt while out of power, only to increase them with abandon once in power. As FDR had put it with characteristic verve in a speech to attendees at a Jackson Day dinner in 1939, Republican leaders sought "to run with the hare and hunt with the hounds, talking of balanced budgets out of one side of its mouth and in favor of opportunist raids on the Treasury out of the other." In 2009, former Vice President Dick Cheney complained about the $600 billion projected cost of Obamacare, even though in 2002 he had deflected Treasury Secretary Paul O'Neill's objection that a second round of Bush tax cuts would cost $674 billion, famously asserting that Reagan had proved deficits don't matter.[15]

Reagan ran up budget deficits that Clinton later paid off. George W. Bush increased them again through tax cuts, wars, and Medicare Part D (which added free prescription drug coverage). Yet here was Obama volunteering that he would be willing to serve only one term to bring the debt under control. By then, evidence from the Reagan- and Bush-era tax cuts was incontrovertible: They don't bring in enough revenue to pay for themselves, and Republicans had contributed disproportionately to the deficit and debt for the better part of three decades. Obama could talk tough—declaring

Figure 4.1 Changes in Budget Deficits in the United States, 1975–2019

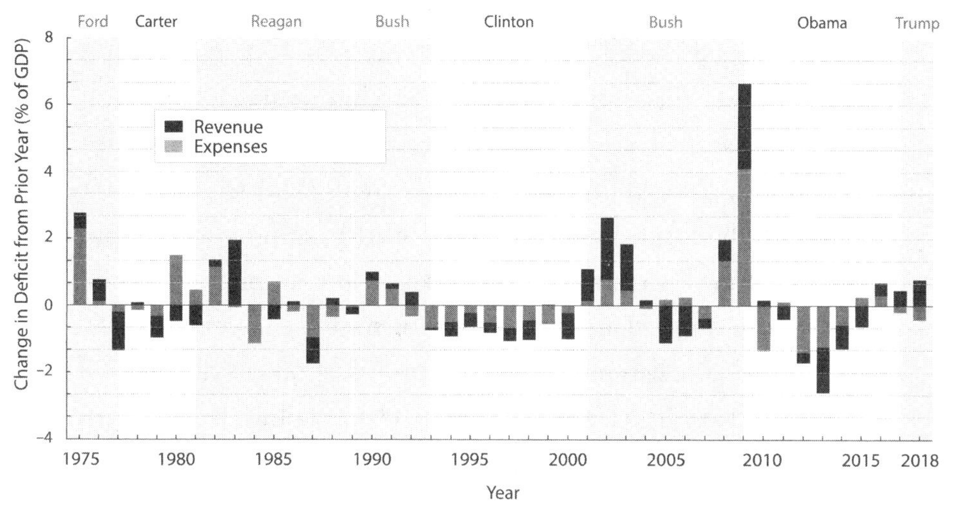

Sources: US Bureau of Economic Analysis, US Office of Management and Budget. Most data retrieved from FRED, Federal Reserve Bank of St. Louis.

that Republicans "drove the economy into a deep ditch" and complaining that they stood by "sipping on a Slurpy" while Democrats worked to push it out—without recognizing the irony his own metaphor underscored. The same dynamic would recur with Trump and Biden. Excluding COVID relief, Republicans who had happily added $4.8 trillion to the debt between 2017 and 2020 instantly became deficit hawks once Biden took office—only to enact the One Big Beautiful Bill in 2025, projected to add $4.1 trillion to the country's $36.2 trillion debt.[16]

The Rich Versus the Rest

The financial crisis of 2008 brought about a sea change in macroeconomic management. The Bush and Obama administrations responded to it with alacrity, preventing it from escalating into a full-blown depression. The trillions they spent to stave off a financial disaster and restart the US and global economies made it incontrovertible that no government can operate in today's world without deploying Keynesian tools. Regardless of political rhetoric to the contrary, the supply-side era was over.

But so was the technocratic conceit that financial regulators were adept at deploying tried and true techniques to manage the economy in the public interest. The extent to which they were manifestly blindsided and then scrambled to improvise solutions was staggering. They hurled arbitrary amounts of money at problems whose dimensions they could not measure, and they relied on personal connections for access and influence. In March 2008 they subsidized JP Morgan's purchase of the failing Bear Stearns with $30 billion in federal funds to take toxic assets off its books. Yet six months later they let Lehman Brothers fail, citing the moral hazards of government bailouts, only to reverse themselves within days and bail out American International Group with $85 billion (the cost would eventually grow to $182 billion). Regulators were picking winners among banks and other institutions, and, whether by default or design, they favored economic elites over Middle America. Nowhere was this more obvious than in their response to the subprime mortgage crisis that was at the heart of the collapse.

The proliferation of low-quality securitized mortgages that threatened the financial system was a perfect storm that had been decades in the making. It began in the 1980s when Fannie Mae and Freddie Mac, government-sponsored enterprises that bought mortgages from originating banks to increase liquidity in the mortgage market, started bundling the loans into mortgage-backed securities—financial products that could be sold to investors. Investment banks and hedge funds soon copied the practice, seeing lucrative opportunities in this new market for mortgage debt. Political pressure on Fannie and Freddie from the Clinton administration and congressional Democrats to relax underwriting criteria and prioritize low-income borrowers incentivized private lenders to write increasing numbers of subprime mortgages in order to remain competitive with the government, secure in the knowledge that they would pass the risk of default on to others. Traders who dealt in subprime mortgages fostered the illusion of safety by dividing them up and recombining them into tranches that mixed low- and high-quality loans, seemingly diversifying risk.[17]

George W. Bush embraced the cause of expanding home ownership to low-income borrowers with the zeal of a convert. In 1989, his father's secretary of housing and urban development, Jack Kemp, had proposed selling public housing to tenants as a way of expanding the American dream—imitating Margaret Thatcher's initiative to create a "property-owning democracy" by selling off government-owned council houses in the UK. Kemp's program had floundered on practicalities. George W. Bush pressured Fannie and Freddie to continue softening underwriting criteria as another path to the same goal, hoping to expand his party's appeal to low-income voters. This kept the dynamic going, with the result that owner-occupied households reached an all-time high of 69.4 percent at the end of his first term. The lucrative securitization of subprime mortgages also grew rapidly during the Bush years. It was helped along by deregulation and by the Fed's low interest rate policies following the burst of the dot-com bubble in 2000, which kept cheap money flowing into the market. Because the packaged mortgages were publicly traded as securities, real estate's traditional function as a hedge against equities was undermined. By 2007, the major investment banks had all become highly leveraged, holding tens of billions in subprime debt, so that when the bubble burst, everything collapsed at once.[18]

The scale of the threat to the US and global financial systems forced Western governments to prevent proliferating failures and then to pour hundreds of billions of dollars into recapitalizing the banks. It worked. Banks began recovering; many paid back the government in full and were soon making record profits once again. Similarly, investors and other well-to-do Americans—through the revival of their 401(k)s, stock portfolios, and other investments—quickly regained and even expanded their wealth. The Dow Jones Industrial Average, which lost more than half its value between its peak in October 2007 and its low point in March 2009, had recovered three-quarters of the loss a year later and went on to enjoy a decade-long bull market, which ended—and then only briefly—when the COVID pandemic hit in 2020. Financial elites and other white-collar workers, especially in California and the Northeast, suffered the least and recovered fastest. Despite the cliff-hanger in 2008, for many of them the financial crisis was soon in the rearview mirror, as they took advantage of the Fed's cheap money to rebuild their lifestyles and exploit new opportunities in the tech economy.

Not so the distressed homeowners. Millions found themselves struggling to make their mortgage payments or, once they got laid off, unable to make payments on homes that were worth less than what they owed on them. This stress was built into the subprime mortgages, which had required little to no down payment and had been given to borrowers who failed to meet conventional underwriting requirements. Many featured balloon payments or low teaser rates that staved off higher payments, based on dubious assumptions: either that the borrower's income would rise or that the home's value would appreciate enough to allow refinancing. Seven years before the crisis, economic commentator Joshua Rosner, among others, had warned proponents of expanding homeownership to borrowers with little or no down payment that a home without equity is essentially a rental with debt, and the borrowers would run into trouble as soon as real estate prices fell.[19]

Unsurprisingly, subprime borrowers began defaulting on their mortgages in droves. Yet Obama stuck to the early avowal he had made to congressional leaders two weeks before taking office: There would be no aggressive government intervention to help them. This meant resisting the arguments of numerous economists and even some heavily exposed banks and hedge fund investors whose losses would be curtailed if homeowners could be prevented from defaulting. Some of them even testified in Congress in support of programs to write down mortgage principal so that underwater homeowners would have incentives to begin repaying their mortgages. The administration ignored these proposals, offering only modest help such as temporary reductions in their mortgage interest rates. But a distressed borrower with an underwater property has little more incentive to pay at, say, a 4 percent rate than at an 8 percent rate, so even those who took advantage of the program to begin repaying soon defaulted again. Eventually more than 9.3 million homeowners were foreclosed on, forcing over 28 million people out of their homes.[20]

Obama's approach was all the more stunning in view of commitments he had made during the campaign. In September 2008, the Bush administration's $700 billion TARP request was initially voted down by the House, throwing markets into free fall at the prospect that the government was not going to stabilize the banking system. Candidate Obama persuaded liberal congressional Democrats who had voted against the bill to switch their votes after he promised them a major antiforeclosure initiative if he won. Once elected, however, he made no effort to build support for ambitious proposals to do just that sponsored by Senator Dick Durbin and others. He did commit $75 billion in TARP funds to forestall foreclosures, but less than $20 billion of it was spent on the program, and the administration delegated its implementation to the banks. This amounted to putting foxes in charge of henhouses. Widespread abuses would eventually result in a $25 billion consent decree between the five largest lenders and the government to address foreclosure abuses, but the small amounts of money that eventually made their way to distressed borrowers typically arrived too late to prevent foreclosure. African Americans, who were disproportionately represented among subprime borrowers, were almost twice as likely to face foreclosure as white borrowers. "It's a terrible irony," commented Damon Silvers, deputy chair of the Congressional Oversight Panel for TARP, that Obama, "who represents so much to people of color has presided over more wealth destruction of people of color than anyone in American history."[21]

Why did Obama fail the homeowners so dramatically? It seems that he was running scared of potential backlash, exemplified in economic commentator Rick Santelli's famous rant on the Chicago Mercantile Exchange—credited by some for galvanizing the Tea Party movement into existence—in which he declared that helping distressed homeowners would create a moral hazard. He demanded, "Who wants to pay for the losers' mortgages?!" But worrying about the moral hazard associated with helping "losers" who had taken on mortgages that they could no longer pay ignored the much bigger moral hazard of bailing out "loser" banks and Wall Street executives, exemplifying the administration's double standard.

Preemptive capitulation also marked Obama's approach to tax policy. His retreat was gratuitous, because it was the one area in which the inertia built into the American political system gave his administration a tactical advantage. George W. Bush had enacted his tax cuts through the budget reconciliation process, which cannot be filibustered and therefore requires only fifty-one votes in the Senate. Yet under the Byrd Rule—named for West Virginia Democratic Senator Robert Byrd and adopted in 1985—a bill could not increase the deficit beyond a ten-year window. The Bush administration had been able to conform to the rule only by inserting a sunset clause stipulating that the cuts would expire in 2010 unless new legislation was adopted to extend them. That gave Obama the upper hand. He could veto an extension that was not to his liking, with the effect that the Bush tax cuts would expire and the rates would return to their higher 2001 levels.

There was near universal agreement when Obama came into office that a short-term extension of some or all of the cuts was warranted in view of the fragile condition of the economy. Obama's initial position—strongly endorsed by many congressional Democrats, including the leadership—was to refuse to extend the cuts for the two highest income brackets, some 2 percent of taxpayers, which would net the Treasury $800 billion over the next decade. But Obama backed down after Democrats lost control of the House in November 2010, agreeing with Speaker-elect John Boehner during the lame duck session to extend all the cuts for two years in return for a one-year extension of unemployment insurance and the two-percentage-point reduction in the payroll tax that had been enacted after the financial crisis. This would give about $1,000 in tax relief to each of 159 million workers. The projected $168.5 billion cost of the two measures would obviously be stimulative, since beneficiaries would spend the money, with multiplier effects throughout the economy.[22]

But at what price? As well as throwing away his leverage and forgoing billions in revenue by extending the cuts for the wealthiest Americans, Obama capitulated further by adding generous estate tax provisions that would benefit a mere ninety-five hundred wealthy families over the next two years. Without new legislation, that tax would have been reinstated at a 55 percent rate with a $1 million exemption ($2 million for a married couple). Instead, Obama agreed to a 35 percent rate with a $5 million exemption

($10 million for a married couple), at a cost to the US Treasury of $68 billion. This was on top of the hundreds of billions that extending the income tax cuts for the wealthy would cost. It was as if he was heeding the advice Newt Gingrich offered on CNN: that Obama should learn from Gingrich's example with Clinton about how to work productively with Republicans who showed scant interest in compromising with him. Even Nancy Pelosi, generally a loyal supporter of the Obama administration, was sufficiently dispirited that she told Geithner confidant Gene Sperling that she wouldn't sell the deal to House Democrats—the White House would have to do it themselves. The final bill was steeply regressive, with the great bulk of the $858 billion extension in tax cuts going to the wealthiest Americans.[23]

Obama, who took some flak for throwing in the towel on the two-year extension, vowed he would rectify things when it expired. But it is a measure of how far triangulation had moved him that the American Taxpayer Relief Act of 2012, which he signed in January 2013, made 82 percent of the original Bush tax cuts permanent. Obama insisted that he was protecting the middle class with the legislation because it restored modest increases in taxes on dividends and long-term capital gains, as well as the 39.6 percent top marginal rate for individuals earning over $400,000 ($450,000 for a married couple). Yet $400,000 was more than eight times the median household income in the United States, scarcely middle class by any plausible definition. Even the $250,000 threshold that Obama had spent much of the previous year defending as his limit was not plausibly middle class at a time when more than 87 percent of Americans were earning less than $100,000 per year. What better way to humiliate the great majority of voters than to declare that people earning more than two or four times what they made were middle class? What did that make them? Yet the Republicans had by then reshaped the terrain so extensively that, after months of stonewalling every proposal that allowed any Bush cuts to expire, Obama's last-minute acceptance of the $400,000 threshold was heralded as a statesmanlike compromise. Icing on the cake for the superwealthy was the estate tax reform. The threshold was raised to $5.25 million ($10.5 million for a married couple) and indexed for inflation—something that has never been achieved for the minimum wage—and a 40 percent rate was made permanent. This was at a time when the median estate in the US was worth $40,000.[24]

More remarkable than the fact that Obama blinked was that he didn't need to. The recession had been over for three years by then, so any countercyclical reason for concern about the effects of letting the Bush tax cuts expire was moot. At the time, commentators debated whether he or the Republicans would be blamed for allowing the cuts to expire, but Obama and the Democrats had by then gained additional leverage. Two months earlier Obama had won reelection, handily defeating Mitt Romney by 126 Electoral College votes and almost five million in the popular vote. The Democrats had increased their Senate majority by two and picked up eight House seats, winning the national popular vote by more than 1.3 million. This was not a world in which Republicans could claim an electoral mandate, let alone pass anything unilaterally. Democrats had no reason to roll over for them. Obama, who would never be running for national office again, certainly did not. Yet the Senate passed the bill by 89 to 8 and the House by 257 to 167, with most votes coming from Democrats in both chambers. The smoking-gun evidence that Republicans had gotten what they wanted was Speaker Boehner's decision to bring the bill to the floor in violation of the Hastert Rule, which bars a vote on any measure lacking majority Republican support. Triangulation had led the Democrats to talk themselves into making almost all the regressive Bush tax cuts permanent, underscoring the reality that they were in the tank for America's elite. Eventually, perceptions would catch up.[25]

Obama's Legacy

Eight years before the financial crisis, Bob Woodward published a laudatory paean to Federal Reserve Chair Alan Greenspan entitled *Maestro*. Other journalists would go further, insisting that the Fed chairman was a rock star. Despite the savings and loan crisis that destroyed nearly a third of the nation's thrifts and the burst dot-com bubble that wiped $5 trillion—78 percent—off the value of the NASDAQ, Greenspan had widely been credited with limiting the US economy to two brief, mild recessions during his nineteen-year tenure. He seemed to have perfected the science of soft landings: prudently adjusting interest rates in anticipation of the peaks and troughs of business cycles. Apparently, he had tamed the boom/bust dynamic of American capitalism into what came to be called the Great Moderation. An admirer of the libertarian Ayn Rand and a strong advocate of financial deregulation, Greenspan had been appointed and reappointed by Republicans and Democrats from Ronald Reagan to George W. Bush. More than anyone, he had embodied the neoliberal hegemony that came unstuck in 2008.[26]

A month after the crisis hit that year, Greenspan was forced to admit at a congressional hearing that the implosion had left him "in a state of shocked disbelief." No longer anyone's maestro or rock star, he went on to confess his distress at discovering that the "whole intellectual edifice" he had relied on for decades to price financial risk had collapsed. He even conceded to Congressman Henry Waxman that he had "found a flaw" in his "free market ideology." It was a stunning admission that the era ushered in by Ronald Reagan's endlessly repeated declaration that "government is not the solution to our problem; government is the problem" was over. By then, no one could contest that without massive government intervention to reopen frozen credit markets, recapitalize insolvent banks, and finance enough demand to prevent a recession from turning into a depression, the US economy and the global financial system would have collapsed along with Greenspan's ideology. Not only was government the solution; it was the only solution.[27]

Obama took office amid the worst financial crisis since the Great Depression, yet his response differed notably from FDR's seven decades earlier. President-elect Roosevelt ignored lame duck President Herbert Hoover's entreaties to embrace a bipartisan response to the crisis, leaving Hoover twisting in the wind for the then-four-month interregnum. Obama did the opposite, reinforcing the impression that the emergency had fallen out of the sky rather than resulting from reckless deregulation of mortgage and financial markets pursued under relentless lobbying by leaders of the big banks—including Bush's Treasury Secretary Hank Paulson when he was head of Goldman Sachs—that were now desperately seeking bailouts.[28]

Roosevelt's first term was marked by far-reaching banking and securities reform, establishing the main components of the New Deal—the Federal Housing Administration, the Public Works Administration, Social Security, robust protections for organized labor, farmers, homeowners, and consumers—and steeply progressive tax reforms. Obama bailed out the banks, paid bonuses to executives who had led their companies and the country to financial disaster, and curtailed regulatory reform to accommodate the banking lobby, while doing comparatively little for millions of others who were harmed during the financial crisis. FDR responded to attacks that he was a traitor to his class by declaring, "I welcome their hatred" and winning reelection by the biggest landslide in over a century. Democrats retained control of both Houses of Congress throughout FDR's twelve years in office. Obama's accommodationist response didn't prevent his losing the House to Republicans in 2010—hamstringing the rest of his presidency. In 2014 he lost the Senate as well.[29]

There were, to be sure, significant differences. FDR was elected during the depths of the Depression, three years after the Wall Street crash. By contrast, Obama ran for office and became president as financial markets were imploding—more like 1929 than 1932—with the key difference that global credit markets were much more tightly intertwined than they had been in 1929. It was clear to all that without immediate, decisive action by the Fed and the US Treasury, the world's major economies would collapse with horrific knock-on effects across the globe. The results would most likely have been incomparably worse for hundreds of millions of people than the Great Recession that actually occurred, and it would have lasted a lot longer than it did. Moreover, the US was the dominant global player in a way that had not been true in 1929. No other government had the power and resources to act on the scale and with the speed and decisiveness that was needed to forestall the imminent catastrophe.[30]

But this circumstance also gave Obama leverage. Like many among America's financial sector leaders and mainstream political elites, he seemed not to grasp how much had changed. It was as if he was mesmerized by their comfortable confidence that, once the crisis was over, voters would continue deferring to leaders who had been so spectacularly and destructively wrong. Most Americans had lived for decades in an unforgiving economic order in which the rich kept getting richer while secure middle- and working-class jobs disappeared. Family incomes were maintained, when they were, by adding second earners or borrowing against their homes—eroding their main source of wealth. They had accepted this world because no leader of either political party challenged the expertise of the elites who both ran it and insisted there was no viable alternative to it. Like them, Obama and the advisors he listened to failed to appreciate that once their reckless incompetence had been exposed, the decades-old conventional wisdom about the dearth of alternatives would be vulnerable as well.[31]

Obama's central failure was his reflexive acceptance of the ideological terrain that Republicans had shaped since the 1980s. In that regard he was working from Bill Clinton's playbook, but by 2008 this was clearly a disastrous strategy for Democrats for the obvious reason that it left larger numbers of their traditional voters behind than it helped. Moreover, the Republicans, led by George W. Bush, together with enabling Democrats, like Summers and Emanuel, had been so thoroughly discredited that an opportunity beckoned to confront them head on. The deregulation, privatization, and supply-side agenda—known as neoliberalism at home and the Washington Consensus abroad—had brought the world's most powerful economy to its knees.

The time was ripe for a long-overdue reckoning, because the supply-side revolution had gained its ascendency and legitimacy from a misdiagnosis of 1970s stagflation. The stubborn persistence then of high inflation, high unemployment, and low growth was not a repudiation of Keynesian analysis or policy. The inflation had mainly been driven by OPEC's sudden increases in oil prices—which tripled after the 1973 Yom Kippur War and more than doubled again after the 1979 Iranian Revolution—at a time when Western economies depended decisively on Middle Eastern oil. Richard Nixon's 1971 abandonment of the Bretton Woods exchange rate regime, in place since World War II, also made it harder for governments to resist inflationary pressures. The oil price shocks fed the slowdown in economic activity in large sectors of the economy, a blow that hit at the same time as

Japanese and German firms, having recovered from World War II, were mounting new competitive challenges to American ones. Increasing pension costs were cutting into corporate profits as retirees' life expectancy rose, fueling a shift from defined-benefit to defined-contribution schemes that took off at the end of the 1970s—a change that would eventually leave tens of millions of retired Americans vulnerable to the vicissitudes of financial markets.[32]

This combination of external shocks and demographic changes meant that the government faced growing fiscal pressure to fund public obligations to the elderly, notably Social Security and Medicare, as a shrinking workforce supported an expanding retired population.[33] Even with the increase in immigration after the adoption of the Hart-Celler Immigration Act in 1965, immigrants as a proportion of the US population remained significantly below early-century levels, leaving too few to offset the growing ratio of retirees to employed workers. Mounting budgetary pressures made it all but inevitable that major political battles over taxation and public spending would erupt in the coming decades. Leading proponents of free-market economics such as Ludwig von Mises, Friedrich Hayek, James Buchanan, and Milton Friedman had been incubating anti-Keynesian arguments in places like the Mont Pèlerin Society, the American Enterprise Institute, George Mason University, and the University of Chicago since the 1940s, but they had not yet had much influence on public policy. The 1970s gave them their opening. The supply-side revolution drew its ideological resources from these intellectual currents and its political momentum from the antitax movement, fueling the Reagan revolution against big government and the welfare state.[34]

The wisdom of "starving the beast" was always a fiction, as we have seen. Starting with Reagan himself, Republicans replaced taxation with deficit spending. They had different spending priorities than Democrats, but they did not reduce the size of government.[35] The crowning irony of triangulation was that Democrats, back on their heels since the 1970s and even more so after the collapse of communism, bought into the neoliberal worldview that Republicans were trumpeting even as they themselves flouted it. Democrats from Carter to Obama governed as though their job was to prove to voters that they were the more responsible neoliberals than the Republicans. But they were sawing off the branch that they sat on, because the benefits of the growth produced by neoliberal policies were not widely shared. The returns from productivity gains accrued almost exclusively to people at the top, fueling their astronomical wealth expansion, as scholars including Emmanuel Saez, Gabriel Zucman, and Albena Azmanova have documented.[36] As jobs moved offshore and then, increasingly, to technology, the incomes of the bottom 90 percent stagnated. By aligning themselves with neoliberal orthodoxy, Democrats were

Figure 4.2 Cumulative Change in Real Annual Wages, by Wage Group, 1979–2010

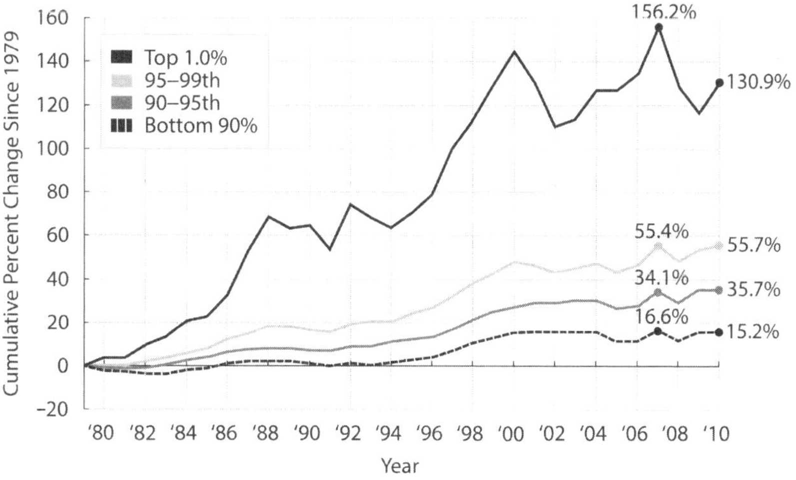

Source: Irwin Kirsch and Henry Braun, eds., *The Dynamics of Opportunity in America: Evidence and Perspectives* (New York: Springer, 2016), 241 (open access).

abandoning their traditional voters in the complacent belief that, lacking an alternative, those voters would remain loyal. In the short run, the Democrats were right, but the 2008 financial crisis scrambled that reality.

This was Obama's moment not just to declare that the emperor had no clothes, but to insist that the condition for deploying trillions of dollars of public money to revive the financial sector was thoroughgoing public investment in the broader economy in ways that had been lacking since the 1980s. High unemployment was obviously inevitable in the short term, but the recession would accelerate the structural changes to the labor market that had been in process since the 1980s, away from well-paid, secure, long-term employment toward lower-paid and increasingly precarious service-sector jobs. One study by the US Department of Labor documents that people born between 1957 and 1964 will change jobs between twelve and fifteen times during their working lives.[37] For the fortunate few, this involves going from one lucrative opportunity to the next, but for the great majority it involves downward mobility.[38] The contrast can be seen in Figure 4.3, which distinguishes the increased earnings of people who stay in their jobs or move directly from one job to the next with the falling earnings of those whose new job follows a brief (less than six months) period of unemployment—and an even larger drop when the new job follows a persistent period (more than six months) of unemployment.

It was Obama's chance to address these developments with long overdue investments to replace the blue-collar jobs that had been disappearing. Yet the great bulk of his stimulus program focused on short-term relief: tax breaks for individuals and corporations, and fiscal help for state and local governments, mostly used to plug gaps in health care and education budgets and to extend unemployment benefits. Much of that was necessary, but as the Keynes biographer and economics reporter Zachary Carter notes, the core

Figure 4.3 Earnings Comparisons Before and After Job Flows, 2001–2019

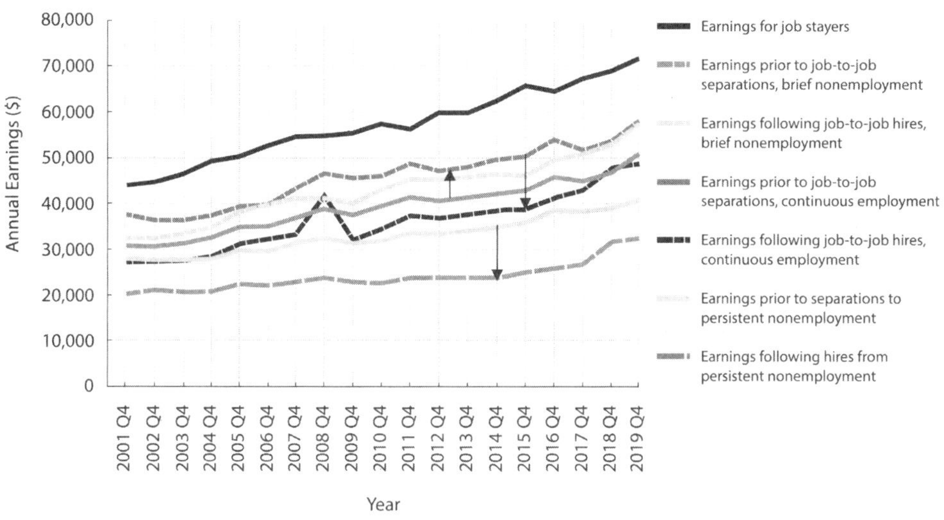

Source: United States Census Bureau, J2J Explorer.

of Keynesian stimulus is direct public investment in the economy. Infrastructure and energy accounted for only $147 billion of Obama's stimulus bill.[39] And it was a countercyclical bill aimed at ending the recession, not one aimed at changing the labor market.

This is all the more remarkable considering that before taking office, Obama clearly understood the structural changes in the labor market that were underway and the political dangers they posed for Democrats. In a 2006 speech at the Brookings Institution, then-Senator Obama stressed that the recent decades of economic growth had created losers as well as winners: people whose jobs had been eliminated, who had lost their health care and retirement security, and who expected their children to face an even bleaker future than theirs. Despite plenty of talk about retraining these people for the new economy, Obama argued, little had actually been done. If more wasn't done, the result would be the growth of "nativist sentiment, protectionism, and anti-immigration sentiment."[40] The following year, competing in the Democratic presidential primaries, Obama posed a prescient question to his economic team: "In year two of my administration, when the housing bubble finally bursts, I come to you as my economic advisers and say, 'What do we do!' Well, what *do* we do?" This led to a discussion in which Alan Krueger, Obama's future chair of the Council of Economic Advisors, walked him through the changes in the labor market that had been occurring since the 1970s, away from well-paid industrial jobs toward less secure and lower-paid service-sector jobs. Krueger particularly emphasized the impact of those changes on the heavily indebted, underinsured, male workers who were dropping out of the labor market in large numbers. Obama dismissed as unrealistic suggestions by some in the room that displaced workers would move into health care and related service-sector jobs, concluding instead that the centerpiece of his policy should be a large enough infrastructure initiative to create ten million jobs.[41]

In office, Obama missed the opportunity the crisis created to go down that path. TARP, combined with the Fed's low interest rates and quantitative easing policies to increase the money supply, flooded the economy with liquidity that predictably revived financial markets—but no one believed these measures would head off a major recession in the broader economy. (It turned out to be the longest recession since the Great Depression.) Beyond the low-hanging fruit of spending the $75 billion that he had committed to distressed homeowners and restoring significant progressivity to the tax code, Obama could have pressed hard for more ambitious programs to address the inevitable foreclosure epidemic and to invest in rebuilding the economy beyond the financial sector. Part of this could have been done directly, through a modern version of FDR's programs: something akin to the Works Progress Administration—which employed some 8.5 million people during its eight-year existence at the cost of $11 billion ($250 billion in

2009 dollars)—to rebuild America's collapsing roads and bridges, and the Civilian Conservation Corps, which recruited another three million workers between 1933 and 1942 and planted 3.5 billion trees at a cost of $3 billion ($50 billion in 2009).[42] Part could have been done through private-sector incentives and public-private partnerships. Yet Obama never attempted anything remotely comparable. Indeed, he froze out advisors, like Christina Romer, who pressed him to rethink.[43]

Likewise with taxation. Whereas Obama rolled over to make almost all of Bush's regressive tax cuts permanent, FDR's revenue acts of 1934 through 1937 raised the estate tax rate from 45 to 60 percent, increased the top income tax rate—on incomes above $1 million ($15 million in 2009 or $23 million in 2025)—from 63 to 79 percent, imposed a 27 percent surtax on undistributed corporate profits in addition to the normal corporate profits tax, and cut back on loopholes that had made tax evasion easy for wealthy taxpayers.[44] This revenue funded major relief for farmers, who had been struggling since the end of World War I, through the Emergency Farm Mortgage Act, which helped hundreds of thousands of them avoid foreclosure. It also funded the Home Owners Loan Act, which did the same for over a million distressed homeowners. FDR's measures also addressed the chronic problem of old-age poverty by designing Social Security, which began paying out in 1937, creating a windfall for the first cohort of beneficiaries, who had not themselves contributed. This was brilliant politics not only because it broadened support for the policy, but also because the funding mechanism protected the program into the future. As George W. Bush discovered when trying to privatize Social Security in 2005, the cost for doing so was prohibitive because it would have involved funding two systems for the transition: one to pay current retirees, and one that current workers could invest in their private accounts. Reflecting on the design years later, FDR remarked that he had structured it that way intentionally, so that "no damn politician can ever scrap my social security program."[45]

Obama's failure to rise to the occasion seems best explained by his triangulating adherence to what by then had become Democratic orthodoxy. This amounted to ceding the terrain of possibilities to a Republican Party that had long made clear it would respond by dragging politics to the right. He failed to see that the orthodoxy he continued reaffirming once the financial crisis was over now rested on quicksand for political legitimacy. He missed the opening—indeed, the imperative—to reject that orthodoxy and start rebuilding the Great Society coalition that Democrats had abandoned since the 1970s. Doing so would have meant responding to the needs of millions of voters who continued suffering the effects of the crash long after the financial elites had recovered. Instead, by acting as though nothing had changed, Obama revealed his blindness to the new reality that Republicans were also missing. If they continued embracing policies that gave short shrift to the interests of millions of voters, others would seize the chance to mobilize those voters in ways that would upend their comfortable world.

Obama's experience illustrated another cost to triangulation. Signaling a willingness to cooperate with adversaries who have no intention of cooperating with you is bound to be seen as weakness. Sensing blood in the water, they will go after you—as they did most dramatically in the fight over extending the Bush tax cuts. FDR is instructive here as well. By pressing his agenda to the point of welcoming his adversaries' hatred, he sometimes overreached, but he also undermined their efforts to disrupt his agenda. In his first term, FDR was frequently frustrated by a conservative Supreme Court that struck down major pieces of New Deal legislation as unconstitutional, including minimum wage legislation, the National Industrial Recovery Act, and the Agricultural

Adjustment Act, which gave relief to struggling workers and farmers. Following Democratic gains in the 1934 midterms and his landslide reelection two years later, which expanded his already overwhelming majorities on Capitol Hill, FDR proposed a plan to expand the Supreme Court that would have undercut its conservative majority. The plan was eventually rejected by Congress, but in the interim the court backed down, upholding major pieces of New Deal legislation that previously had been in doubt, such as the Wagner Act—which created extensive protections for unions—and the Social Security Act, and reversing its previous rejection of state minimum wage laws.[46]

American politics always involves a blend of cooperation and conflict, but as in the prisoner's dilemma, if you signal that you will keep cooperating when your adversary does not, you are asking to be played for a sucker.

Chapter Five

Harvesting Disaster

Obama's missteps would play into Donald Trump's hands in 2016, but he was hardly alone in setting the stage for a populist backlash. Across much of the democratic world, left-of-center parties had been failing their traditional constituencies for decades while secure long-term employment was disappearing to globalization and, increasingly, to technology. Tony Blair didn't limit himself to wresting control of the Labour Party from hard-line Marxists and abolishing Clause Four of its constitution, which had promised to nationalize the commanding heights of the economy. His New Labour mimicked Clinton's triangulation, pursuing more aggressive privatization than had Margaret Thatcher's governments of the 1980s, granting operational independence to the Bank of England, and expanding on Thatcher's deregulatory Big Bang with a stripped down Financial Services Authority, which diluted financial regulation so extensively that New York City Mayor

Mike Bloomberg and Senator Charles Schumer found themselves lobbying Congress to do likewise—arguing that otherwise Wall Street couldn't compete. Blair compounded New Labour's alienation of the party's traditional base by clambering aboard George Bush's Global War on Terror. His initial commitment of seventeen hundred troops to Afghanistan would grow to ten thousand under his successor, Gordon Brown, during Obama's military surge there in 2010—more troops than any country except the US. But it was Blair's full-throated support for the Iraq War, to which he committed forty-six thousand British troops, that garnered him the moniker "George Bush's Poodle" and, eventually, scathing condemnation for misleading Parliament in the exhaustive report published by Sir John Chilcot in 2016.[1]

Most European social democrats shunned American military adventurism, but not the neoliberal triangulation of economic policy. Soon after his decisive victory in France's 1981 presidential elections, François Mitterrand jettisoned his socialist program, devalued the franc twice, embraced harsh austerity measures, including wage and spending freezes, declared price stability rather than employment to be his top priority, and dispatched the left-wing members of his government. The French also led the charge on European monetary integration and the creation of a European Central Bank in the 1990s, hoping to limit the dominance of a newly unified Germany and its Deutschmark in setting the terms of intra-European trade and monetary policy.

In Germany, it was a coalition of the Social Democrats and the Greens that implemented the pro-business Hartz reforms starting in 2003. Brainchild of Volkswagen executive Peter Hartz, they were designed to restore labor market flexibility by forcing the long-term unemployed into low-paid service jobs—replicating the American pattern in which Germany's dramatic productivity gains were accompanied by working- and middle-class wage stagnation.

Even when the coalition between the Social Democratic Party (SPD) and the Greens that had ruled Germany since 1998 lost to Angela Merkel's ascendent Christian Democratic Union (CDU) in 2005—relegating the SPD to junior partner status in her grand coalition—it was the SPD finance minister Peer Steinbrück, a deficit hawk, who ramped up Germany's anti-Keynesian supply-side reforms. The result, as Adam Tooze put it, was that the SPD and the CDU found themselves "huddling together" at the shrinking center of Germany's fragmenting political landscape.[2]

By then, the SPD was hemorrhaging votes to the reconstituted former East German Communists and other left parties, which in 2007 consolidated themselves into the neo-Marxist Die Linke. It garnered about a tenth of Germany's vote for the next decade. The SPD, which had commanded between one-third and 40 percent of the vote until 2005, would never win more than a quarter thereafter. Yet aside from a brief stint in opposition from 2009 to 2013, successive SPD leaders clung to Merkel in a series of grand coalitions, during which their electoral support continued to dwindle. They eventually broke this pattern in 2021, but not for long. In February 2025 they suffered a devastating defeat, winning a mere 16.4 percent of the vote—their worst result in well over a century.[3]

Comparable stories can be told across much of Europe. Italy's center left abandoned Keynesian thinking in favor of debt reduction and inflation fighting as they triangulated toward the technocratic center under the leadership of Romano Prodi. In Spain it was Felipe González's Socialists who privatized state firms, devalued the peseta, and enacted financial sector deregulation as the country adapted to the demands of European integration. The Labour Party in the Netherlands talked about a third way and campaigned against austerity in the 2012 elections, but like Germany's SPD, it then joined a conservative government and got behind €40 billion in austerity measures that included brutal cuts to social security, social care, housing, and education. Despite its electoral implosion in the 2017 elections, from which it has yet to recover, its leaders continued insisting that they had done the right thing, even though, as Finance Minister Jeroen Dijsselbloem lamented, "We weren't able to take our electorate along with us." In this they echoed the Swedish Social Democrats under Olof Palme in the 1980s, whose anti-Keynesian third way had quickly morphed into devaluation, tight budgets, supply-side tax cuts, financial deregulation, and partial privatization of social services.[4]

For a time, Portugal seemed to be the exception that proved the rule. The confusingly named center-right Social Democrats governed from the 1980s through the mid-1990s, pursuing strongly promarket policies as the country's already high levels of inequality escalated still further. Between 1995 and 2024, however, the center-left Socialists were in government continuously except for seven years, usually governing alone—if with implicit backing from other left parties. They were out of office between 2011 and 2015, so they were not saddled with implementing the austerity reforms demanded by the European Commission, European Central Bank, and International Monetary Fund in return for a €78 billion bailout in the wake of the European sovereign debt crisis. When in office they invested in education for those at the economic bottom, protected and even encouraged collective bargaining, and increased the minimum wage. As a result, both pre- and posttax inequality fell over the first two decades of the new century when it was rising almost everywhere else. After 2016, Portugal outperformed the EU averages in economic growth and employment rates, leading some commentators—including Paul Krugman—to herald the performance as an economic miracle. The Socialists managed to hold on to their economic base when their sister parties were fragmenting across Europe, and no far-right party emerged until 2019, when the new Chega ("Enough") won a single seat. By 2022, it had expanded to a modest 7.2 percent of the vote and twelve seats. The Socialists and Social Democrats always accounted for more than 60 percent of the vote between them, making it seem that Portugal was defying the political fragmentation that was working its way across the rest of Europe—a political miracle as well.[5]

But appearances can be deceptive. The very high levels of inequality inherited from the 1990s mean that even with the subsequent reductions, Portugal remains one of the most unequal countries in Europe. Ditto with education. Portugal started so far behind that literacy and numeracy rates remain among the lowest in the Organisation for Economic Co-operation and Development (OECD). Portugal's reductions in its public debt were achieved via brutal austerity programs, starving an already slim welfare state. The comparatively good economic growth has mostly been in tourism and housing. It has done little for Portugal's struggling industrial north, once prosperous towns like Abrantes, or the dilapidated Lisnave shipyards in Margueira. Employment growth is mostly in low-paying, insecure service-sector jobs. The real estate boom has been concentrated in Lisbon, Porto, and a few large towns, creating some instant millionaires but driving up rents and putting home ownership out of reach for most people. Economic stress became more widespread in the wake of the COVID pandemic, so that by 2023 inequality was increasing again and more than a fifth of the population was at risk of living either in poverty or in severe material and social deprivation. The Socialists were living on borrowed time.[6]

A sea change began in 2024. Historically, both mainstream parties had been relaxed about immigration, which had not been contentious in Portugal, but as the economic stress intensified, particularly for young people, Chega leader André Ventura saw his opening. In the 2024 election, his party won 18.1 percent of the vote and 50 seats in the legislature, while the Socialists dropped precipitously—from 41.4 percent of the vote and 120 seats to 28 percent and 78 seats. Any question that the Chega movement was a flash in the pan was laid to rest in the snap election fourteen months later. Chega jumped into second place, with 22.8 percent of the vote and 60 seats, while the Socialists had their worst showing since the 1980s. The Social Democrats picked up 11 seats to a total of 91, forcing them to continue as a precarious minority government since they were unwilling to form a coalition with Chega. The Portuguese exception was no more.

Bearing the Costs

As in the US, many right-of-center European parties responded to the left's triangulation by shifting the goalposts. Britain's Tories got a running start at this while Neil Kinnock, John Smith, and Tony Blair were reinventing the Labour Party in opposition. By 1990 Margaret Thatcher's remaking of the Conservative (Tory) Party seemed to have run its course. Despite the fact that she was the first prime minister in 160 years to win three consecutive elections, her cabinet dumped her that year in a palace coup when her popularity plummeted over her regressive poll tax and what had by then become her relentless hostility to the EU. The final straw was a fight over joining the Exchange Rate Mechanism, which required members to align their currencies in the run-up to the anticipated introduction of the euro at the end of the decade. The cabinet muscled the ERM through over her objections, some because they wanted Britain eventually to adopt the euro and some because they saw it as a source of fiscal discipline. Thatcher's successor, John Major, was a staunch ERM proponent who appeared vindicated when he led the Tories to an unprecedented fourth consecutive win in April 1992. The Thatcher era, it seemed, was over.

But everything changed five months later. George Soros shorted the British pound just as the Bank of England began hiking interest rates in a desperate—and what turned out to be futile—effort to maintain the pound's peg to the Deutschmark, forcing the UK to crash out of the ERM and netting Soros a billion-pound profit. It was a watershed moment in British politics that shattered the Tory reputation for competent economic management. This helped Labour reinvent itself as the party of competent technocrats, but it also set up the revenge of the Euroskeptic Thatcherites in the Conservative Party, which began under the leadership of William Hague and Iain Duncan Smith. In 2013, they badgered Prime Minister David Cameron into promising the Brexit referendum that would become the hinge for the hard-right takeover of the party.[7]

Brexit brought the Tories full circle. In 1973 Prime Minister Edward Heath had taken Britain into Europe, fulfilling a long-standing Conservative aspiration—Harold Macmillan's application a decade earlier had been vetoed by Charles de Gaulle. Long before the move toward monetary union would appeal to mainstream Tories as a source of fiscal discipline at home, they expected that joining what was then the European Economic Community would force Britain's sclerotic industrial economy to become more competitive. In those days Labour was divided over Europe, with its left wing virulently opposed for the same reason that the Tories were in favor: Membership would erode Britain's strong union protections and give employers greater labor market flexibility. It was not until Thatcher's governments decimated those protections in the 1980s and Europe adopted its Social Chapter as part of the Maastricht Treaty in 1992 that this rationale disappeared.

Thatcher's approach to Europe had been to run it or ruin it. Initially, she made significant strides with the former. In 1984 she won substantial UK tax rebates as compensation for common agricultural and fisheries policies that worked to Britain's disadvantage. Two years later she succeeded in replacing the Community's unanimity rule with qualified majority voting on tariffs and other barriers to trade—effectively ending the French, German, and Italian veto power that had locked in their advantages before Britain joined. But as post-Maastricht Europe moved toward more intrusive regulation from Brussels, monetary integration, and talk even of fiscal union, Thatcher and her followers slammed on the brakes—not least because by then Britain's unions had been successfully cowed.

And then there was nativism, that potent—if sometimes latent—ingredient of Tory ideology that dates back at least to Britain's imperial heyday. Always a tempting card to play to mobilize voters, it comes with the added appeal of diverting attention from distributive inequities and focusing economic anxieties on antipathy for foreigners and immigrants—however spuriously. So it was unsurprising that resurgent Thatcherites discerned an elective affinity between anti-Europeanism and their supply-side agenda to limit taxation. Still, this alignment carried risks—most notably, as former Tory Cabinet member and Deputy Prime Minister Michael Heseltine never tired of pointing out, the potential to threaten the free trade agenda favored by many business conservatives. That danger would mostly remain submerged so long as the bogeyman was the EU, lending plausibility to the expectation that casting off its yoke would improve wages and conditions for British workers—notwithstanding the reality that much of the growth in immigration to the UK in recent decades has been from the Indian subcontinent. Fueling anti-immigrant sentiment would turn out to be a mixed bag for the Tories, as it would for center-right parties elsewhere once they discovered that others were better than they were at nativist politics—but that challenge lay in the future.[8]

The Brexit referendum did not spell out what the post-EU British economy would be like, but most Tory Euroskeptics and the United Kingdom Independence Party, led by the ascendent populist Nigel Farage, envisaged a low-regulation, smaller state—a kind of Singapore-on-the-Thames—as senior Tory ministers began intimating in the media. Farage helped shift their center of gravity even further to the right by forming the single-issue Brexit Party (subsequently renamed Reform) to push for a hard or "no-deal" Brexit, and threatening either to run candidates in Tory constituencies or to mount "entryist" challenges to individual members for renomination as Tory candidates. The result was to push most former Remainers (including Cameron's successor as prime minister, Theresa May) into the hard Brexit camp and pave the way for Boris Johnson, Liz Truss, and Rishi Sunak to continue rebranding the Conservative Party as an anti-immigration, supply-side party. This came on top of the tens of billions of pounds in spending cuts that Tory Chancellor George Osborne had implemented as a proud champion of austerity between 2010 and 2016. The cumulative effect was to reduce public spending from 41 percent of GDP in 2010 to 35 percent of GDP in 2019, decimating the court system, prisons, the police, schools, care for the elderly, youth programs, and investments in public health and local government services.[9]

In July 2024, Labour won a landslide 174-seat majority while the Tories collapsed, losing 251 seats, which left them with 121—their worst rout ever. But these numbers masked the degree to which the ideological terrain had shifted. Reform won more than 4 million votes and came second in 89 constituencies that Labour won, effectively displacing the Tories, for the moment, as their main challenger on the right. Labour won only 9.7 million votes, amounting to a historically low 33.7 percent of the electorate for a winning party. But instead of capitalizing on this windfall benefit of Britain's two-party system—which made him the envy of center-left parties all over the democratic world—the new prime minister, Keir Starmer, opted for a scatter of small-bore measures that signaled he was triangulating rightward. He rejected widespread calls to get rid of the two-child benefit limit instituted by Theresa May in 2017, despite the Archbishop of Canterbury pointing out that it kept half a million children in poverty. By the end of Labour's first hundred days, Sam Knight was writing in *The New Yorker* that the government's most notable accomplishment had been to cut a home heating program for the elderly, a measure that was so unpopular Starmer would be forced to abandon it a year later. The baffling question was why, with his enormous majority and a five-year parliament ahead of him, Starmer was frittering his advantage away.[10]

Within six months of the election, Labour's support had collapsed to 26 percent, putting it neck and neck with the Tories and Reform. Starmer's approval rating was by then trailing Farage's by five percentage points, and some three million disgruntled Labour supporters had signed a petition demanding new elections in view of Labour's failure to deliver on its election pledges. Even Starmer's sympathetic biographer Tom Baldwin likened him to someone trying to navigate a minefield who "takes one step forward, two steps to the side, one step back, two more steps to the side." Despite the fact that it had been obvious for at least a year before the 2024 election that Labour would likely win big, Starmer's government appeared to have no appetite—let alone a plan—to deploy its huge majority to reverse the cumulative effects of thirty-two years of Tory austerity punctuated by the thirteen-year New Labour interregnum that had greased the skids of neoliberal reform.[11]

In Europe, Angela Merkel had led the charge to double down on austerity in the wake of the 2008 financial crisis. She began at home with the "debt brake," which limited Germany's federal deficits to 0.35 percent of GDP. In 2009 she and her SPD finance minister, Peer Steinbrück, embedded it into the German constitution by winning a 68.6 percent vote in the Bundestag—just above the necessary two-thirds threshold. They were appealing to the backlash that had been building in former West Germany after more than a trillion euros had been poured into the East following reunification. Not content to impose austerity on Germans, Merkel declared her ambition to export balanced budget amendments to Eurozone members whose governments had, in her judgment, been profligate borrowers at Germany's expense. As Tooze notes, the stance that German taxpayers were tired of paying for other people's debts ignored the vast benefits German industry had derived from the government's investments in the former GDR and the intra-European trade financed by southern European borrowing.

Merkel and French President Sarkozy achieved her goal in March 2012 by orchestrating a new fiscal compact that required Eurozone members to reduce public debt to 60 percent of GDP and restrict structural deficits to 0.5 percent of GDP—a formula that amounted to "the German debt brake vision transposed to the European level."[12] And it ensured that, as in the US, austerity would be imposed on those who had borne the brunt of the financial crisis on top of three decades of wage stagnation since the 1970s. When the European Central Bank was finally cajoled in 2010 into behaving more like the US Federal Reserve by intervening in financial markets to stem the Eurozone crisis, Merkel and ECB president Jean-Claude Trichet insisted that ensuring price stability would remain its exclusive mandate—unlike the Fed, which since 1977 has also had an explicit mandate to sustain full employment. As the economist Mark Blyth has pointed out, what Merkel and Trichet billed as long-overdue discipline for decades of profligate social spending by spendthrift governments was accurate, if at all, only for Greece. Elsewhere in Europe, the expansion of public debt after the crisis resulted from backstopping banks that turned out to be even more heavily leveraged than their American counterparts. The difference was that the move to the euro meant that European governments could neither devalue currencies nor print money. Merkel and Trichet could in effect force their populations to internalize the costs of the banking crisis by embracing austerity.[13]

There had been warning signs as early as 2005 that large numbers of European voters felt abandoned by the social democratic parties, which triangulated their way rightward in line with the neoliberal consensus euphemistically labeled "modernization." That year had widely been expected to mark a giant leap forward in the project of creating an "Ever Closer Union" with the ratification of a European constitution. Designed by a convention led by former French President Giscard d'Estaing, it was approved by the European Parliament in a vote of 500 to 137, with 40 abstentions, and endorsed not only by Europe's center-right parties but also across the mainstream left. The European Trade Union Confederation (ETUC) endorsed it, as did major trade unions, such as France's Confédération française démocratique du travail and the Union nationale des syndicats autonomes. The proposed constitution would have strengthened the European Commission and reduced the veto power of national governments by expanding the use of qualified majority voting in the service of creating "a highly competitive social market economy aiming at full employment and social progress." Yet in ratification referendums, first French and then Dutch voters rejected the draft constitution by decisive margins, sending shockwaves through Europe's political establishments. Panicked governments in Britain, Ireland, Portugal, Denmark, and Poland canceled scheduled referendums, and ratification procedures elsewhere were abandoned.[14]

European elites scrambled to find another way to adopt the core provisions of the draft constitution. Angela Merkel declared that she would lay out a vision to accomplish it during Germany's six-month presidency of the European Council in 2007. Her foreign minister, Frank-Walter Steinmeier, a member of the SPD, agreed, declaring that "if it is to be saved, and we urgently need it, everyone has to move their position."[15] They achieved the resuscitation by reconstituting the main provisions of the constitution as an intergovernmental treaty. It was signed in Lisbon later that year. But this Band-Aid approach failed to come to grips with the message that farmers, the unemployed, and disadvantaged workers—mostly in the service sector, often unprotected by unions—had sent them in the failed referendums. In France, decisive majorities of "no" voters came from households with incomes below €3,000 per month, whereas 63 percent of households voting "yes" earned above that threshold. Dutch "no" voters also came predominantly from economically vulnerable groups: the less well educated and the lowest paid.[16]

A decade earlier, the historian Tony Judt had warned that significant populations within EU countries were being left behind by the "modernizing" project that was the darling of European elites, and that they would eventually be mobilized in a nationalist backlash against that project. Judt's prescient warning was not about whether the EU would be governed by a single constitution or an intergovernmental agreement enshrined in the Lisbon Treaty, but about the populations whose stagnating circumstances had been ignored since the 1970s. The same parties that had abandoned these voters in national politics were now champions of transferring more control to European institutions whose well-known insularity had spawned the term "democratic deficit" decades earlier. It is perhaps understandable that the elite champions of "modernization" would ignore their constituents' defiant foot-stamping in the giddy years before 2008, despite the warnings of commentators like Judt. That they would keep doing so once the financial crisis and its aftermath had shattered their reputations for competence is more striking.[17]

Yet that is exactly what they did. European government after European government continued capitulating to the Franco-German consensus on supply-side budgeting and fiscal austerity. Even when François Hollande replaced Sarkozy in 2012 as the first Socialist to win the French presidency since Mitterrand's departure in 1995, little changed. Hollande had campaigned on a progressive socialist platform, but—like Mitterrand before him and despite the decisive Socialist victory over the center-right Gaullists in the June 2012 legislative elections—he was soon cleaving to Berlin's mantra. Before his first hundred days were up, he had infuriated the French left by enacting only modest increases in the minimum wage, deferring his proposed tax increases on high-income earners, and reneging on his popular campaign commitment to renegotiate the EU fiscal compact—which, unsurprisingly, he declared would not be put to a referendum. This meant buying into the compact's austerity mandate by committing to raise €7.2 billion in new revenue to meet its deficit targets, while proposing no significant investments in the economy. In case there was any doubt about where he stood, Hollande went out of his way to warn Greek voters that electing the antiausterity coalition led by the progressive Syriza party in their upcoming elections could get them banished from the Eurozone.[18]

Hollande's neoliberal turn failed to ignite significant economic growth in France, but it succeeded in making him so unpopular that he became the first sitting first-term president in the Fifth Republic not to seek reelection. Nor could his badly fractured party get behind any other plausible candidate. In effect, Hollande's about-turn did for the French left what Gerhard Schröder's and Peer Steinbrück's embrace of the Hartz reforms and Project 2010 had done for Germany's left a decade earlier. Hollande underscored this in a keynote speech at the 150th-anniversary celebration of Germany's SPD in Leipzig in 2013, when he lauded Schröder's courage for having adopted the reforms while a beaming Angela Merkel looked on from the front row of the audience. Similar patterns prevailed across many older democracies as industrial jobs disappeared and voters abandoned the center-left parties they traditionally had supported.[19]

Also as in Germany, fragmentation on the left was mirrored by fragmentation on the right. This isn't surprising in view of the broad consensus among mainstream parties on the policies that had been leaving so many people behind for decades. If voters were fleeing the left-of-center parties as they scrambled to embrace neoliberal orthodoxies that had been set by the center right, there was little reason to think that they would gravitate to those parties either. In Germany's four elections between 1990 and 2002, the CDU, together with its affiliated Bavarian Christian Social Union (CSU), and the SPD had won more than three-quarters of the German electorate between them. By 2017, their combined vote share had plummeted to just 53 percent. In 2021 it fell below 50 percent, requiring a three-party government for the first time in decades, and in 2025 their combined share of the vote dropped to a new low of 44.9 percent. This fragmentation of mainstream parties reflects a broader pattern across twenty-six OECD democracies. Whereas in 1960 their legislatures had fewer than six parties on average, by 2020 they had more than eight.[20]

The remarkable thing was how few leaders of mainstream parties showed any sign of grasping that the financial crisis and its aftermath had obliterated their credibility. In the years after 2008, as the fortunes of elites recovered along with equity and other financial markets, orthodox political leaders continued insisting—echoing Margaret Thatcher from the 1980s—that There Is No Alternative to their supply-side policies and austerity mandates. But at what would become a bellwether meeting in Bad Nauheim in the German state of Hesse in September of 2012, a group of journalists and intellectuals demurred. They declared that there was indeed an Alternative für Deutschland—the name they gave their new party. The following year, the party fell just short of Germany's 5 percent threshold to win seats in the Bundestag, but in 2017 the AfD exploded onto the scene with 12.6 percent of the vote, winning 94 seats. Its share of the vote did not drop below double digits thereafter, even as mainstream parties rejected its participation in governing coalitions due to its members' neo-Nazi sympathies—a pattern later repeated in Austria, Italy, and the Netherlands as similar parties emerged and quickly grew.

This shunning strategy turned out to be little more than a holding pattern. In 2022, Giorgia Meloni became Italy's prime minister after her Brothers of Italy party came first in its parliamentary elections. In May 2024, Geert Wilders's Party for Freedom joined a governing coalition in the Netherlands following six months of tortured negotiations after it had more than doubled its vote to become the largest party in the Dutch parliament. The far-right Freedom Party of Austria also placed first in the 2024 elections. It was kept out of power only after four months of wrangling yielded a fragile coalition of Christian democrats, liberals, and social democrats who agreed on little besides their antipathy for the far right. It was as if they saw themselves as the sensible chaps who were waiting for angry voters to calm down and realize how unreasonable they were being. But as Germany's traffic-light coalition of Social Democrats, Greens, and libertarian Free Democrats, cobbled together in 2021, discovered, coalition governments that don't agree on anything can't govern—further antagonizing voters. Support for all the governing parties fell precipitously in the February 2025 Bundestag election, while the AfD doubled its vote to 20 percent. By October, it was polling at 26 percent, ahead of all Germany's other parties.[21]

What establishment politicians seemed incapable of grasping was that support for right-wing populist parties had little to do with the policies they propounded or whether the policies were likely to address the problems they identified. Their blood-and-soil nativism, hostility to immigration and globalism, and virulent anti-elitism made them potent conduits for voter rage directed at the consensus the establishment had embraced for more than four decades—a consensus that had left those voters behind. As television host Tucker Carlson, one of Donald Trump's earliest and most vocal champions, put it in the wake of his presidential victory in 2016, "Trump's election wasn't about Trump. It was a throbbing middle finger in the face of America's ruling class. It was a gesture of contempt, a howl of rage, the end result of decades of selfish and unwise decisions made by selfish and unwise leaders." "Happy countries," he insisted, "don't elect Donald Trump, desperate ones do."[22]

Dismissing these parties wouldn't make them go away. Yet establishment political leaders displayed surprisingly little interest in coming to grips with why their fragmenting parties were hemorrhaging voter support, or why populist figures like Trump, Farage, Meloni, and Wilders were gaining so much political traction.

Macron's Blown Opportunity

Nowhere was this more dramatically evident than in France. Marine Le Pen, daughter of the openly anti-Semitic and Islamophobic Jean-Marie Le Pen, who had led France's right-wing National Front from 1972 to 2011, took over the party that year and began rebranding it as a working-class nationalist party in what would become a model for Europe's emerging right-wing populist parties. In addition to its racism and xenophobia, her father's National Front had taken a hard-right stance on economics. Channeling Ronald Reagan by saying he was determined to "get the state off my back and take its hand out of my pocket," Jean-Marie had called for rolling back the welfare state and greater protection of shareholder interests, and he'd endorsed the large-scale privatization pushed by Jacques Chirac's government in the 1980s. He also pushed for corporate tax cuts, greater labor market flexibility for employers, and abolition of the wealth tax and even the income tax—policies the National Front continued advocating throughout the early 2000s. It combined supply-side neoliberalism with nativist xenophobia, limiting its electoral appeal in an era when that brand of identity politics appealed only to fringe populations.[23]

But Marine Le Pen reoriented the party. In stark contrast to the blinkered leaders of mainstream parties, who kept right on keeping right on with supply-side austerity policies, she realized that their response to the financial crisis was creating new constituencies of alienated voters that she potentially could mobilize. Soon after taking the helm, she began calling for more steeply progressive taxes on the rich to "rebuild" the state as "the first condition of justice," railing against "the dogmas of ultra liberalism" and the "unleashed rein of King money," and denouncing the "proliferation of unchosen part-time work and the untamed spread of short-term contracts" that threw sectors of the workforce "into precarious financial straits." "Shock precarity," she insisted in a press release in December 2012, "did not have to happen!" Most important, she started forging links between class politics and French ethnic identity by attacking "the super-rich who sell our work, our heritage." She also shed her father's anti-Semitism and the extreme biological racism that antagonized many on the left. As Cécile Alduy put it, Le Pen devised "a clever balance of triangulation toward the Left on economic and republican questions and securing voter loyalty on questions of culture and identity."[24]

Le Pen's strategy soon began paying dividends by broadening the National Front's appeal. An early sign was that in the run-up to the first-round regional elections in 2015, polls showed the party winning 46 percent support from blue-collar workers as compared to 41 percent from white-collar employees, 35 percent among the self-employed, and 33 percent among farmers. It even garnered 30 percent support among public-sector workers. Support from economic elites, by contrast, remained low, with only 18 percent of managers, 15 percent of voters with a college degree, and 19 percent of voters with a monthly income above €6,000 supporting the party. The National Front's growing popularity first became manifest in presidential elections. In 2012 Le Pen had been eliminated after the first round, having placed third behind Hollande and Sarkozy with 18 percent of the vote. Five years later she finished second with over 21 percent, rising to over a third of the vote in round two. She lost to Hollande's former minister of the economy Emmanuel Macron, who had reinvented himself as an independent once the Socialists' electoral prospects dwindled.[25]

Le Pen was by then obviously ascendent, and the fact that her party—soon to be renamed National Rally—had yet to gain much traction in the National Assembly was no measure of voter confidence in France's mainstream parties. They were utterly decimated in 2017. The center-right Republicans and their allies lost over 40 percent of their seats, and the center left was hammered even harder—winning just 45 seats as compared with 331 five years earlier. But instead of hemorrhaging disaffected voters to fringe parties, as was happening elsewhere in Europe's multiparty systems, the quirks of France's two-round system enabled Macron to create an ersatz party—En Marche! ("On the move!")—that capitalized on this tidal wave of voter discontent. En Marche! won a stunning majority: 350 out of 577 seats. It was the most far-reaching repudiation of establishment parties in any Western democracy since the 1930s.

The 2017 election results created an unparalleled opportunity for Macron. No French politician had been handed a carte blanche of this magnitude since 1958, when the Algerian War was tearing the country apart and the National Assembly recalled Charles de Gaulle from retirement to take the helm. De Gaulle ended the Algerian crisis, founded the Fifth Republic, which he led for the next decade, and bequeathed a political mantle that French conservatives continue vying over to this day. Macron was analogously placed. He had run a maverick—almost oxymoronic—campaign as a kind of populist centrist, creating widespread expectations that he would address the crisis in voter confidence and restore voters' shattered faith in French institutions. This made him the envy of mainstream politicians across the democratic world, many of whom found themselves fighting rearguard actions against the antiestablishment and even antisystem extremists who were hijacking their voters. Macron was beholden to no one. The left's traditional constituencies had deserted the Socialists en masse, but while Jean-Luc Mélenchon's new La France Insoumise ("France Unbowed")—inspired by Spain's far-left Podemos ("We Can")—picked up 5 percent of the vote and 17 seats, the vast majority of traditional Socialist supporters either stayed home (turnout overall was less than 50 percent) or bet on Macron and En Marche! At the same time, the right found itself split between Gaullists and Le Pen's resurgent National Rally, which took almost 9 percent of the second-round vote, further strengthening Macron's hand. No politician in recent decades—except, perhaps, for Donald Trump in 2016—has had as much freedom to reset the political agenda.[26]

Even more unusual in view of his role as a principal architect of Hollande's economic policies, voters gave Macron a second chance. After all, the economy had floundered throughout the Hollande years, with wages stagnant, GDP growth hovering stubbornly between 0.2 percent and 1.1 percent, unemployment close to 10 percent, and youth unemployment at 25 percent. Macron probably wouldn't have made it at all but for the scandal that enveloped the center-right candidate François Fillon. Fillon had been the front-runner until he was placed under formal investigation for embezzlement a month before the election, leading to his elimination after he came in third in the first round. This left supporting Macron as the only way to stop Le Pen, which most supporters of the center right, as well as many on the left, did, giving Macron his easy victory. It would have taken staggering hubris for the beneficiary of this political windfall to believe that voters loved him or the policies that had destroyed Hollande's presidency.[27]

At a minimum it should have been imperative for Macron to engage in a searching analysis of why France's establishment parties were in such serious trouble, and in particular why the Socialists had suffered their worst defeat in the party's history. It was more devastating even than in 1993, when—in a result that could have been instructive for Macron—they lost 209 seats to win only 53 seats in the National Assembly. That implosion had been fallout from Prime Minister Michel Rocard's decision in 1988 to appoint four cabinet members from the center-right Union for French Democracy in an effort to reduce the Socialists' dependence on the left. His triangulating gambit blew up in his face three years later, when they all resigned to form an alliance with the Gaullist Rally for the Republic. The magnitude of the Socialists' collapse was amplified by the political ineptitude of Rocard's successors, Édith Cresson and Pierre Bérégovoy, but there was ample evidence at the time that his love affair with the center right had infuriated the

Socialists' traditional base, which deserted them in droves in the 1992 regional elections. As with so many efforts at triangulation by center-left parties, Rocard's strategy had backfired.

In fact, Macron appeared to have learned nothing from this precedent or from the realities behind Fillon's inadvertent gift to him in 2017. This was even more striking because by then mounds of evidence were accumulating that voters who had been left behind by supply-side policies were deserting "modernizing" center-left parties and their agendas. Germany's SPD had lost more than a third of its supporters in the elections since getting behind the Hartz reforms and Project 2010 and was projected to do even worse in the upcoming September elections. Britain's Labour Party, which had been turfed out in 2010 following Gordon Brown's response to the financial crisis, was even more badly defeated five years later. The Labour leadership and most Labour supporters voted to remain in the EU in the Brexit referendum the following year, but these were predominantly high earners in London and in the so-called home counties, which border London. Voters earning less than £20,000, low-skilled and manual workers, the unemployed, and those whose believed they had been left behind were most likely to vote to leave the EU.[28] The American Democrats' shedding of low-income and less well-educated voters that had been underway since the 1990s went into overdrive in 2016, giving Donald Trump his shocking victory. In the Netherlands, Wilders's populist Party for Freedom was on a similar trajectory to Le Pen's National Rally, having taken second place and twenty seats in the March elections. Austria's Freedom Party was on track to make comparable gains in October. Everywhere anyone cared to look, populist political entrepreneurs were capturing economically vulnerable voters and those who believed that they had been left behind. It was obvious that for mainstream politicians to have any chance of winning back these voters, they would have to come up with policies to address their vulnerability and alienation.

Yet Macron kept right on just keeping right on. He picked a center-right prime minister in Édouard Philippe, who quickly announced a raft of supply-side reforms that included a flat tax on capital income, elimination of the wealth tax on financial assets, and a phased reduction in corporate taxes from 33 percent to 25 percent. Philippe announced major cuts in public spending to meet the EU's fiscal compact rules at the same time as he promised to spend €50 billion on infrastructure. His government cut back on worker protections to make it easier to fire employees and weakened unions by shifting wage bargaining to individual firms, ensuring greater labor market flexibility.[29]

The Macron-Philippe "Go for growth" strategy garnered applause from French business and international organizations such as the OECD, the World Bank, and the World Economic Forum. Corporate profits were restored to levels that had not been seen in over a decade. Ernst and Young declared in a report that by 2018 France had become the most attractive European destination for foreign investment. The macroeconomic numbers seemed to support the cacophony of applause. GDP growth climbed to 2.4 percent before the COVID pandemic hit, outperforming Germany's and in line with that of the overall euro area. Ditto with unemployment, which was whittled down to 7.7 percent. France, long lambasted as the sick man of the major European economies, had a credible claim to indeed being on the march.[30]

But the reforms did little for France's most vulnerable workers. The fall in unemployment made minimal inroads with the long-term unemployed and unemployed older workers. Moreover, the new jobs were low paying and more precarious, reflecting greater use of short-term (often less than one week) labor contracts and increased reliance on "independent contractors" in the new gig economy. Real wages fell. Six months into his presidency, Macron was being lampooned as the "president of the rich," not just in predictable media outlets and by figures on the left like François Ruffin and Thomas Piketty. Even Emmanuelle Ménard, a far-right politician affiliated with Le Pen's National Rally, complained that creating more rich people would do nothing to reduce poverty. The distress they were tapping into was well captured in a 2019 study by the European Council on Foreign Relations, which found that more than three-quarters of French workers reported having no money for discretionary spending at the end of each month—a percentage that was exceeded in Europe only in Romania, Hungary, and Greece.[31] Twenty-one percent of the population remained in poverty, the same as in the mid-2000s. By the fall of 2018 consumer confidence was falling, growth was slowing, and street protests were erupting against the reforms. Amid collapsing approval ratings and after three ministers resigned in six weeks, Macron added €6 billion in tax breaks for middle- and low-income voters, but he also doubled down on his supply-side reforms. He sent ministers on a media blitz to sell his variant of There Is No Alternative. Emblematic was his finance minister Bruno Le Maire, who conceded they had to do a better job at explaining "that this new model will be successful," while insisting that the alternatives to their reforms would lead to "a dead end."[32]

But they had more than a messaging problem. Six weeks after Macron insisted to *Le Journal du Dimanche* that "je ne changerai pas de politique" ("I will not change my policy"), the Yellow Jacket protests erupted. Triggered by a planned increase in fuel taxes—and named after the yellow vests that motorists are required by law to carry—tens of thousands of protesters began occupying roundabouts and other access points to cities and towns, demanding the abandonment of the fuel tax, restoration of the wealth tax, minimum wage increases, tax concessions for overtime and retirees, and Macron's resignation. The weekly protests quickly began snowballing, sometimes morphing into violent confrontations with police that were decried—sometimes plausibly—as having been instigated by the authorities. The heavy-handed response boosted the already high levels of public support for the protesters while a defiant Macron hunkered down in the Palais de l'Élysée. Comparisons to 1968 abounded, though as a diverse movement that included workers, farmers, truck drivers, and commuters who were united by their economic distress, the protests unleashed by the Yellow Jackets were potentially more destabilizing than the student-centered ones of half a century earlier.[33]

As the size and intensity of the protests grew, it became obvious that waiting for them to peter out was not going to work. The government balked. In a rambling speech to the nation on December 10, a visibly shaken Macron waxed contrite, acknowledging that the anger motivating the protests had been building for decades, that it was "deep and in many ways legitimate," and that he had been cavalier in ignoring it. He declared that the government was rescinding the fuel levy and a proposed tax on low-income retirees, abolishing taxes on overtime and bonuses (which he urged private employers to award before Christmas), and implementing an immediate €100-per-month increase in the minimum wage—to be borne by the state rather than businesses. But he also went out of his way to reaffirm his supply-side philosophy, declining to reimpose the wealth tax on the grounds that doing so would be inimical to job creation. Pointedly, he did not signal any additional measures beyond these reactive changes, asking instead for patience and reaffirming that improvements would materialize in due course.

Like the Occupy Wall Street protests that had erupted in American cities seven years earlier, the Yellow Jackets had neither leaders nor an identifiable organizational structure. As a result, there was no one for the government to negotiate with. But if Macron hoped that his measures would extinguish the protests or restore his popularity, he was wrong on both counts. His plea to businesses to award bonuses to their workers was widely lambasted as comical wishful thinking, and the protesters dismissed his concessions as crumbs, a charade, smoke and mirrors, a drop in the ocean. Polls revealed that while the French public strongly supported Macron's individual measures and half wanted the protests to stop, 66 percent said they continued to support the Yellow Jacket movement. The protests continued for much of 2019 and into 2020, often marked by violent clashes with police. They finally ended with the COVID lockdown.[34]

Macron would never regain the popularity that had swept him to power in 2017. France's two-round voting system ensured his reelection in 2022 (though Le Pen increased her second-round vote to over 41 percent), but his party—renamed La République En Marche! and then Renaissance—lost 101 seats and its majority, while National Rally picked up 82 seats and Mélenchon's La France Insoumise picked up 74. The precipitous collapse came two years later. National Rally cleaned up in the European elections, winning 31 percent of the vote and 30 seats, while Macron's coalition garnered a mere 22 percent and 13 seats, with left-wing parties and the Greens picking up 29 percent of the vote and 27 seats between them. Devastated, Macron tried to regain the initiative by calling a snap election for the National Assembly, but his coalition lost 86 seats—winning less than a quarter of the second-round vote. They were left with 159 seats, barely more than the far right's 20 percent and 142 seats. This left Macron scrambling to form a government. After months of tortured negotiations with a broad alliance of left-wing parties whose only common ground was their hatred of the far right, he eventually endorsed a minority government led by the Gaullist Michel

Barnier, whose party had also taken a massive hit in the election. Unsurprisingly, it collapsed less than three months later after a successful no-confidence vote. Barnier had tried to ram an austerity budget—with more than €40 billion in spending cuts and €20 billion in tax increases—through the National Assembly by means of a procedural gimmick, sidestepping a vote that everyone knew would have failed.[35]

Macron and Barnier were trapped in the straitjacket that Angela Merkel and Jean-Claude Trichet had created twelve years earlier. The budget cuts and tax increases were mandatory because, at 6.1 percent, France's budget deficit was well in excess of its EU fiscal compact requirement. But Barnier's policies scarcely boded well for an economy that had eked out only 1.1 percent GDP growth in 2024, after narrowly avoiding recession the previous year. Forecasts pointed to growth of just 0.8 percent in 2025 and 1.4 percent in 2026, with inflation projected below 2 percent and unemployment stuck at 7.5 percent. As Mark Blyth had pointed out at the height of the Eurozone crisis more than a decade earlier, countries that bought a one-way ticket to the euro were doing something akin to rejoining the gold standard. With devaluation and control of their own money supply off the table, European governments are forced to adopt austerity levels that verge on internal deflation. These policies will lead to growth only under the extravagant assumptions built into the "rational expectations" economic models championed by Alberto Alesina and others.[36]

We can leave it to the economists to debate the merits of the heroic assumptions behind these models (Blyth provides an excellent review of that literature). Politically, it is hard to escape the conclusion that they are disastrous invitations to return to the distributive conflicts not seen in Europe since the 1930s because, when they do promote growth, its benefits don't reach most of the population. Barnier's three-month debacle left Macron an emasculated lame duck: prohibited from calling another election for at least six months, unable to work with a divided left, and dependent on fellow centrist François René Bayrou to manage what was essentially a caretaker minority government that was as hamstrung as Barnier's had been. Unsurprisingly, Bayrou's government fell apart less than nine months later when his proposed austerity budget became a no-confidence motion that he lost by 364 to 194. Macron responded by appointing yet another center-right prime minister who lacked parliamentary support, this time the former Gaullist Sébastien Lecornu. Lecornu managed to avoid becoming the shortest-serving prime minister in more than seven decades only by agreeing to suspend Macron's planned increase in the retirement age until after the 2027 presidential elections. By then the moratorium on calling new parliamentary elections had passed, but with National Rally polling at its highest level yet, 34 percent—ten points ahead of the alliance of left parties, more than double Macron's Ensemble, and almost three times the support for the center-right Republicans—Macron found himself reeling from makeshift solution to makeshift solution to avoid calling the elections that Marine Le Pen was insistently demanding.[37]

Trump Without Trumpism?

The forces that fostered populism in the United States were far from unique, as we have seen, but they played out distinctively because of America's weak parties. Low-turnout primaries in safe seats gave organized congressional expression to the Tea Party via the Freedom Caucus in 2015, and the primary and caucus systems made Trump's hostile takeover of the Republicans against sixteen other presidential candidates possible despite trenchant opposition from the entire party establishment. Once nominated, he squeaked to victory by 80,000 votes spread across three swing states, while losing by more than 2.8 million votes nationwide. This perfect storm was helped along by an opponent in Hilary Clinton who was compromised by her elite connections, her wooden persona, and FBI Director James Comey's damaging last-minute investigation of her use of a personal email server while secretary of state. The improbable outcome left Trump, once elected, in an unprecedented spot: He had triumphed over implacable opposition from Republican leaders inside and outside Congress, as well as many major donors and business leaders who routinely supported Republican candidates.[38]

House and Senate Republican leaders were shell-shocked. Trump's brand of scorched-earth campaigning had taken the politics of personal destruction to levels not seen in the living memory of anyone in Congress. Yet every prediction that "this time he has gone too far!" in shattering norms and disparaging iconic Republican figures as fools, corrupt, suckers, and worse was belied by his relentless upward trajectory. Likewise with the stream of shocking revelations about his personal conduct that would have destroyed any other politician, culminating in the lurid *Access Hollywood* tape released by *The Washington Post* a week before the election. His opponents had been convinced that he would never secure the nomination and, when he did so against all expectations, that he would lose the general election. Trump's response to all criticism was to unleash outrageous ad hominem assaults on his critics and refuse to back down, a tactic that never failed him. The result was that when he finally won, he owed them nothing—as he never tired of repeating. The spectacle of figures like Mitt Romney, Chris Christie, Marco Rubio, and Ted Cruz—all of whom he had repeatedly denigrated and belittled—prostrating themselves before the president-elect in search of positions in his administration made it clear that they agreed. He had hijacked their party. They had to fall in line or leave.

Trump's win gave him a huge opportunity. His terrifying effectiveness left Republican leaders on Capitol Hill—who controlled both houses of Congress—so far back on their heels that it would have been unthinkable for them to oppose him. As a result, he had more freedom to set the congressional agenda than any American president in at least a century, with the possible exceptions of FDR in 1932 and Lyndon Johnson after his landslide win in 1964. Roosevelt had used his political capital to enact the New Deal. Johnson had deployed his to enact voting rights and the Great Society. Having redefined electoral politics, Trump was now free to reshape public policy with comparably far-reaching implications. Despite the polarized political environment that he had done more than anyone to create, the fact that Republican leaders were in no position to oppose him meant that he was in a unique position to legislate across the aisle.

What might he have done? The obvious way forward was to announce a legislative agenda that would have appealed to Democratic leaders on Capitol Hill and many moderate Republicans. This would have given House Speaker Paul Ryan a powerful incentive to get behind it and enabled him to garner enough Democratic support to face down the Freedom Caucus. The caucus's power would in any case have been diminished, because the main instrument of that power, the threat of primary challenges, would have been blunted if it involved opposing Trump's agenda. It is difficult to achieve legislative successes in the American system without bipartisan support. Trump was in an unusually strong position to cultivate that support and build on it to achieve a legislative legacy that might indeed have rivaled the New Deal and the Great Society. This would have meant rejecting the supply-side policies that had produced four decades of wage stagnation and economic distress for the tens of millions of Americans he had mobilized, and investing instead in an agenda designed to foster the type of growth whose benefits are widely shared. The fact that he had been a Democrat for most of his life—and one who famously lacked political convictions—would have helped. It was his ticket to the greatness that he craved.

The distinctive thrust for the New Trump Deal could have been public-private partnerships. In 2016 the US federal deficit was running at $587 billion, or 3.2 percent of GDP, with the debt closing in on $20 trillion.[39] Trump and the Republicans would soon escalate these numbers dramatically, so that by 2019—before COVID hit and without a recession—the debt would top $22.7 trillion, with the deficit closing in on $1 trillion and running at 4.6 percent of GDP. They did so behind the usual smoke and mirrors, insisting—against mountains of evidence accumulated since the Reagan era—that the 2017 tax cuts would pay for themselves by increasing government revenue. Still, it stretches credulity to suppose that even moderate Republicans could have supported large outlays on federal initiatives unless there was substantial private-sector involvement, not least because large sectors of organized business would have opposed them. The answer was to create incentives for business to participate in fostering economic growth whose benefits would extend to those who had been excluded from it for decades. This would have had to look more like an industrial strategy than supply-side breaks for business, the benefits of which had so manifestly failed to trickle down for so long.

One way to do this would have been aggressive and targeted expansion of the Earned Income Tax Credit (EITC). First floated by Richard Nixon as a negative income tax and then enacted by the Ford administration in 1975, the EITC is a refundable tax credit that was initially a modest wage subsidy aimed at low-income workers with children who were living in or close to poverty. It paid $400 ($2,400 in 2025) to workers earning less than $4,000 ($24,000 in 2025) per year and then phased out as income grew, disappearing at an annual income of $8,000 ($48,000 in 2025). It has since grown into a major expenditure program paid to some twenty-seven million workers that costs the Treasury between $65 billion and $75 billion a year. It begins phasing out at $21,560 and disappears at between $46,560 and $56,838, depending on the number of children, providing a maximum credit of between $4,328 and $8,046 a year. Because this is a credit (deducted from taxes owed) rather than a deduction (taken off income before taxes owed are computed), the full amount of the credit is paid to the worker. Some thirty states now have state EITCs as well.[40]

The EITC has enjoyed bipartisan support since its inception. Originally proposed by Louisiana Democratic Senator Russell Long (who shepherded much of Johnson's Great Society and War on Poverty legislation through the Senate), it was expanded during the Reagan, Clinton, George W. Bush, Obama, and Biden administrations. Republicans support it because it promotes work, is pro-business, and requires no new bureaucracy (it is administered by the IRS). Democrats like it because it is a progressive antipoverty program and, though a subsidy to business, is paid directly by the government to the worker. Unlike corporate tax cuts, which can easily vanish into executive bonuses or stock buybacks, the business doesn't get the EITC subsidy unless it actually hires the worker whose income is subsidized by the government. Economists, who typically object to all subsidies as distorting markets, support the EITC in surprisingly large numbers. A 2020 survey of American Economic Association members found some 90 percent agreeing that it should be expanded.[41] Even such conservative economists as Gary Becker and Robert Barro like it. This broad support might reflect the fact that, unlike a minimum wage, the EITC does not decrease employment or invite a race to the bottom. On the contrary, by reducing labor costs to firms, it operates as a capital magnet.

Expanding the EITC had figured in every significant tax reform since its inception—until Trump. Republicans writing his 2017 tax bill rejected numerous proposals to expand it. The White House made no effort to move them, despite the fact that by then some 14 percent of *employed* Americans were living in poverty—a percentage exceeded only in Spain, Colombia, and Mexico among the OECD countries. In fact, the new law reduced the EITC's value by adjusting the way in which the inflation adjustment was calculated. This was a major missed opportunity. Trump could have owned the EITC and run with it to fund significant parts of his agenda that never got off the ground—most obviously infrastructure. His "infrastructure weeks" became a running joke in Washington because of the frequency with which he announced them without ever producing any concrete proposal, let alone enacting anything. A big part of the reason was Republican hostility to funding a major infrastructure bill.[42]

As Trump's tax cuts subsequently revealed, plenty of offshore capital was available for repatriation to the US. The reduction in the corporate tax rates from 35 to 21 percent in the 2017 tax bill was predicted to produce about a trillion dollars in repatriated profits held abroad, and unlike the predictions about the impact of the tax cuts on federal revenue, they were largely accurate. In 2018 alone, the Federal Reserve estimated that some $777 billion was repatriated, roughly 80 percent of the estimated offshore stock of cash holdings at the end of the previous year. This arguably led to a modest increase in investment by the repatriating firms—the ratio of assets to investment for the top fifteen cash holders rose from 2.3 percent in 2017 to 2.8 percent in 2018, while it remained flat at 1.5 percent for other nonfinancial S&P 500 firms. However, this was dwarfed by stock buybacks, which almost tripled among those firms, rising from $86 billion in 2017 to $231 billion in 2018, while dividend payments to shareholders remained flat. The increase in buybacks was two to three times greater than for other nonfinancial S&P 500 companies. The top fifteen cash holders also paid down debt at higher rates, cutting their aggregate debt by $84 billion, while other nonfinancial S&P 500 cash holders increased theirs by $157 billion. One study of the 2017 tax cuts found that for every $1 reduction in corporate tax receipts, there was a modest $0.44 gain in output, 80 percent of which flowed to the richest 10 percent of earners and 20 percent to the bottom 90 percent. Within firms, the tax cuts produced substantial increases in executive compensation and benefits for the highest-paid 10 percent of employees, but had no impact on workers in the bottom 90 percent.[43]

This repatriable capital was low-hanging fruit for generating infrastructure investment by conditioning all or some of it on taking advantage of an expanded and targeted EITC.[44] Trump could have announced an ambitious plan not only to rebuild America's airports, bridges, and highways but also to begin meeting the infrastructure requirements of the new tech economy—telecommunications, networking, and high-speed internet access for all—by including the sorts of projects the Biden administration would fund through its CHIPS program in 2022. He could then have conditioned the benefits of the reduced corporate tax cuts on spending a portion on hiring workers for those projects, with wages subsidized through a significantly expanded EITC targeted at the designated infrastructure projects. It would have been a variant of schemes in Peru and Colombia, where corporations receive tax breaks in return for building infrastructure projects they have bid on, with the added incentive of doing so with subsidized labor. The Treasury Department could have modeled different mixes of EITC subsidies and corporate tax breaks to produce the optimal return. The infrastructure program could have created employment in every state, deployed to projects that are widely recognized as necessary, like rebuilding America's thousands of dilapidated roads and corroding bridges and replacing obsolete airports. Funding it this way would have been a vastly more effective use of tax breaks to create employment than Trump's approach. It would have provided a way to spend a trillion dollars on infrastructure that could appeal to centrists in both parties, business, and organized labor.[45]

Trump could have announced a thoroughly revamped system of retraining and unemployment support to replace America's dysfunctional Trade Adjustment Assistance program and its outmoded patchwork of state unemployment programs, which rely on ad hoc federal add-ons during times of crisis. Administrations since FDR's have been tinkering ineffectually with this legislative and administrative mess. This was Trump's chance. America's TAA program—for workers whose jobs have gone offshore—has never been well funded or well run since its creation by the Kennedy administration. It is in any case obsolete, now that technology is replacing trade as the main source of long-term job loss. Rather than seeing young and middle-aged workers leave the labor market entirely, it would be much better to retrain them for new roles in the knowledge economy, perhaps funded by a tax on windfall gains from automation, as Bill Gates and others have proposed. Workers who leave the labor market are not counted in employment statistics, but they are a major drag on the economy—whether they rely on Social Security Disability Insurance, as growing numbers of dependent adult children do, or worse. This is to say nothing of the lost productivity and political alienation that make them easy to mobilize for virulent, extremist politics. Rather than continue threatening businesses with tariffs for producing offshore, Trump could have led the charge to create an American workforce that American businesses would want to hire.[46]

Trump could also have proposed a replacement for Obamacare that expanded coverage, rather than following the Republican approach of trying to repeal it and, when that failed, chipping away at it through the courts and the tax system. Like Obama, Trump had campaigned on renegotiating drug prices for Medicare Part D. This multibillion-dollar giveaway to Big Pharma originated in 2006, when the George W. Bush administration instituted free prescription drugs for seniors. Obama's efforts to change the program came to naught when it became clear that the drug companies would lobby the Affordable Care Act to death unless he backed off. Trump could have joined the battle, as he had promised to do on the stump and as the Biden administration eventually did for drugs like insulin, but as with so many of his other commitments, he punted. And instead of trying to destroy Obamacare, Trump could have used his political capital to enact universal health insurance by expanding Medicare to younger Americans. The big obstacle is the multitrillion-dollar sticker shock of introducing Medicare for All overnight—a tough political sell in a country where most people already have employer-based coverage. But there are creative solutions. Begin by including twenty-six- to thirty-five-year-olds, who are cheap to insure because they are generally healthy. Allow others to buy into Medicare voluntarily when they lose their jobs or when the falling quality and rising cost of their employer-based plans make them unattractive enough to opt out. These numbers will surely grow as rapid improvements in AI continue hollowing out the middle-class workforce.[47]

Instead of seizing the moment in these ways, immediately on taking office Trump embraced the standard Republican congressional diet. True, he kept up his attacks on the North American Free Trade Agreement (NAFTA), China, and NATO, but unlike the trade policies he would pursue in his second term, much of this was bluster. On the domestic front he quickly signaled conformity. Goldman Sachs had been his poster child for elite villainy during the campaign, yet he appointed three former Goldman executives to his first cabinet and reached for the standard Republican governing playbook: Cut taxes for the wealthy, appoint ultraconservative judges to the federal bench, eviscerate Obamacare, Dodd-Frank, and other regulation, attack green energy in all its forms, and wage relentless war on House and Senate Democratic leaders. These moves obliterated his opportunity to achieve the status he craved: that of a great president for the history books.

Nothing is guaranteed in politics, but it is hard to imagine a political and policy agenda that would have made reelection likelier for Trump in 2020. As the country emerged from COVID, he could have capitalized on his windfall 2016 win by starting to entrench a centrist policy agenda that would have forced both parties to keep converging on the middle. Instead, he boosted the terrifying polarization he has fueled with dishonest claims about winning in 2020 and with his even more divisive 2024 campaign and the presidency that began in 2025. This was the most consequential missed opportunity by an American president since Lyndon Johnson reversed John Kennedy's decision to ramp down the US's fledgling military commitment in Vietnam in late 1963 and instead scaled up the disastrous war, despite strong advice not to do so from major figures on the left and the right.[48] Johnson's Vietnam debacle thwarted the possibility of a second term in which he might well have expanded the Great Society, creating the possibility of holding the traditional Democratic coalition together and perhaps even growing it. That would have been the best bet for heading off what eventually became Richard Nixon's Southern strategy—a deliberate effort to wean political support from Democrats in the South by appealing to racial resentment—and the corrosive politics that followed. Trump's missed opportunity became an accelerant of divisive politics in a comparable—though even more destructive—way. How costly that choice will prove remains to be seen.

Chapter Six

Taking Stock and Looking Forward

The year 2024 was a bumper one for democratic elections. Half the world's population spread over more than seventy countries went to the polls, sweeping away incumbent governments almost everywhere. Even when they survived, as in Japan, India, and South Africa, governing parties lost their majorities, forcing them into coalitions. The exception was Mexico, where the ruling Morena party gained votes and seats, but did so in an unusual context where rising real wages, robust economic growth, and significant investments in the welfare state over the previous five years shielded the government from the voter rage that was visited upon ruling parties elsewhere.[1] In country after country, voters—stung by inflation and angry about immigration—rebelled. The insurgent Chega's furious declaration that Portuguese voters had had

"Enough!" reverberated across the democratic world. In February 2025 German voters continued the trend, delivering devastating losses to the governing Greens, Free Democrats, and Social Democrats. In July, Japan's governing Liberal Democrats followed up the previous year's lower-house losses with their worst-ever performance in the upper House of Councilors.

The anti-incumbent fervor partly obscured the more consequential story of these elections: that right-wing populists made huge gains almost everywhere. Japan's ultra-right-wing Sanseitō, which previously had held a single seat in the upper house, won over 15 percent of the vote and fifteen seats. Germany's AfD doubled its vote over the previous election to become the second-biggest party in the Bundestag. Austria's FPÖ had placed first in its elections six months earlier with 28.8 percent of the vote. It was kept out of office only by an improbable three-party coalition stitched together after months of tortured negotiations among Christian Democrats, Social Democrats, and the "liberal" but fiscally conservative NEOS. Poland's Law and Justice party had lost power following a no-confidence vote the previous December, but it remained the country's largest party in the April elections. Portugal's Chega more than doubled its vote, quadrupling its seats in the legislature. In France, Marine Le Pen's National Rally and its allies won more than a third of the vote and a quarter of the seats in the National Assembly. Giorgia Meloni and her Brothers of Italy–led coalition quadrupled their vote and tripled their seats in the European elections, having taken power with an absolute majority in Italy's national elections two years before. This performance reflected the overall trend of dramatic far-right gains in the 2024 European elections.

In the US, Donald Trump grew his vote by more than three million over 2020 and fourteen million over 2016, becoming the first Republican in two decades to win the popular vote. Republicans kept the House of Representatives and won control of the Senate, despite having doubled down on hard-right policies since 2020 and in the face of the Biden administration's major investments in the workforce and infrastructure, as well as robust economic growth that normally protects incumbents. Even in Britain, Keir Starmer's historic landslide was made possible only by Reform's savaging of the Tory vote in scores of constituencies, handing the Conservative Party its largest decline in history. If Britain had a proportional representation system, Reform's 14 percent of the vote would have yielded more than ninety seats instead of five—which was in any case a record. The populist surge that had seemed aberrational to so many commentators when it first erupted with Brexit and Trump's election eight years earlier appeared now to be baked into the landscape of democratic politics. Traditional center-left parties continued imploding, and center-right parties scrambled toward the far right in vain efforts to staunch the bleeding.

The world had come a long way since the jubilation of 1989. In place of cheery prognostications about a liberal-democratic end of history, ominous comparisons to the 1930s abounded. That decade, too, had been an era of major economic dislocation and widespread insecurity, when countries that were drowning in debt were devastated first by inflation and then by deflation as they crashed off the gold standard in the wake of the Great Depression. Instead of returning to the golden era of globalization that had prevailed from the 1870s to 1914, the post–World War I era descended into destructive trade wars, ushered in by unilateral American tariffs during Warren Harding's administration and accelerated by the Smoot-Hawley Tariff Act under Herbert Hoover. By the mid-2020s, a comparable dynamic was a looming possibility.

Today's fragmenting parliaments also seem like an eerie replay of the 1930s, when socialists, social democrats, and communists squabbled with centrist parties and with one another over how to confront the emerging fascist threat. Then, as now, it was an era of virulent identity politics, tolerated and all too easily normalized by conservatives and business elites because it served up convenient scapegoats to blame for the economic malaise afflicting vulnerable voters who might otherwise make demands on them. The identity politics of the 1930s revolved around demonizing Jews and other ethnic minorities more than immigrants, but the effect was similar: to mobilize support for blood-and-soil nationalism by attacking outsiders. It helped the Nazis, who had won just 2.6 percent of the vote in 1928, become the second-largest party in the Reichstag in 1930 and then the largest one in the two elections held in 1932—a status they retained until they seized power the following year. Mussolini had by then been in power in Italy for more than a decade. Franco would follow in Spain three years later. Even in Britain, where the electoral system kept third parties out of Parliament, Oswald Mosley's British Union of Fascists signed up fifty thousand members by 1934. The pace at which far-right parties were growing in the mid-2020s made it hard to discount the comparison as fanciful.[2]

Tragic Choices

Whether a dynamic that rhymed with the 1930s would continue unfolding into its centenary remained to be seen. That this was a distinct possibility was the result of disastrous choices made by multiple leaders detailed in the preceding chapters of this book. They weren't tragic choices in the sense invoked by Mary Sarotte in connection with NATO enlargement, where an agent faces conflicting imperatives that cannot be satisfied simultaneously, or in the sense sometimes invoked by moral philosophers to mean that all available options are bad. On the contrary, our circumstances are tragic in that we didn't have to be here. Choices were made that could have been made differently. We can't know for sure where they would have led, but it's reasonable to believe they could have opened up better possible futures. There was unusual scope for agency because the institutions, ideologies, and constellations of interests that had constrained political leaders so tightly in the last years of the Cold War suddenly loosened up. Nor is this a retrospective judgment. People whom the decision-makers had good reason to regard as credible made powerful cases for choosing different and better directions.

Some of these missed opportunities arose as soon as the Soviet Union collapsed. The most consequential one for the global order revolved around NATO enlargement. Instead of building on the disciplined, farsighted decisions he made when Iraq invaded Kuwait in 1990, George H. W. Bush created much rougher sledding than necessary for his New World Order by refusing to make major economic investments in the new Russia. Such investment might have helped it become a thriving, diversified trading partner in the post–Cold War era as it attempted the unprecedented transition from a collapsing, sclerotic communist system to market-based capitalism. Bill Clinton followed Bush's lead, effectively ensuring that post-Soviet Russia would be an economic basket case throughout the 1990s. This strengthened the hands of Russian reactionaries, who undermined economic reform and threw Boris Yeltsin into the arms of the corrupt oligarchs as his only economic lifeline to beat back resurgent communists in the mid-1990s. Clinton compounded his error by scuttling the Partnership for Peace and adding Poland, Hungary, and the Czech Republic to NATO, even after his electoral constraint had become moot following his reelection in 1996, and in defiance of powerful arguments made by Brent Scowcroft, Sam Nunn, George Kennan, Bill Perry, and others that he was missing a historic opportunity. The net effect was to scuttle the possibility of a major redesign of the East/West security infrastructure that Yeltsin, François

Mitterrand of France, Hans-Dietrich Genscher of Germany, and others had been pressing for since 1990, and to revert instead to an antagonistic relationship with Moscow.

A revival of the Cold War was not yet inevitable, but George W. Bush and European leaders missed the chance for a reset in the early years after Putin came to power in Russia. They rebuffed his repeated overtures to join NATO and develop close ties with the European Union at a time when he was not objecting to NATO enlargement or European integration for others in the former Soviet bloc, including Ukraine, and when he was going the extra mile to be helpful to the US in Afghanistan. Previous declarations by German, British, and Italian leaders about the overriding importance of integrating Russia into Europe's economy and security arrangements were forgotten or brushed aside, even though Russia was obviously getting back on its feet and would soon become more assertive internationally. Bush's backing of a slew of new NATO members in 2004 was a thinly disguised quid pro quo for their joining his Coalition of the Willing to invade Iraq the previous year, and it destroyed the last vestiges of Russian goodwill toward the US.

The decline in US-Russian relations became all but irreversible at Munich in 2007, when Bush thumbed his nose at Putin's warnings about American unilateralism. The following April, in both Bucharest and Kiev, Bush publicly endorsed NATO membership for Georgia and Ukraine, making it undeniable that the alliance Russia could never join would expand deeper into former USSR territory. Putin went into Georgia four months later. He abandoned his aspiration to expand Russia's economic ties with Europe and began developing plans for a Eurasian economic and political bloc instead. Putin might have become an aggressive nationalist anyway as his economy got into trouble after 2010, but it is hard to see how any Russian leader would not have gone down this path after 2008—as Richard Nixon had so presciently predicted sixteen years earlier when urging major economic, political, and diplomatic engagement with the new Russia.

If the first strike against the elder Bush's New World Order was NATO's unilateral bombing of Kosovo in 1999, and the second was the Iraq invasion in 2003, the third was the decision by Barack Obama, Nicolas Sarkozy of France, and David Cameron of Britain to flout international law by destroying Gaddafi's regime in October 2011 in open defiance of UN's SC 1973, which had authorized NATO's limited intervention seven months earlier. The action in Libya ushered in a failed state with competing capitals and a civil war that remained unresolved into the mid-2020s, and it compounded the regional devastation that had begun with the US-led invasion of Iraq in 2003. It also obliterated the last remnants of any notion that NATO might evolve into a disinterested backbone for a new rules-based international order, leaving in tatters the hard-won doctrine that governments have an enforceable responsibility to protect the populations in their countries. As a naked defender of Western interests, NATO would endure only so long as its members regarded their interests as aligned. Once that assumption started becoming unstuck after 2016, and especially after 2024, its days as a viable alliance were likely numbered as well.

Apart from the economic and human costs of the failed wars in Afghanistan and Iraq and the ongoing civil war in Libya, with its regional fallout across North Africa and the Middle East, the price in lost prestige paid by the US would be hard to exaggerate. The defeats in Iraq and Afghanistan amounted to the largest display of American weakness on the world stage since Marine helicopters had evacuated the last seven thousand desperate Americans from Saigon when it was about to be overrun by North Vietnamese forces in April 1975. It was a long way to fall. The US had squandered huge amounts of military, diplomatic, and moral capital and backed itself into a renewed Cold War that might well have been avoided. Beyond this, it had trapped itself into spending much of the new century mired in the Middle East, with the result that Barack Obama's much-trumpeted pivot to Asia turned out to be little more than a slogan. The pace of Chinese development had indeed become staggering. Its new assertiveness across East Asia and through its Belt and Road Initiative into the developing world marked it as America's emerging geopolitical and economic rival. Yet the US had backed itself into a pointless replay of the Cold War as it staggered from Middle East crisis to Middle East crisis with no end in sight.

There was one benefit gained from the quixotic American catastrophes of the first two decades of the twenty-first century. They finished off the neoconservative fantasy that pro-American democracies could be installed by toppling regimes willy-nilly without regard for their viability, American voters' willingness to sustain them, or whether they would ultimately be friendly to the US. Important as this victory is, it is hardly a cause for celebration, because the reaction it has fostered—disengaged if muscular America Firstism—is no less damaging. Any notion that the US might deploy its economic, military, and diplomatic heft to stop bullies without itself becoming one was obviously risible in light of the second Trump administration's early actions toward Panama, Greenland, and Canada.

Lurching from neoconservatism to America Firstism, as the Republican Party has done, will be costly and damaging, but the Democrats, who reflexively bemoan Trump's brand of unilateralism, have either forgotten or failed to grasp the implications of their own complicity in closing off paths to a better future. It was Bill Clinton who made the decisive early moves to grow NATO, forestalling the possibility of an alternative post–Cold War international security order. Obama and Biden followed his lead with the backing of both center-left and center-right parties in Europe, most of which saw tactical benefits in humoring—or at least acquiescing in—American military adventures, as this allowed them to continue outsourcing the costs of their own defense. It was only a matter of time until someone like Trump would see the domestic political mileage that could be gained from attacking this arrangement.

As this system crumbled in the mid-2020s, forcing the Europeans to ramp up investment in their own security, Democrats wrung their hands about the disappearance of a rules-based international order that they had been as active as Republicans in undermining. All the way back to the Global War on Terror, when they attacked the George W. Bush administration for tactical incompetence without offering any alternative to the Bush Doctrine, they have followed their triangulating instincts to present themselves as more competent managers of the conventional wisdom, as Bush had redefined it, than proponents of an alternative.[3] Barack Obama opposed the Iraq invasion, which 40 percent of House Democrats and 58 percent of Senate Democrats voted to authorize. But by backing intervention in Libya—alongside the French, the British, and unilateralists in his own administration—he joined the club of Democrats who lacked the restraint George H. W. Bush had modeled in 1991, rendering any hope of embedding a rules-based international order little more than a distant memory. Continuing to blame everything on Trump, as Democratic leaders repeatedly did, revealed a troubling degree of denial or amnesia that did not bode well for the future. Having destroyed the fledgling post–Cold War order without pursuing or even articulating an alternative, they were left with nothing. In politics, you can't beat something with nothing.

America's tragic choices in domestic politics also sprang from a myopia about the conventional wisdom emanating from Washington, DC. Neoliberal economics dates to the 1930s, when

Friedrich Hayek and others began challenging John Maynard Keynes's emerging framework for managing capitalist economies. For decades, their ideas remained on the fringes, confined to institutions like the Mont Pèlerin Society and a few universities—notably James Buchanan's Jefferson Center at the University of Virginia (subsequently reconstituted at Virginia Tech) and George Mason. Their political influence started growing in the 1970s at think tanks like the Heritage Foundation and the Cato Institute as Keynesian policies were declared to be impotent in the face of stagflation. But it was Margaret Thatcher and Ronald Reagan who gave supply-side neoliberals direct access to the corridors of power.

Neoliberal economic ideas would have faced a tougher fight to displace Keynesian thinking as the new conventional wisdom had it not been for the triangulating embrace of center-left parties. The neoliberals were pushing against an open door. Jimmy Carter's administration in the US and Prime Minister James Callaghan's government in the UK began embracing austerity as the solution to stagflation even before Reagan and Thatcher came to power, and Mitterrand made similar moves in France in the early 1980s. The accelerating troubles of communism added momentum to the shift because, unlike the 1930s, there was no alternative system competing for the hearts and minds of workers in the West. Part of the impetus for business elites' and center-right parties' acceptance of the New Deal and Great Society in the US, and of the growth of postwar European welfare states, came from a desire to prevent workers from concluding they had nothing to lose but their chains. Indeed, Marxists like Ralph Miliband had criticized the welfare state precisely because it undermined that possibility. Once communism no longer posed a competitive economic threat, Western elites could ignore disgruntled workers, making it easy for center-right parties to keep shifting the goalposts in response to the left's triangulation.[4]

Communist economic models were in manifest trouble long before the Soviet bloc began imploding. Mao Zedong died in 1976, opening the way for market reform in China. Within two years, Deng Xiaoping was introducing private incentives and opening the economy to foreign investment. Companies like Caterpillar and Cummins opened offices in China in the late 1970s and started producing engines and equipment there, soon to be followed by retailers like Nike, Apple, and Walmart. In 1978, the state-sponsored Progress Publishers in Moscow released *The USSR: A Guide for Businessmen* in English, a sign that Soviet leaders were starting to recognize that Western capitalism was the wave of the future well before the fiscal strains of the 1980s set in. That recognition was confirmed for me in a March 1991 meeting between Soviet Politburo member Vadim Zagladin and a visiting Yale delegation, when Zagladin volunteered that he, Gorbachev, and other aspiring Communist Party leaders had concluded in the late 1970s that their command economic model was doomed.[5] The giddy momentum of market reform across the collapsing Soviet bloc after 1989 fed the self-confidence among Western elites that Western democratic capitalism did indeed represent the end of history on which the whole world was converging. That center-left parties in the established capitalist democracies decided to get with the program was perhaps unsurprising in this context, cementing the displacement of Keynesian orthodoxy by the neoliberal one as they embraced the new consensus.

But they missed the extent to which the financial crisis changed things. The neoliberal technocrats' hegemony was indissolubly linked to their reputation for competence. All the talk of the self-reinforcing virtues of financial deregulation and the supposed capacity of central bankers to fine-tune interest rates and monetary policy to produce soft landings blew up in the fall of 2008.

The crash and the Great Recession that followed inevitably gave way to a tortured and many-sided debate among economists and commentators about what caused it. Financial deregulation? The housing bubble? If housing, was it government pressure to write subprime mortgages, securitization, or collateralized debt obligations? Was it the shadow banking system? Was it a perfect storm of all these factors? What mattered politically was that the Fed, the regulators, and the Bush and Obama administration officials—many of whom had for decades been moving through the revolving door between Washington and Wall Street—were so utterly blindsided and visibly panicked by the crisis.

It wasn't just that politicians gave the regulators and financial players implicated in causing the crisis a free ride—letting them keep their jobs and bailing them out—which fueled voter anger that intensified as the downstream effects of the crisis dragged on for millions. Nor was it only that their solution—to bail out the banks with hundreds of billions in public money—violated fundamental tenets of their professed approach. That they did so in ways that benefited themselves and their associates while imposing austerity on so many others was, at minimum, terrible optics—adding to the rage of those left behind. Those decisions were bound to be costly for incumbents, but by themselves they wouldn't have been enough to upend electoral politics as most Western countries have known it since World War II. They wouldn't have made parties like the British Tories or the US Republicans vulnerable to wholesale takeovers. They wouldn't have been enough to cause long-established multiparty systems to splinter, with center-left parties imploding and center-right ones hemorrhaging support to new populist parties with nativist agendas aimed at dismantling the postwar economic and political architecture. And they wouldn't have been enough to produce a precipitous collapse of trust in representative institutions, leading academic commentators and the chattering classes to fret about democracy's viability for the first time in living memory.[6]

For all that to happen, there had to be a more fundamental rift between voters and established parties and politicians. Beyond the stunning scale of the crisis and the mainstream politicians' failure to see it coming—and beyond their self-serving response to it—was their failure to grasp how thoroughly it had destroyed the legitimacy of the neoliberal order that they had championed for decades as the One True Way, to which there was no alternative. The crisis was, after all, at least as damning an indictment of neoliberal orthodoxy as persistent stagflation had been of the Keynesian orthodoxy in the 1970s. Indeed, the crisis revealed the neoliberals to be closet Keynesians—but only for themselves. As Björn Bremer has documented, once the period of "emergency Keynesianism" between 2008 and 2010 was over, center-left parties joined the center right in quickly reverting to austerity. This added the whiff of hypocrisy to the bipartisan moralizing over deficits and embrace of austerity measures justified as being in the national interest. The hypocrisy was most brazen in the US, where Republicans routinely excoriated Democrats for deficit spending and flatly opposed raising taxes in all circumstances, yet when in power they ran up deficits with abandon to pay for unfunded wars and giveaways to Republican interests.[7] In 2025, Senate Republicans went even further when they showed themselves willing to abandon the strictures of the budget reconciliation process, which hitherto had required the budget bill to avoid adding to the debt beyond a specified period as a condition for exempting it from the filibuster. This allowed them permanently to extend $3.8 trillion in expiring 2017 cuts, without finding offsetting spending reductions.[8]

While most political leaders failed to grasp that their legitimacy was irretrievably compromised, some did. As the fortunes of elites and most voters continued diverging in the years following the financial crisis, innovative populists like Donald Trump, Nigel Farage, Giorgia Meloni, Jair Bolsonaro, and Marine Le Pen saw openings to mobilize new constituencies to challenge the basic terms of the neoliberal consensus with an anti-elitist nativism geared to rejecting free trade and the institutions that went with it. And some mainstream politicians who sensed that the foundations of politics were shifting—notably Boris Johnson, Viktor Orbán, and Tayyip Erdoğan—began reinventing themselves to ride the populist wave. It did not matter that they lacked coherent programs. They saw what others could not or would not see: The shopworn consensus and global order that sustained it had become a tottering edifice that was waiting to be pushed over.

Just how exceptional the new populists were was underscored by the reactions they elicited from mainstream politicians and commentators. The predominant impulse was to reach for idiosyncratic explanations or otherwise diminish the significance of their successes. David Cameron was a fool to have called the referendum, and the Remainers botched their campaign. Farage was an opportunist who would remain sidelined by Britain's two-party system. Ditto for Le Pen, who, like her father, would be kept out of power by the Fifth Republic's two-round voting system. Trump lost the popular vote and sneaked to victory in 2016 by fewer than eighty thousand votes spread across three states. Hungary had weak democratic traditions pre-1989. It was wracked by violence and elite manipulation in the interwar years, making it more susceptible to backsliding than the other Central European countries. Turkey had never been integrated into the European Union despite a decades-long on-again, off-again accession process that eventually alienated Erdoğan. There was always a story to tell that allowed establishment politicians to minimize the significance of what was happening, or to address it via gentlemen's agreements to avoid coalitions with the new far-right parties while triangulating toward the anti-immigration policies that were integral to their support. But these tactical responses obscured the strategically vital question: Why were tens of millions of voters across the democratic capitalist world available to be mobilized by these populists in the first place?

The Biden Interregnum

Joe Biden was a partial exception, if a star-crossed one. He was an accidental president, initially a beneficiary but ultimately a victim of the COVID epidemic. By 2020, his political career was waning. Having failed in efforts to win the Democratic presidential nomination in 1988 and 2008, he had also been sidelined in 2016 when, ambivalent about running in the wake of his son Beau's recent death from brain cancer, he was nudged aside by Barack Obama, who declared it to be Hillary Clinton's turn. Once she lost, it seemed that Biden's time had passed. He would be seventy-eight in 2020, four years older than Donald Trump was in 2016 and five years older than Ronald Reagan had been when reelected in 1984 as the oldest president in US history. Before the pandemic hit, Trump looked hard to beat. Two-thirds of sitting presidents are reelected. The economy was doing well enough, and whatever the demerits of his chaotic governing style, Trump was a brilliantly charismatic campaigner. More than two dozen Democrats threw their hats into the primary ring. Most were hoping to get lucky or auditioning for the future, so the field winnowed quickly. But 2020 was Biden's Hail Mary shot, so he clung on despite disastrous showings in the early contests in Iowa and New Hampshire. His victory in the South Carolina primary on February 29 revived his flagging campaign. Three days later he won ten of the fifteen Super Tuesday contests, all but clinching the nomination just as the scale and seriousness of the COVID crisis were becoming clear. His only remaining serious challenger, Bernie Sanders, dropped out a month later, after which Biden coasted to the nomination.

The pandemic turned a long shot into a credibly winnable race. By midsummer, the country was on full lockdown, millions of workers had been laid off, and millions more were working from home while struggling with children who were themselves struggling with remote schooling. The economy was heading for recession, and although the financial markets had bottomed out, they were still in bear market territory with the Dow more than five thousand points below its prepandemic high. President Trump's haphazard response to the crisis—marked by manifestly implausible predictions that it would soon go away, and risible proposals for homespun remedies like ultraviolet light and ingesting bleach—caused his approval ratings to plummet from around 50 percent before the virus hit to 39 percent by June. His Operation Warp Speed program to fund the hunt for a vaccine would ultimately be judged an impressive success, but emergency-use vaccinations were not authorized until after the election. Perhaps most important, the lockdown deprived Trump of his best weapon: massive rallies where he pumped up crowds and mobilized supporters. Biden, at best an indifferent campaigner, ran a low-wattage effort from his basement, promising to be a competent manager who would deliver the vaccine to hundreds of millions of Americans and end the chaos. On Election Day, despite losing thirteen House seats, the Democrats retained control of the chamber, and they also won the Senate, albeit with a razor-thin majority that depended on Vice President Kamala Harris's tiebreaking vote to pass any legislation. They could govern, just.

And they tried. In contrast to Macron's En Marche! party in 2017 and Starmer's Labour in 2024, the Democratic administration that took office in the US in January 2021 quickly differentiated itself from the New Democrats who had dominated the party in government from Jimmy Carter to Barack Obama. Emblematic—and to some extent an architect—of the rethink was Jake Sullivan, a Yale graduate and Rhodes Scholar who had served in various senior roles in the Obama White House and Hillary Clinton's 2016 campaign. Sullivan spent the years of the first Trump administration as a corporate consultant, licking his wounds while conducting a postmortem on the 2016 Democratic defeat. The results of his soul-searching were summed up in an article entitled "The New Old Democrats," at once a mea culpa for inattention to traditional Democratic voters who had long been alienated from the party and a manifesto for the party's renewal that would inform much of the Biden administration's governing agenda.[9]

Bernie Sanders's strong showing in the 2016 primaries had rattled Sullivan to the point that he pushed Clinton to distance herself from the Trans-Pacific Partnership trade agreement, which Sullivan had assisted her in negotiating, and to campaign harder in the Rust Belt during the last weeks of the campaign. Though careful not to repudiate the triangulating strategies of Bill Clinton and Barack Obama, Sullivan called for a renewal of New Deal and Great Society thinking, "to marry the principles of Roosevelt and the ambition of Johnson with updated understandings of how the job market works, how families live, and how corporate and political power are exercised in the globalized, technology-driven landscape." This meant focusing centrally on the increasingly precarious middle- and working-class populations of contract and freelance workers who must often change jobs and will comprise 40 percent of the workforce by 2030. Most of them, he noted, will continue to be service-sector workers who are not unionized and so lack leverage in negotiating with employers and navigating the vicissitudes of the business cycle.

Sullivan then sketched the policies a Democratic administration must prioritize to win and retain the support of this increasingly vulnerable class. His proposals had affinities with the Sanders campaign proposals, but they were tailored to this population and tempered by political realism. Whereas Sanders had called for universal health care, a tough political sell in the US, where tens of millions still have employer-subsidized health insurance, Sullivan argued that the self-insured should be able to buy into Medicare or a comparable public insurance scheme. Whereas Sanders had called for free college tuition for all, Sullivan prioritized debt-free lifelong learning geared to a world in which adult workers must expect to retool multiple times. He also called for incentives to encourage businesses to provide apprenticeships, similar to the programs that are widespread in Britain and that send half a million people into Germany's workforce each year. And because so many families depend on two wage earners or are headed by a single adult who often cares for aging parents as well as children, he argued that affordable child care and elder care should be central priorities for sustaining a viable workforce.

He proposed a mix of sticks and carrots to restructure the government's relations with business. The sticks were geared to breaking up concentrations of corporate power with aggressive antitrust enforcement and redressing inequality by reversing the 2017 Trump tax cuts. On the incentives front, he called for leveraging public investment with private capital by expanding the Earned Income Tax Credit and introducing place-based incentives geared to breaking "the cycle of economic unraveling and social unraveling in cities and regions that have fallen behind." In effect, this was a call for a return to an industrial policy of the sort that had been fashionable in Western democracies in the 1960s and 1970s but had since been denounced by neoliberals as a form of government interference that inevitably distorts market-based capital allocation. It was a measure of how much the bloom was off the rose for reflexive appeals to the market that Sullivan was echoing a recent paper coauthored by Larry Summers. Whatever the economic costs of interfering with market-based allocations, which had concentrated 75 percent of all US venture capital in three states, the social and political costs of not doing so were no longer viable.[10]

The Biden administration that took office in January 2021 was drinking out of a fire hydrant. It had to manage the logistical challenges of delivering the vaccine to hundreds of millions of Americans during a nationwide lockdown with much of the government working from home, sustain support for tens of millions of distressed workers who had been or were in danger of being laid off, help tens of thousands of businesses avoid bankruptcy, and do what was needed to end the recession and mitigate its aftermath. Cognizant of the widespread consensus that Obama's stimulus after the 2008 financial crisis had been too small and prolonged the Great Recession unnecessarily, the administration supplemented the $4 trillion the Trump administration had already spent in response to the pandemic with the $1.9 trillion American Rescue Plan, which consisted mostly of emergency relief and other countercyclical measures. It also had to manage the US withdrawal from Afghanistan that the Trump administration had negotiated with the Taliban. The plan called for the final departure of all American troops by May 2021.

Both these actions turned out to be costly. Republicans would effectively blame the Biden stimulus for the price increases that began accelerating as soon as he took office and peaked at 9 percent in mid-2022, even though inflation was a worldwide phenomenon, most of it driven by supply-chain shocks associated with COVID and the Russia-Ukraine war.[11] In Afghanistan, the rapid collapse of Ashraf Ghani's regime and his flight to the United

Arab Emirates as the Taliban was seizing control of Kabul led to a hectic American withdrawal that limited the United States' capacity to remove military equipment and evacuate refugees. The chaos was dramatized when an ISIS suicide bomber blew himself up at Hamid Karzai International Airport as the Americans were leaving, killing 182 people including 13 US soldiers. The perception of a botched withdrawal shattered Biden's image for competence, contributing, however unfairly, to a rapid decline of his popularity from which he never recovered.

Given these handicaps, it is surprising that the administration enacted as much of its positive agenda as it did. With the economy in recession, rescinding the Trump tax cuts was not an option. Nor would there be an aggressive campaign against concentrations of corporate power, though the administration did ramp up antitrust enforcement. But before the Democrats lost control of the House in the midterms, they made a down payment on an industrial policy geared to twenty-first-century economic realities. Whereas Trump had talked endlessly about infrastructure but done nothing, in November 2021 Biden signed a $1.2 trillion bill—four times the size of Obama's 2015 law that had done little more than keep pace with growing congestion. In addition to major commitments for repairing crumbling highways, bridges, and railways, the infrastructure law provided $65 billion for broadband access, clean water, and electric grid renewal. Then, in two successive weeks in August 2022, Biden signed the $280 billion CHIPS and Science Act, and the $891 billion Inflation Reduction Act, both comprising investment incentives and provisions to mitigate economic vulnerability and reinvigorate America's workforce.[12]

The Inflation Reduction Act was a greatly scaled-down substitute for Biden's $3.5 trillion Build Back Better plan, which was to have accompanied the infrastructure bill. It had been derailed by Democratic Senator Joe Manchin from West Virginia, whose support was essential to its passage and who objected to the cost and pace of its transition to clean energy—coal mining being a major part of the West Virginia economy. These constraints meant that provisions in the Inflation Reduction and CHIPS acts were bound to be small-bore. Most of the funds were spent on climate change initiatives, with some tax benefits tied to hiring workers from apprenticeship programs. The CHIPS Act was the main vehicle for place-based industrial policy and workforce investment. By late 2024, the government had committed some $60 billion in CHIPS funds to seventeen companies, with an expected yield of 38,000 new manufacturing jobs and over 78,000 construction jobs—a drop in the bucket for America's workforce of 170 million. Ditto for workforce development, for which some $200 million was given out to Samsung, Intel, GlobalFoundries, Micron, TSMC, and Texas Instruments. The administration committed about $373 million in subsidies for apprenticeships in 2023 and 2024, and added $109 million to the Workplace Innovation and Opportunity Act, the federal government's largest program of direct funding for workforce programs. As with the employment subsidies, the administration's intentions were good, but none of this could make a significant dent in restructuring the workforce for the new economy.[13]

Timing isn't everything in politics, but it is a great deal, and for Biden it was brutal. Most of his constructive measures were not implemented until the second half of his term, when perceptions of him as an ineffectual drifter were already fixed. Part of these perceptions stemmed from factors beyond his control, but part reflected his ineptitude as a salesman for his policies—especially by comparison with the consummate showman Trump. Emblematic of the difference was that by the 2024 election, voters remembered that Trump had sent them stimulus checks but not Biden—even though Biden's had been more recent. The reason: Trump's name appeared on the checks issued during his administration, and Biden's did not appear on his. By the time Biden left office, Democratic Party websites featured long lists of his achievements that would have been news to most voters. The Biden administration increased the child tax credit and the Earned Income Tax Credit. It helped millions of renters and homeowners stay in their homes and kept hundreds of thousands of retailers and small businesses afloat during the lockdown. It presided over a quicker and stronger economic recovery than other G10 economies—a recovery that was also impressive by historical American standards. Yet Bidenomics, a term Biden coined early on to signal his innovative agenda, had become a pejorative label of failure by the time of the 2024 election season.[14]

By then, the Democrats were inescapably on the defensive. Biden's manifest frailty and disastrous performance in his June 2024 debate with Donald Trump left an indelible image of creeping senility, triggering a palace coup three weeks later to replace him as the presumptive Democratic nominee with Vice President Kamala Harris. With two-thirds of Americans believing that the country was on the wrong track, Harris was saddled with the impossible task of defending an unpopular administration while also trying to differentiate herself from it. And she had to do so while leading a truncated campaign, her legitimacy as a candidate in doubt because she had not won the nomination herself. She ran a surprisingly well-coordinated campaign under the circumstances, marked by a unified convention in Chicago and unprecedented fundraising. The race tightened to the point that many reputable polls had her within the margin of error in the battleground states, but in the end, she lost them all—and the national popular vote—decisively. Rather than marking an end to the Trump era, the Biden administration would instead go down in history as an interregnum.

Could the Democrats have won with a different candidate or a tidier handoff to Harris? Possibly. The economy was in good enough shape, growing faster than that of any other country in the G10, unemployment was at a fifty-year low, and more than sixteen million new jobs had been created. Despite a terrible year for sitting governments internationally, US Democrats shed less support than incumbents in every 2024 election in developed democracies except Belgium. And as the Canadian and Australian elections the following April and May underscored, center-left incumbent governments *can* defeat insurgent right-wing populists in comparable countries and circumstances. So it is possible to conjure scenarios in which the Democrats could have won the presidency, though with Harris it was bound to be a heavy lift.[15]

More concerning for the future was that the Harris campaign was terrifyingly similar to Hillary Clinton's in 2016, suggesting that Sullivan's call for strategic redirection of the party had been ignored or forgotten. Clinton's campaign had been tone-deaf to the economic vulnerabilities of working- and middle-class Americans. Trump, by contrast, had made them central from the start of his 2016 campaign and never wavered. The difference was captured in their slogans: "America's best days lie ahead!" versus "Make America great again!" Both slogans were cribbed from Ronald Reagan, but when he declared in the early 1980s that the country's best days lay in the future, it was when four decades of wage stagnation and erosion of middle-class wealth were just getting started. Trump's slogan was backward-looking, aimed at the Americans who had endured that stagnation. He was tapping into a feeling of loss—which social scientists have known for decades is more potent than the prospect of future gains.

Amos Tversky and Daniel Kahneman initiated the behavioral revolution in economics in 1979 by showing, against conventional orthodoxy, that people are loss-averse: Losing a dollar causes more unhappiness than gaining a dollar brings happiness.[16] It's a robust finding, perhaps traceable to the fact that for millennia most people lived so close to starvation that even a small loss was potentially catastrophic. Whatever its origins, Trump played into it by promising to reverse the changes that he blamed on the neoliberal consensus, especially the loss of traditional American industries to globalization, which had devastated communities. Attacking Hispanic immigration reinforced that message by layering the threat of ethnic and cultural displacement—dubbed the Great Replacement theory by far-right conspiracy theorists—on top of economic loss. Trump promised to restore 1950s Middle America.

Harris walked into the same trap. Her trademark slogan "We're not going back!" resonated with what had become the Democratic base—people with college degrees, bicoastal celebrities, cosmopolitan internationalists, and party activists—all of whom saw the Trump years as an aberration. She supplemented this appeal with speech after speech decrying Trump's negativism, insisting that her campaign was about optimism and above all "Joy!"—which she enlisted Oprah Winfrey to scream at the top of her lungs at the Democratic National Convention—and dubbing herself and her running mate, Tim Walz, "joyful warriors." Trump doubled down on MAGA, supplementing it with more frequent appeals to "America First" than in his previous campaigns. His message to Middle America was that the Biden administration had failed them just as previous administrations had, a message the Harris campaign never took seriously because the macroeconomic indicators were good by comparative and historical standards. The Harris team seemed flummoxed that polls consistently showed majorities of Americans believing that Bidenomics was a failure, and that Trump would be better for the economy.[17]

Inflation, which became *the* proxy in voters' minds for the condition of the economy, was emblematic. Most of the inflation was imported. It peaked in June 2022, the same month that wages—which had been falling since the start of the pandemic—turned around. By mid-2023, wage growth, especially among lowest-paid workers, was outpacing inflation, so that over the course of the Biden administration, changes in wages and prices came close to canceling each other out, with prices growing a total of 21.3 percent while wages grew 19.4 percent. The Harris campaign could arguably have done a better job of explaining these facts, but to believe that this would have made the decisive difference is to miss the psychology of loss aversion. People who know they are paying more for gasoline and groceries than they were four years ago will not be mollified by being told that their wages have grown an equivalent amount, even if it is true. They focus on what they must shell out now versus what they had to shell out then. Before prices took off in 2021, some 20 percent of Americans thought they were worse off than a year earlier. By 2022, that number had increased to 35 percent. In 2023, by which time wage growth was outpacing inflation, over 30 percent still said they were worse off than a year earlier.[18]

Talking about joy and focusing on future gains also signals tone-deafness to the economic strains millions of Americans live with. Almost 20 percent of households cannot pay their monthly bills. A quarter believe that they are not doing "at least okay" financially. Over 45 percent do not have three months' worth of emergency savings. More than a third say that they could not find $400 to meet a medical emergency without borrowing it. In the wake of the pandemic, consumer loan and credit card balances rose to their highest levels in two decades, at the same time as higher interest rates (not counted in measures of inflation) made that debt more burdensome. Unsurprisingly, credit card delinquency rates surged to their highest levels in over a decade. Ditto with auto loan balances and delinquency rates, which by the end of 2024 stood at their highest rate since 2010. Nor was the stress limited to the lowest paid, whose incomes have grown relative to middle-income workers in recent decades. Focusing on those gains can be misleading, because the middle class is in decline. As Daniel Markovits has documented, the rich have pulled away from the middle class, and many middle-class jobs are disappearing. They typically face downward mobility, and half of them belong to the "sandwich generation"—people who are supporting both their children and their aging parents. These are not people who will likely resonate with politicians preaching optimism and joy.[19]

Like Clinton in 2016, Harris featured long lists of policies on her website that could help vulnerable families, from increasing the child tax credit, to subsidizing first-time homebuyers, to regulating rents and outlawing price gouging—all of which polled well individually. But most voters didn't know that they were Harris's policies, a reality that was ironically underscored in a *Washington Post* op-ed contending that most voters "unknowingly" preferred Harris's agenda to Trump's. Trump won the messaging war through endless repetition of a small number of initiatives aimed at providing tangible relief to the economically stressed voters he was trying to reach: Abolish taxes on tips and Social Security, and make interest on car loans tax deductible. It didn't help that Harris ducked media opportunities, notably failing to appear on Joe Rogan's podcast, which reaches between sixteen million and twenty-four million people, where she could have pitched her proposals to groups among whom they would resonate. Rogan's demographic was disproportionately young males, whose most important concern was unaffordable housing. Her $25,000 in down-payment assistance for first-time homebuyers was tailor-made for them. It was campaign malpractice to skip opportunities of that kind. Harris was preaching to her choir while flaunting the endorsements of Hollywood celebrities like Julia Roberts, Beyoncé, and Taylor Swift.[20]

Harris also signaled that she was living on a different planet by failing to grasp that vulnerable voters see the world in zero-sum terms, where one person's gain is another's loss. In her speech accepting the nomination at the Chicago convention—to which 28.9 million viewers tuned in—her central theme was to decry Trump's negativism and insist that America is a country where "anything is possible," where "nothing is out of reach," where "none of us has to fail for all of us to succeed."[21] She seemed oblivious to a truth about economic psychology that Trump grasped intuitively: People's propensity to see the world in zero-sum rather than positive-sum terms varies with their experience. A significant body of research by economists and psychologists shows that older voters, who grew up in an era of high economic growth, are more likely to see the world as positive-sum than younger voters, who have come of age in slower-growth conditions and are more likely to see it as zero-sum. Moreover, two distinct increases in zero-sum attitudes have coincided with two slowdowns in economic growth: during the 1970s and over the past two decades. People with zero-sum outlooks are less likely to think that wealth can grow enough for everyone and more likely to believe that people can only get rich at another's expense. This lesson should have been learned from Hillary Clinton's loss in 2016. Self-identified Democrats who voted for Trump that year had strongly zero-sum beliefs.[22]

Failure to heed this lesson helps make sense of why Harris underperformed with younger voters, winning the usually safe Democratic demographic by only 52 percent, compared with Trump's 46 percent—a ten-point jump for him over four years earlier. It also helps explain why Trump won 56 percent of young men. Consider the lived experience of working- and middle-class Americans born in 2004, the midpoint of the Gen Z cohort. They were four years old at the time of the financial crisis, likely the start of a multiyear period of economic stress for their parents. They were ten when Iraq collapsed back into civil war and sixteen when the

Taliban retook Afghanistan, bookends to the multitrillion-dollar foreign-policy failure that brought no tangible benefit to the US. They were high school sophomores when COVID hit. They finished school under lockdown with the economy in free fall, and one or both of their parents had likely been laid off. And they were twenty, coping with the residue of post-COVID inflation and still eighteen years away from the median age of a first-time homebuyer, at the time of the 2024 election. It is hardly surprising that young voters report substantially higher levels of stress, worry, and loneliness than the rest of the population. Yet Harris was peddling optimism, hope, and a positive-sum vision in which nothing is out of reach. She denounced Trump for "denigrating America" and "talking about how terrible everything is." He was meeting them where they were. She was speaking past them.[23]

Attending to the difference between positive- and zero-sum worldviews also helps account for why millions of Americans could identify with Trump as "one of us" when plainly he was not. As a New York billionaire who inherited what today would be hundreds of millions of dollars from his father, endlessly flaunts his wealth, and travels in his private jet between his luxury properties and golf courses, he had nothing in common with the tens of thousands of MAGA supporters who turned out to his rallies and the tens of millions who voted for him. But his ideology is unremittingly zero-sum. It shapes his approach to trade and geopolitics as well as his America First nativism and relentless hostility to immigration. Even if Trump's supporters don't agree with everything he says, or they know that particular claims he makes are exaggerated or false, his worldview resonates. A trade deficit with China means they are taking advantage of us. An immigrant who gets a job is taking it from an American. NATO is freeloading off the US. Money spent on Ukraine's defense is a rip-off unless they give us mineral rights in return.

For people who see the world as zero-sum, Trump is looking out for us, and that makes him one of us. Harris is not, and she isn't.

The Populists and the Future

The zero-sum outlook that was such fertile terrain for Trump has become widely prevalent across many older democracies.[24] This can scarcely be surprising given the fiscal strain with which so many in their populations are living. One poignant snapshot taken in 2019 revealed fewer than a third of Europeans reporting cash left for discretionary spending at the end of the month, and in no country did that number exceed 50 percent.[25]

It would be misleading to say that the prevalence of a zero-sum outlook is the cause of the nativist and anti-immigrant sentiment that right-wing populists appeal to so successfully, but it seems clear that the electoral appeal of those sentiments is unlikely to diminish among voters who see the world in zero-sum terms. This creates a dilemma for mainstream parties and politicians who are

Figure 6.1 Most Europeans Have No Money for Discretionary Spending

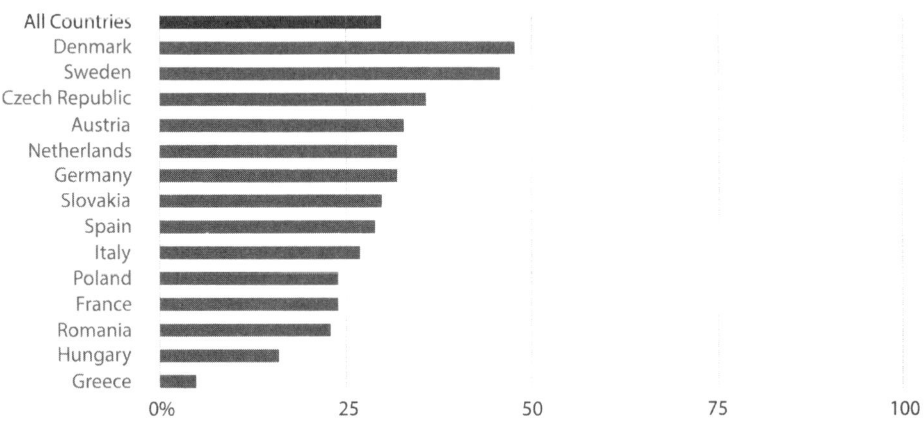

Source: European Council of Foreign Relations survey. Reproduced with permission from ECFR/Datapraxis.

losing support to the far right. One option is triangulation: Adopt their policies with the hope of staunching the hemorrhaging. The alternative is to try to address the conditions that give rise to the zero-sum outlooks that the far right feeds on and reinforces.

The triangulating course is powerfully tempting. Politicians whose time horizon is the next election understandably run scared of being outflanked on the right if they don't. This dynamic is exemplified by center-right parties like Britain's Tories and Germany's CDU adopting strong anti-immigration platforms to head off the respective threats from Reform and the AfD. Whether this tactic can do any better for center-right parties chasing the far right than it did for the center left chasing the center right in the 1990s and 2000s is an open question. The 2024 UK and 2025 German elections are obviously not encouraging.

Pursued as a strategy in the OECD countries, clamping down on immigration will increase fiscal strain on governments, because the old-age dependency ratio (the ratio of retired to working-age people) is growing in all of them. For the OECD as a whole, in 1980 there were twenty people aged sixty-five and over for every hundred between ages twenty and sixty-four. By 2020, that had increased to thirty, and it is projected to double to fifty-nine by 2060. There is significant variation in those projections among OECD countries, but it is growing in all of them due to increasing longevity and declining fertility rates. All else equal, steadily shrinking working populations are going to find themselves supporting steadily expanding retired ones.

Some far-right parties and politicians aspire to ameliorate this stress by reversing the decline in fertility rates. Hungary's Viktor Orbán, who declared in 2022 that Europe is committing "civilizational suicide" due to the combination of immigration and declining birth rates, champions this view and has acted on it. Hungary spends around 5 percent of its GDP trying to increase

Figure 6.2 Old-Age Dependency Ratios for the OECD, 1980–2060

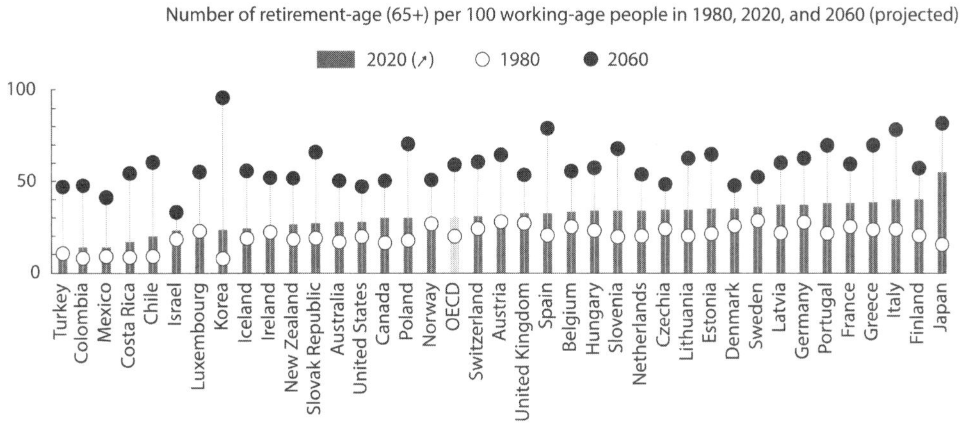

Number of retirement-age (65+) per 100 working-age people in 1980, 2020, and 2060 (projected)

Source: Calculations from United Nations, World Populations Prospects, 2022 Revisions. Some of the values are provisional or estimated.

its birth rate, including government loans that are written off for couples that have at least three children, subsidies for first-time homebuyers with children, government-run fertility clinics, and lifetime exemptions from taxation for women who have four children. Polish parents receive around €120 per month for every child after the first, up to the age of eighteen. Echoing this impulse, in 2025 the Trump administration was exploring a $5,000 "baby bonus" for American mothers to combat the alleged Great Replacement of Americans by immigrants. But whatever their ideological appeal, there is no evidence that such measures have much impact on fertility rates. Hungary increased its birth rate slightly from a low of 1.2 births per woman in 2013 (the lowest in the EU) to 1.6 a decade later, still below even a population-sustaining level. Poland saw a slight uptick in the birth rate after it introduced its program in 2016, but the rate soon reverted, reaching its lowest level since World War II in 2023, even though the program was covering four million children (55 percent of all Polish children) by 2017.[26]

Figure 6.3 Number of Children per Woman in the European Union, 2022

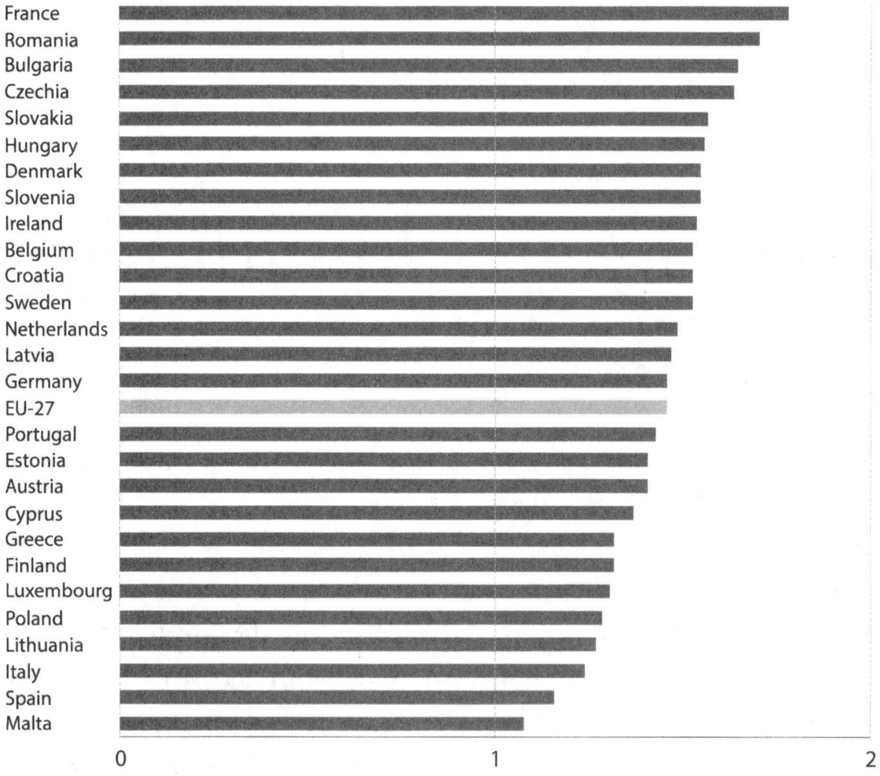

France
Romania
Bulgaria
Czechia
Slovakia
Hungary
Denmark
Slovenia
Ireland
Belgium
Croatia
Sweden
Netherlands
Latvia
Germany
EU-27
Portugal
Estonia
Austria
Cyprus
Greece
Finland
Luxembourg
Poland
Lithuania
Italy
Spain
Malta
0 1 2

Source: Eurostat.

This isn't surprising. Declining fertility rates and rising old-age dependency ratios are not aberrational. They are by-products of a global transition that demographers have studied since the 1920s.[27] Until the mid-eighteenth century, populations remained stable. Birth rates were high, but few children made it to adulthood, and those who did died young. Populations then started growing in the Global North because death rates fell due to improved living conditions, sanitation, and nutrition, while birth rates remained high—known as phase 2 of the transition. Population growth began slowing in the late nineteenth century—phase 3—because fertility rates fell as women's status and education improved and access to contraception became widespread. Most countries in the Global North are now at the end of phase 4, marked by low birth rates and death rates. Populations stabilize as women average 2.1 children, but the old-age dependency ratio grows along with longevity. Shrinking working-age populations are supporting expanding retired populations. Once fertility falls below replacement rates—as is happening in all OECD countries today, except Israel—a country enters phase 5, exacerbating the problem.

The demographic transition doesn't follow an inexorable path. The discovery of antibiotics, starting with penicillin in 1928, increased longevity in many countries, accelerating phase 2. Labor shortages during World War II led to the rapid influx of millions of women into the workforce, about a third of whom continued working after the war, accelerating phase 3. Likewise with the move from one to two wage earners per family and the growth of single-female-headed households in the late 1960s and early 1970s, which reduced fertility rates further in most Western countries. China is joining phase 4 countries much faster than it would

Figure 6.4 Five-Phase World Demographic Transition

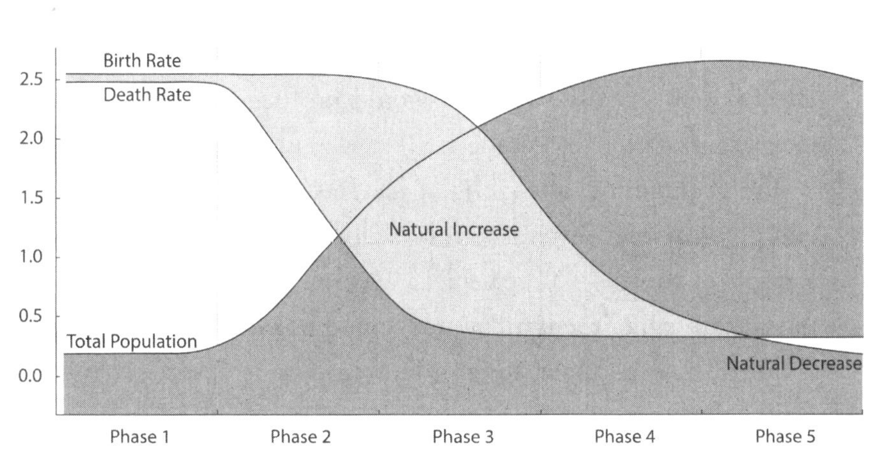

Source: Our World in Data.

otherwise have done because of its one-child policy, which was enforced from 1979 to 2015. That brought fertility rates down dramatically, increasing its old-age dependency ratio from about 6 percent of the working-age population to more than 20 percent.[28]

While societal changes and government policies affect the pace and shape of the demographic transition, reversing it would require a social revolution of gargantuan proportions. Far-right parties aspire to do it by rolling the clock back. Their appeals to tradition and Europe's Judeo-Christian heritage signal that they want to see a return to nuclear families in which wives stay at home as full-time mothers. As Orbán put it in a declaration signed by leaders of sixteen far-right parties in mid-2021, "In a time when Europe is facing a serious demographic crisis with low birth rates and an ageing population, pro-family policy making should be an answer instead of mass immigration."[29] Fertility rates would have to increase dramatically to four or more births per woman to address the fiscal challenge. On its return to power in 2021, Afghanistan's Taliban government banned girls from most employment and schooling beyond the sixth grade. A measure that draconian might have an impact on family structure and fertility rates if enforced over time, but any policies a democratic government could adopt are unlikely to have a meaningful effect. Even successful reforms would not begin to alter old-age dependency ratios for decades.

The economic challenge is at least as daunting as the social and political ones. Even if tens of millions of twenty-first-century European women—70 percent of whom are in the labor market, more than half of them full-time—could be induced to have more children, huge subsidies to families would be required, given how financially strained most people are. Few two-earner families can sacrifice one of their salaries any more than single-female-headed households can, and in any case, far-right parties typically advocate work requirements as conditions for social support. This approach would also exacerbate old-age dependency ratios in the short and medium run as millions of women left the labor market, intensifying the fiscal strain on their governments. Contemplating these possibilities underscores the extent to which far-right populists are inherently oppositional. They rail against the status quo without having viable alternatives.

Some mainstream governments have tried subsidies to sustain fertility rates while parents remain in the workforce. The Nordic countries have led the way, with half of all children under the age of two enrolled in nurseries—almost double the EU average. In Sweden, heavily subsidized day care limits parental contributions to 11 percent of the cost—the lowest in the developed world. These countries also provide generously subsidized parental leave, ranging from seven months in Finland to a year divided between two parents in Sweden. Whatever the desirability of these measures on other grounds, they have had a negligible effect on fertility rates. Sweden's rate has actually fallen from 1.9 children per woman to around 1.5 since 2013, the same level as Denmark and Finland. France has tried a mix of subsidies for day care, cash payments to parents that increase with the number of children, and other benefits like larger pensions and cheaper train travel for large families. It has the highest fertility rate in the EU, but at 1.8 children per woman, it has not even reached the replacement rate. Nor do cultural factors have an impact. The Catholic church's hostility to abortion and birth control notwithstanding, Europe's Catholic countries have among the lowest fertility rates—1.5 births per woman in Ireland, 1.3 in Italy and Poland, and 1.2 in Spain. Women in phase 4 countries delay having children and have fewer of them. Nothing that governments do greatly changes this fact.[30]

Some governments have tried to limit the costs of supporting their growing retired populations by increasing the retirement age, but as Emmanuel Macron discovered in 2023—when his decision to raise it from sixty-two to sixty-four provoked some of the largest demonstrations in decades and had to be rammed through via a procedure that avoided a vote in the National Assembly—there are political limits to this solution. Even in the US, proposals for gradual phase-ins of modest increases to the retirement age face trenchant opposition, underscoring how hard and unrewarding most jobs are. The other logical possibility is to limit longevity. Anyone contemplating that option should read Anthony Trollope's *The Fixed Period*, a dystopian satire set in the 1880s about a country formed by young adults who adopt a policy of euthanizing sixty-eight-year-olds. It collapses into acrimony as the people who enacted the law approach their terminal age. There is no avoiding the reality that the fiscal strain on governments of countries in phase 4 of the demographic transition will continue to grow if they refuse substantial immigration.[31]

The remaining option is to bite that bullet by dealing with the costs domestically. The Danish Social Democrats have enjoyed some success with this approach. In 2015, in the wake of the refugee crises spawned by the Libyan and Syrian civil wars, they embraced one of the most restrictive immigration policies in Europe under the new leadership of then thirty-eight-year-old Mette Frederiksen. Heavily criticized for selling out by other center-left politicians and activists, she was successful at leading the left to victory in 2019 and again in 2022 with an increased 28 percent of the vote—the party's best showing in two decades—while defusing the appeal of the right-wing populists, whose support fell from 21.8 percent in 2015 to 14.3 percent in 2022. Bucking the austerity trend in the rest of Europe, her Social Democrats have poured money into health care, education, and the welfare system. They reduced the retirement age for blue-collar workers (while increasing it to seventy for white-collar workers), adopted rent controls to protect tenants, and instituted carbon taxes to fight climate change. They did this while sustaining Denmark's free education through university and one of the most generous unemployment and retraining programs for displaced workers in the world, amounting to 2 percent of GDP—twenty times what is spent in the US. But they have held fast on immigration restrictions, with Denmark's foreign-born population at 12.6 percent in 2025—well below the 20 percent in Germany and Sweden.[32]

These programs come with a hefty price tag. Denmark is among the most heavily taxed of the advanced democracies, comparable only to Belgium and France. It has income tax rates that rise to 55.9 percent, an 8 percent labor market tax, a 25 percent value-added tax (VAT), and various other indirect taxes that combine for a tax-to-GDP ratio of over 43 percent. That compares with a 34 percent average for the OECD and 25 percent in the US. Moreover, the cost of sustaining Denmark's system will continue to grow. The European Commission projects that Denmark's old-age dependency ratio will increase from 34.1 percent in 2019 to 53.8 percent by 2070. As in the rest of Europe, without significant increases in its working-age immigrant population, Denmark will have to tax itself at ever-higher rates to sustain this system in anything like its present form.[33]

Significantly higher taxes are not without precedent in the older democracies. From World War II until the supply-side revolution of the 1980s, many of them had notably more steeply progressive tax systems, with top marginal rates above 80 or even 90 percent. Moves toward re-creating that world would sharpen conflicts between the populist left and populist right, who agree on their hostility to technocratic elites, immigration, and free trade, but not on distributive politics. Whereas left populists and parties like Denmark's Social Democrats support high taxes to fund redistribution and a welfare state, provided their benefits are shielded from immigrants, right populists want low tax regimes. Germany's AfD advocates radical cuts in income, corporate, and energy taxes, as well as the abolition of taxes on wealth, inheritance, and property. France's National Rally wants to exempt taxes on households and local businesses and on people under thirty, and reduce the VAT on energy and necessities. Yet these parties want to retain and even expand their welfare states. The AfD favors a robust minimum wage and family subsidies. National Rally wants to reduce the retirement age to sixty for long-term workers, index pensions for inflation, and reverse Macron's cuts in unemployment benefits. Britain's Reform party advocates tens of billions of pounds in tax cuts while increasing winter fuel subsidies, scrapping the two-child benefit cap, and adding billions in National Health Service (NHS) spending. Left-populist agendas in these countries court intergenerational class warfare as their populations age. Right-populist agendas are fantastical.[34]

Voters' preferences don't fall out of the sky. Economic stress predisposes people to see the world in zero-sum terms, but they must be mobilized. It's not as if sixty-three million American voters were looking for a candidate who would advocate building a wall along the southern border before Trump came along. These voters had not been available in anything like these numbers until the 2008 financial crisis and its aftermath made them receptive to attacks on immigrants and free trade. To be sure, there had been rumblings before then. In 1992, Ross Perot won almost twenty million votes in the presidential election—the best performance by a third-party candidate since Teddy Roosevelt in 1912—by predicting a "giant sucking sound" of American jobs leaving for Mexico in the wake of the newly negotiated NAFTA. That year, Patrick Buchanan won almost three million votes (23 percent) in the Republican primaries against incumbent President George H. W. Bush, denouncing NAFTA and immigrants in thinly veiled racist terms, and four years later, he won over three million primary votes (20.8 percent) in a three-way race against Steve Forbes and Bob Dole. Significant as those numbers were, there was never a serious prospect of someone like Buchanan or Perot winning the nomination of a major party or winning the election as an independent.

The mainstream political response to the financial crisis and its aftermath changed that. Bailing out financial elites while imposing austerity on the rest of the population expanded the pool of potential voters who could be mobilized by populist candidates. Mainstream politicians with their heads in the sand about what had changed set themselves up to be marginalized by fringe candidates peddling arguments that resonate with people who have zero-sum worldviews. This was starkly evident in tariff debates, where long-accepted appeals to comparative advantage and mutual gains from trade increasingly fell on deaf ears, while Trump's insistence that trade deficits mean Americans are being ripped off gained traction. Telling people with zero-sum worldviews that the US derives benefits from free trade just doesn't work. Either they don't believe it, or they believe that the benefits must be accruing to someone other than themselves. Telling them that consumer prices will be higher with tariffs becomes a tough sell once Trump's message resonates with, and reinforces, their worldview.

And they are at least partly right. It is true, for instance, that in 2025 the $235 billion US trade deficit in manufacturing with Europe was partly offset by a $76 billion trade surplus in services, but the services in question were mainly financial and digital. The winners were financial and tech companies, mostly in New York and California. Europe exports more than four times as many cars to the US as it imports from the US, and it enjoys substantial trade surpluses with the US in machinery, chemicals, and other manufactured goods that are produced in Middle America. This difference is emblematic of why the combination of globalization and supply-side austerity has been disastrous politics for mainstream parties, especially the center left, which abandoned voters in the hardest-hit industries while currying favor with the winners. "Governments aren't good at picking winners" was the standard neoliberal mantra. Its proponents heaped scorn on industrial policy in all its forms and demanded that government get out of the economy. What they missed, and what the new populist politicians saw, is that economic losers can be mobilized to pick governments.

The results are not pretty. Because almost all far-right parties have not yet been in government, they have had the freedom to push policies that are at best impractical and at worst likely to aggravate the problems they identify. The one instance in which such a policy has been unambiguously implemented—Brexit—is instructive. As the costs of leaving the EU (anemic growth and costly red tape for doing business with Britain's largest trading partner) have mounted, and the promised benefits (more lucrative alternatives to European trade and increased funds for the NHS) have failed to materialize, buyers' remorse has steadily grown. In March 2021, British voters were equally divided, with 44 percent believing that Brexit had been the right decision and 44 percent believing it had not, but by mid-2025, only 32 percent believed it had been the right decision, while 56 percent were convinced it had not. For the most part, far-right populist policies are untested, but as with tax cuts, immigration, and social spending, the basic arithmetic doesn't add up. What happens when populists in power try to square that circle came into focus with the fight over Trump's One Big Beautiful Bill in mid-2025, as Republicans found that they could only satisfy both the tax-cutting and social-spending interests in their coalition by adding $4.1 trillion in debt over the next decade. Other countries don't have that luxury.[35]

Far-right populists are, in any case, fighting the last war. Restoring domestic industrial jobs that have been lost since the 1990s through tariffs and immigration restrictions is a fool's errand because the real challenge of the present and future is robotics and AI. The coming battle with China is going to be over telecommunications, microprocessors, quantum computing, solar energy, nuclear and fusion power, rare earth metals, electric cars, biotech, and pharmaceuticals—not over low-wage industrial manufacturing. What this will mean for the future is radically uncertain, with estimates ranging from massive elimination of good jobs to massive expansion of them.[36] But it is obvious that we are not going back to the past that populists promise. In this respect, those who describe figures like Trump as fascists miss the mark. Fascism was radically forward-looking. Hitler was a high modernist who promised a transformative future in a Thousand-Year Reich that would dominate the world. Likewise with Mussolini's expansive corporatism. Trump wants to retreat behind walls and re-create what is billed as a lost past—however idealized it might be. The same holds for other right-wing populists. Hitler's ethnic politics were about expansion and domination—if not extermination—of non-Aryan races. Mussolini's variant of *lebensraum* was *spazio vitale*. Figures like Marine Le Pen, Viktor Orbán, and Giorgia Meloni are traditionalists. Their commitment to the EU is conditional on turning it into Fortress Europe. If it turns out that they can't, they will likely want to go their separate national ways.

The fantastical policies of right-wing populists aside, zero-sum politics is destructively self-defeating. Engaging in it perpetuates it. As with the prisoner's dilemma, one party's uncooperative behavior provokes the same in others, to everyone's detriment. This is most obvious with trade wars, where tariffs provoke escalating cycles of retaliation. They are hard to break out of not only because of that dynamic, but also because politicians aligned with different domestic interests engage in pork barrel politics with those who want other tariffs. The Smoot-Hawley Tariff Act of 1930 in the US exemplified both dynamics. Initially intended to protect American agriculture, the tariffs proliferated to other industries and were eventually imposed on thousands of imported goods, provoking retaliatory tariffs that undermined Smoot-Hawley's original purpose. Demand—and therefore prices—for US agricultural exports fell, leading to increased farm foreclosures and hampering the nation's recovery. The cycle was broken only when Congress delegated its power to negotiate tariffs to the president in the Reciprocal Trade Agreement Act of 1934, enabling Franklin Roosevelt to negotiate nineteen trade agreements over the next five years without Senate approval. This paved the way for the liberalized trade regime that was enshrined in the General Agreement on Tariffs and Trade after World War II.

Congress was only willing to cede that power to the president five years into the Great Depression, when it had become obvious there was no other path out. It worked. FDR knew what was required, and he had established his credibility with his dizzying swath of New Deal legislation the previous year—a dramatic contrast to the torpor of the Hoover years. But it also set a precedent that President Trump would exploit to produce the opposite result nine decades later. The Trade Expansion Act, adopted at President Kennedy's behest in 1962 as the successor to the New Deal law, which had expired the previous year, empowered the president to negotiate tariff reductions of up to 80 percent, but it also included an emergency provision that allowed him to impose tariffs in response to national security threats. In 2025, by which time the powers of the president—especially in matters of national security—had vastly expanded, Trump invoked this provision to impose tariffs on all American imports and additional "reciprocal" tariffs on scores of countries, many of them confiscatory. Whether and how much Congress or the Supreme Court would rein in this assertion of power was an open question, but the fact that Trump could impose them with the acquiescence—if not agreement—of congressional Republicans, many of whom had traditionally favored free trade, was testimony to how intimidated they were by the zero-sum outlook that resonates so powerfully with his base.[37]

Trump's trade war is the end point in an evolution that marries the two halves of this book. America's return to unilateralism under his leadership calls to mind Ernest Hemingway's line about how he went bankrupt: first gradually, then suddenly. It began with Bill Clinton's expansion of NATO and bombing of Kosovo in 1999, eroding his predecessor's efforts to establish a multilateral post–Cold War regime—mediated through the UN Security Council—to manage international conflict. It accelerated with George W. Bush's Coalition of the Willing in Iraq and went into overdrive with Donald Trump's full-throated America Firstism. This spawned both Trump's economic nationalism—verging on autarky—and his torching of what was left of NATO's credibility as a multilateral alliance by fostering radical uncertainty about whether the US would meet its Article 5 obligations in the event of an attack on a member country. He broadcast his zero sum outlook at every turn and confirmed it with his every action. He would support participation in collective arrangements only if the US controlled them and they offered the largest available transactional benefits. This is why he wanted to dismember the European Union. It is a multilateral institution that he could not control. He would have more leverage negotiating with countries individually than with a twenty-seven-member union representing five hundred million people.

And his zero-sum behavior inevitably prompted the same in others. This became clear in mid-2025, when Trump insisted that NATO members increase defense spending to 5 percent of GDP as a condition for the US remaining in the alliance, whereas in Europe the conversation emphasized increased spending as preparation for the possibility that the US might leave. No longer confident that they could count on the US going forward, Europe's NATO members would have to do it for themselves. Whether they could solve the "herding cats" problem without any obvious alternative to American leadership remained an open question, given the run-down and poorly coordinated state of their militaries, their domestic economic needs, and their governments' differing views of the Russia-Ukraine war. Because Putin would be unlikely to survive in office if he lost in Ukraine, it seemed clear that either Russia would win the war, or it would remain at a stalemate as long as he remained in the Kremlin. Given Trump's relentlessly transactional view of international politics, his determination to decouple the US from China as much as possible, and Xi Jinping's regional ambitions, it seemed unlikely that there would be any chance for a reset among the three great powers until all three leaders had passed from the scene. Then it would depend on who came next and how much damage had been done in the meantime.[38]

The internal politics in many established democracies will continue to be challenged by demographic realities. A logical solution for governments faced with the relentlessly rising old-age dependency ratios would be to take advantage of the labor surplus in emerging-market and developing countries, most of which are between phases 2 and 3 of the demographic transition—with some six hundred million young people expected to enter the working-age population between 2025 and 2030—and accept significant immigration to expand the tax-paying labor force. But that seems unlikely, because most of those governments are either committed to—or running scared of—the anti-immigration political agendas that have been weaponized by the populist right. Combining an anti-immigration agenda with a commitment to low taxes raises the specter of ever-increasing austerity, at least in countries whose governments are unable or unwilling to deploy debt to fund a new era of economic growth. Even governments that are willing to raise taxes to the levels currently prevailing in Denmark and France will not be immune from such pressures as the dependency ratios increase and those who are living from paycheck to paycheck in the shrinking working-age population find themselves required to pay increasing amounts to provide services for the elderly—services that will seem unlikely to be there for them once they retire. The resulting intergenerational conflict might not reach the levels that Trollope satirized in *The Fixed Period*, but it will likely be ugly.[39]

The better and more benign approach would be for governments to make substantial public investments to improve the economic circumstances of the working population. This would reduce workers' propensity to see the world in zero-sum terms, which might in turn make them less resentful of supporting older generations and, eventually, more open to accepting significant increases in immigration. As much as possible, such investment should be in the form of predistribution—investing to produce desirable employment on a wide scale—rather than redistribution to compensate those who fall by the wayside. This is true not only for the obvious economic reasons, but also because most people would rather have good jobs than live off government handouts.[40] There is no blueprint for predistribution in the emerging economies of the 2020s and 2030s any more than there was a blueprint for the New Deal in the 1930s. FDR made much of it up as he went along, sustaining things that worked and abandoning those that did not. Policies that will likely pay dividends are those that foster human capital, like ensuring basic nutrition, education, and retraining for displaced workers; policies that indirectly facilitate labor force participation, like affordable day care; direct public investment in the economy to create employment, as with infrastructure projects and other public works; and indirect investment and regulation to bolster low incomes, such as minimum wages, wage subsidies like the EITC, and health insurance. One thing that more than four decades of supply-side policy has made clear is that waiting for tax cuts to produce growth whose benefits are widely shared is waiting for Godot.

Where will the money come from? Borrowing is an option for countries where the politics and economics are feasible. An encouraging sign in March 2025 was when, in a Nixon-to-China moment, Germany's incoming CDU chancellor, Friedrich Merz, engineered the suspension of Germany's debt brake that Angela Merkel had embedded in the constitution sixteen years earlier. The trigger was the imperative to increase defense spending in the wake of Trump's stepping back, but Merz also planned €500 billion over twelve years for long-overdue investment in Germany's infrastructure as well as in climate change and the green economy. That is a large number, comparable to a $2.3 trillion investment in the US economy. Similar developments became likely across Europe as NATO members committed at their June 2025 Hague summit to raise defense spending to a staggering 5 percent of GDP by 2032, 1.5 percent of which would go toward long-overdue refurbishment of infrastructure. Plans to spend on this scale will likely create pressure from other EU members to revise the Fiscal Compact and perhaps even for the European Central Bank to issue Eurobonds to facilitate new growth—a precedent already set during the pandemic. This could unleash a new era of European growth with the potential to reverse the austerity politics of the last two decades. Governments that are more constrained will have to revisit their historically low tax rates sooner, perhaps with windfall profits taxes on emerging forms of AI to fund workforce retraining for economies that are changing faster than ever before.[41]

Another encouraging sign in mid-2025 was that in the UK, Keir Starmer finally began pursuing a raft of policies that promised better results than those of his first wasted year. This might have been because, by then, Labour had fallen to a dismal 23 percent in the polls—11 points below its performance in the previous July's election, 7 points behind Reform, which now stood uncontested in first place at 30 percent, and only 6 points ahead of the foundering Tories, who polled a historic low of 17 percent. Or it might have been because Labour was inspired by Merz's about-face on Germany's debt brake and the advent of a new era of military Keynesianism in Europe. Or it might have been that Labour saw opportunities to capitalize on the reverse brain drain triggered by Donald Trump's attack on universities and research funding in the US. For whatever reason or combination of reasons, in June 2025, Chancellor of the Exchequer Rachel Reeves set out a £2 trillion spending plan on health, defense, and infrastructure projects aimed at restoring Britain's desultory growth and reversing the relentless slide in Labour's popularity.[42]

A more ambitious manifesto than anything Reeves had previously proposed, it included funding for transportation, upgrades in defense hardware, airport expansion, nuclear power stations, and green energy investments. She promised action on the much-discussed Oxford-Cambridge corridor, which has been billed as Britain's answer to Silicon Valley. She included substantial sums for social housing and regulatory reform to reverse the housing backlog. Significant sums would go to regions beyond London—long overdue investment in places like Blackpool, Cardiff, Teesside, and Kirkcaldy. She promised real NHS spending increases of 2.7 percent per year over four years, some of it front-loaded into the first two. On the funding side, Reeves moderated her characteristic caution by projecting substantial savings from efficiency reforms, without providing much detail on how they would be achieved. She also relaxed fiscal rules to allow the government to incentivize private investment by issuing loans and guarantees that would not appear as debt on the government's balance sheet, and by using other forms of creative accounting to facilitate housing and green energy projects. It was the government's first serious effort to free itself from the fiscal yoke it had inherited from the Tories and give Labour a fighting chance to realize a political comeback.[43]

The big question was whether the benefits would show up soon enough for Labour to get the credit in 2029. Like Biden's Infrastructure Investment and Jobs Act and his CHIPS Act, this was an infrastructure-heavy approach that got off to a slow start. One reason politicians talk about infrastructure more often than they invest in it is that it is slow to implement, so apart from those who benefit from the jobs involved in building it, voters are unlikely to reward them at the next election. FDR understood this during the New Deal, insisting that long-term investments be accompanied by measures that affect voters in the short run. Whereas his secretary of the interior, Harold Ickes, focused on public works and other forms of infrastructure, Harry Hopkins at the Federal Emergency Relief Administration spent hundreds of millions of dollars (some $8 billion today) through the states and $1 billion (more than $24 billion today) of federal money on "quickie" projects through the Civil Works Administration in 1933 and early 1934. Notoriously, he rejected projects that promised long-run benefits, remarking that people "don't eat in the long run—they eat every day."[44] The question was: What would Starmer and Reeves implement that would matter to voters by 2029?

The most important priority was restoring public faith in the NHS, which, as political analyst Sam Freedman notes, is the primary way British voters judge the quality of public services. The NHS used to be Britain's most popular institution, but in 2025 satisfaction levels stood at record lows, with accident and emergency wait times near record highs—partly a hangover from the pandemic, partly because the service has not kept pace with changes in longevity and medical innovation, and partly because of years of systematic underfunding by Tory governments. Whether the £22.6 billion Labour planned to spend in the first two years would make a dent in NHS's problems was an open question, since much of that sum seemed likely to be absorbed by inflation, including pay settlements, population growth and aging, and efforts to reduce long wait times for elective care. This meant that much of the burden of improving public perceptions of the NHS would depend on harvesting major savings from as yet unspecified efficiency gains in the projected 10-Year Health Plan. Failing that—or absent larger up-front investments—the 2025 Starmer-Reeves plan risked turning out to be too little too late, consigning the Starmer government to the same fate as the Biden administration.[45]

Perhaps the most encouraging European democracy at the end of the first quarter of the century is Spain. It has the second-lowest fertility rate in the EU (behind Malta) and is projected to have the highest old-age dependency ratio by midcentury. Yet it has managed to resist the anti-immigration politics sweeping other democracies, despite having one of Europe's largest shares of foreign-born residents and despite the rise of the far-right, anti-immigrant party Vox, which emerged in 2013 and became a political force in the 2019 elections by winning more than 15 percent of the vote and fifty-two seats in the Cortes. Pedro Sánchez's Socialist governments, which have been in office since 2018, have refused to run scared of Vox on immigration. Instead, they have continued the pragmatic policies followed by most Spanish governments this century, marked by openness to immigration from inside and outside the EU, including pathways to normalize irregular migrants and eventually grant them citizenship. This permissive attitude has persisted in the face of Spain's comparatively high levels of unemployment, because, as in Britain and the US, immigrants in Spain's highly segmented labor market work mainly in low-paying sectors with tough working conditions that Spanish-born workers avoid, such as agriculture, domestic service, and catering. Unlike his European counterparts who have been traumatized by the far right, Sánchez has been unabashed in tying the country's economic viability to immigration, insisting, as he did in the Cortes in October 2024, that "Spain needs to choose between being an open and prosperous country or a closed-off, poor country."[46]

Sánchez had been expected to pay a heavy price for his pro-immigration stance in the 2023 elections, when Spain faced post-COVID inflation and social dislocation similar to what had battered many incumbent governments elsewhere. In the event, Vox underperformed predictions, dropping to 12.4 percent of the vote and losing nineteen seats, allowing Sánchez to cobble together a minority government. Spain's comparatively strong economic growth was perhaps one of the reasons Vox's zero-sum message did not gain better traction. This continued in 2024, when *The Economist* cited Spain's high level of immigration as a major factor in its 3.2 percent GDP growth and its ranking as the best performing of the world's thirty-seven richest economies. With the economy predicted to continue outperforming the European average and other signs of reduced economic stress—in 2024, Spain recorded its lowest percentage of citizens living in or at risk of poverty in a decade—the possibility that the country might avoid cycles of self-reinforcing zero-sum politics was at least conceivable, offering a ray of hope in an otherwise bleak European political landscape.[47]

Part of the reason the Socialists were able to prevail with this strategy is idiosyncratic: Spain's blood-and-soil nationalism is fragmented due to the presence of Basque and Catalan separatist movements. Their parties are virulently opposed both by the center-right People's Party and by Vox, whose members hate them viscerally. If a deputy from Barcelona begins speaking Catalan in the Cortes, Vox deputies start screaming and People's Party deputies walk out. This dynamic fragments the political right as well as the natural constituency for anti-immigrant politics, to the advantage of the Socialists, who are more muted in rejecting separatist aspirations. In 2021, the Sánchez government pardoned nine Catalan leaders who had been imprisoned for their role in Catalonia's failed 2017 independence bid, and in 2023 it granted a general amnesty in exchange for separatist support for Sánchez's minority government. The socialists have made good use of this advantage, with the result that Spain stands out as a compelling illustration that governments able to call the bluff of anti-immigration populists can succeed in implementing policies that ultimately benefit their populations.[48]

Shouting at the Wind, Again?

What should we make of these developments in Germany, Britain, and Spain, and the decisions by Canadian and Australian voters in 2025 to resist the populist wave that has swept so much of the democratic world? Are they green shoots that will blossom into a better politics, or will they turn out to be stillborn hopes, unable to escape the bleak legacy of decades of bad political decisions? The answer depends on whether the emerging generation of political leaders understand the errors of omission and commission since the Cold War that have produced today's politics. These errors, born of the dispiriting combination of amnesia and myopia documented in this book, have yet to be widely appreciated.

The amnesia was an almost willful unlearning of painful historical lessons. Despite a promising start in responding to Saddam Hussein's invasion of Kuwait in 1990, Western leaders, once the Soviet empire collapsed, made choices more akin to the disastrous policies of the victorious powers after World War I than to those of their far-sighted counterparts after World War II, who were determined not to repeat past mistakes. Where the League of Nations had floundered and failed, and the return to the gold standard had decimated many economies, post–World War II leaders created the UN and the Bretton Woods system and invested heavily in ancillary institutions to manage international security and prevent war among the great powers. They also worked hard to integrate historical adversaries into cooperative economic and security arrangements through the EU and NATO, and they made huge financial outlays to help former adversaries build thriving capitalist democracies.

But the historical learning that produced the post–World War II order was ignored or forgotten after the Cold War. Leaders of both parties in the US succumbed to the temptation to exploit the country's position as the world's lone hegemon, weakening multilateralism and international institutions and paving the way for resurgent nationalisms. The US also led the way in domestic politics. Keynesian policies were successfully blamed for the stagflation of the 1970s, creating an opening to mainstream the supply-side neoliberalism that had been hovering in right-wing think tanks for decades. Leaders of both parties turned away from industrial policies that had fostered widespread, secure employment in favor of supply-side policies whose benefits did not trickle down as promised. Instead, they rendered millions of voters increasingly vulnerable to the vicissitudes of the business cycle, ever-more-mobile capital that hunts the world for cheap labor, and new technologies that make their jobs obsolete. The pattern was replicated across most of the capitalist democracies, as public sectors were privatized, capital markets were integrated, and taxes, regulations, and social support were cut.

Once the communist economies vanished, the neoliberals found themselves pushing against open doors with variants of There Is

No Alternative. Triangulation strategies led center-left parties to embrace the new orthodoxy and stick doggedly to it, even after the financial crisis had rubbished its legitimacy and as their management of the aftermath decimated their electoral support in country after country. Perhaps the best epitaph for this strategy came from the Dutch Labour Party politician Jeroen Dijsselbloem, who had enforced an austere neoliberal diet as finance minister in a coalition led by the center-right Mark Rutte from 2012 to 2017. Labour's voters responded by deserting the party in droves, leaving it with 5.7 percent of the vote in the 2017 elections, as compared with 24.8 percent five years earlier—an even worse implosion than the French Socialists endured that year. Yet Dijsselbloem insisted that the party had done the right thing while in office, lamenting of his voters, "We have lost them somewhere along the way."[49]

The historical amnesia that led so many politicians to undermine the fledgling post–Cold War order and alienate huge swaths of their electorate was buttressed by a myopic outlook that repeatedly took better possibilities off the table. In 1840, Alexis de Tocqueville had praised Americans for understanding that people will be more likely to thrive if others in their society can thrive too. This was the doctrine of "self-interest rightly understood" that he thought the reactionary French aristocrats of his day must either learn or continue facing revolutionary explosions like those of 1789 and 1830 that would eventually sweep them away. He believed this admonition was vindicated when revolution erupted again in France in 1848, as he pointed out in the preface to the twelfth edition of *Democracy in America*, published that year. By flatly rejecting widespread aspirations for a better life, his peers were sawing off the branch they were sitting on. Like Keynes seven decades later, Tocqueville was shouting at the wind.[50]

Whether or not Tocqueville was right to discern this enlightened self-interest in nineteenth-century Americans, US political leaders have displayed little capacity for it since the Soviet empire collapsed. They had the chance to build on and deepen the rules-based international order that FDR and Harry Truman had begun constructing at the end of World War II, which had stalled for much of the Cold War. Instead, they made decision after decision that undermined that order and all but ensured that the West's decades-long standoff with the USSR would be replicated in its dealings with the new Russia. They did it because they could get away with it, brushing aside missed opportunities and warnings about what their unilateralism would provoke once their adversaries were able to respond.

At home political leaders behaved likewise, imposing neoliberal economic regimes because no one could stop them. With unions on the back foot and Keynesian demand management discredited, they abandoned the prudential considerations that had led political and economic elites to support the New Deal and Great Society in the US and comparable initiatives in European social democracies. Once capitalism was the only game in town, they saw no reason to worry that workers might conclude they had nothing to lose but their chains. The question going forward is whether the rude awakening delivered since 2016 is sinking in. The danger is that political leaders will rely on the eventual failure of populist policies to regain voter support—a risk that came into view six months into the second Trump administration. Voters were souring on Trump's management of the economy and immigration, the signature issues that had won him the election. Democratic leaders and commentators reveled in the schadenfreude, but none of them addressed a more troubling fact: Their own popularity stood at its lowest level since the early 1990s, when Newt Gingrich orchestrated the first Republican takeover of Congress in more than four decades.[51]

Democracies are at an inflection point. The supply-side era that was ushered in after the stagflation of the 1970s and went into overdrive with the collapse of communism has run its course. Its proponents have themselves been discredited by the failures of their macroeconomic management and their opportunistic use of Keynesian remedies to bail themselves and their allies out of trouble while imposing austerity on everyone else. Another piece of conventional wisdom has been shredded since 2016: that everyone must live with the neoliberal project because There Is No Alternative. The rise of far-right populism has revealed that alternatives do exist—ones that people left behind by neoliberalism can be mobilized to support, and that people who celebrated Fukuyama's "end of history" do not want for themselves or their children. It is time for them to wake up to the fact that unless democratic capitalism delivers demonstrable advantages for most citizens, they will have few reasons to support it.

It is not enough to wait for the populists to fail. They might be voted out of office when they don't deliver, but that is far from certain. They might become more repressive, turning recent episodes of democratic backsliding into harbingers of the future. They might involve their countries in foreign conflicts—one of the oldest tricks in the book for governments that are failing at home—with plenty of opportunities to do so in a protracted zero-sum global environment. Or they might simply stumble on in government, particularly if mainstream parties offer no viable alternatives that address the conditions that gave rise to populism. As the forty-two-year-old Franklin Roosevelt told the defeated Democrats in 1924, "Waiting with hands folded for the Republicans to make mistakes" would never be enough. They needed to devise a program that would speak to the interests of most voters, get behind it, and—when the opportunity arose—implement it.[52]

FDR was still hammering away at this theme in the run-up to his fourth victorious presidential election twenty years later. In his January 1944 State of the Union message, he argued that the

Bill of Rights had been appropriate for an agrarian society when the Constitution was written, but more was needed for people to have a viable shot at a good life in a modern industrial economy. He proposed an economic Bill of Rights, beginning with a right to "a useful and remunerative job" that would provide adequate sustenance. He added rights to education, a decent home, medical care, and "protection from the economic fears of old age and sickness and accident and unemployment," rights for farmers to earn a decent living and for businessmen to trade in a world free of domination by monopolies. This was the manifesto for postwar reconstruction that FDR never lived to implement, though parts of it would be realized in Harry Truman's Fair Deal and Lyndon Johnson's Great Society.

FDR's rationale for his Second Bill of Rights was that people cannot be genuinely free without economic security. "Necessitous men are not free men," he insisted. "People who are hungry—people who are out of a job—are the stuff of which dictatorships are made."[53] This was obvious common sense when FDR said it eight decades ago. It remains obvious common sense today.

Acknowledgments

This book grew out of the DeVane Lectures that I gave at Yale in the fall of 2019. My thanks are due to then-President Peter Salovey for inviting me to deliver the lectures, which are distinctive in being a regular Yale course that is also open to the public. The latter mandate was helpfully amplified by the staff of Yale's Poorvu Center for Teaching and Learning, who filmed the lectures and posted them on YouTube, expanding my audience into the millions. The online presence has given the lectures an afterlife and made me the recipient of a steady flow of email commentary from all over the world. This gift that keeps on giving has posed novel questions for me and broadened my horizons in countless ways while I have been writing the book. It has been a hugely rewarding experience for which I am grateful.

Much of the material has also been presented at conferences, workshops, and public lectures, often garnering helpful feedback. My conversations with postdocs Fernando Bizzarro, Maikol Cerda, Christian Cox, William Kwok, Alex Kustov, Elle Pfeffer, and Christian Salas in connection with our collaborative work on political parties and the politics of inclusive growth have been especially valuable, as have the contributions of many scholars who have attended our workshops on these topics. I am indebted to Michael Graetz, David Mayhew, Rogers Smith, and Jonny Steinberg, who read the manuscript and helped me diminish many of its faults, as did my good friend Elizabeth Kaufman. Elizabeth deserves special mention for humoring my grumpiness often enough to be well qualified to testify that I am someone who relishes the condition of having written more than I do the process of writing. I am grateful to my agent, Sebastian Godwin, and my publisher, Lara Heimert, for their enthusiasm for the project from the start and their helpful comments on the manuscript. Joshua Bolchover and Tioné Hoeckner did outstanding work as research assistants, as did Miye Sugino in drawing the figures.

Some material in the introduction builds on arguments I made in *Uncommon Sense* (2024) and is drawn on here with permission from Yale University Press. Ditto for some material in Chapter Three, which expands on arguments I made in *Politics Against Domination* (2016) and is drawn on with permission from Harvard University Press. Financial support for the research was supplied by Yale's Institute for Social and Policy Studies, the MacMillan Center for International and Area Studies, and the Jackson School's Program on Effective Democratic Governance, which is generously funded by Jim Leitner. I am grateful for all this support, and also to the Center for European Studies and Comparative Politics at Sciences Po in Paris, which hosted me as a visiting professor during the spring semester of 2024 while I was writing. Thank you, everyone. The usual caveats apply.

Notes

Introduction

1. Steven Levitsky and Daniel Zieblatt, *How Democracies Die* (New York: Penguin Random House, 2019); Timothy Snyder, *The Road to Unfreedom: Russia, Europe, America* (New York: Crown, 2019); David Runciman, *How Democracy Ends* (London: Profile Books, 2018); and Martin Wolf, *The Crisis of Democratic Capitalism* (New York: Penguin Press, 2023).

2. Adam Przeworski, *Democracy and the Market* (Cambridge, UK: Cambridge University Press, 1991); János Kornai, *The Road to a Free Economy* (New York: Norton, 1990); Jeffrey Sachs, *Poland's Jump to the Market Economy* (Cambridge, MA: MIT Press, 1993).

3. These sentiments were bluntly expressed by Soviet Politburo member Vadim Zagladin to a Yale delegation of which I was a member in Moscow in March 1991.

4. Richard Boudreaux, "Mandela Lauds Castro as visit to Cuba Ends," *Los Angeles Times*, July 28, 1991, www.latimes.com/archives/la-xpm-1991-07-28-mn-519-story.html.

5. Albert O. Hirschman, *A Bias for Hope: Essays on Development and Latin America* (New Haven, CT: Yale University Press, 1971), 6–7.

Chapter One: Waging a Global War on Terror

1. Kyle Fitzgerald, "What Did the US War in Iraq Ultimately Cost?," *The National*, March 17, 2023, www.thenationalnews.com/world/us-news/2023/03/17/what-did-the-us-war-in-iraq-ultimately-cost/; Neta C. Crawford, "Blood and Treasure," Watson Institute for International and Public Affairs, Brown University, March 15, 2023, https://costsofwar.watson.brown.edu/sites/default/files/papers/Costs-of-20-Years-of-Iraq-War-Crawford.pdf; Neta C. Crawford, "Human and Budgetary Costs to Date of the U.S. War in Afghanistan, 2001–2021," Watson Institute for International and Public Affairs, Brown University, 2021,

https://watson.brown.edu/costsofwar/figures/2021/human-and-budgetary-costs-date-us-war-afghanistan-2001-2022.

2. "Timeline: The Rise, Spread, and Fall of the Islamic State," Wilson Center, October 28, 2019, www.wilsoncenter.org/article/timeline-the-rise-spread-and-fall-the-islamic-state; Riazat Butt, "Two-Year Timeline of Events in Afghanistan Since 2021 Taliban Takeover," Associated Press, August 14, 2023, https://apnews.com/article/afghanistan-taliban-second-year-timeline-490bab098864b13d8f8cdb67ae044bee.

3. Virginia Harrison and Daniele Palumbo, "China Anniversary: How the Country Became the World's 'Economic Miracle,'" BBC, September 30, 2019, www.bbc.com/news/business-49806247; "China GDP per Capita," Macrotrends, 2023, www.macrotrends.net/countries/CHN/china/gdp-per-capita; "United States GDP per Capita," Macrotrends, 2023, www.macrotrends.net/countries/USA/united-states/gdp-per-capita.

4. Michael McFaul, "U.S.-Russia Relations After September 11, 2001," Carnegie Endowment, October 24, 2001, https://carnegieendowment.org/2001/10/24/u.s.-russia-relations-after-september-11-2001-pub-840; Jacques deLisle, "9/11 and U.S.-China Relations," Foreign Policy Research Institute, September 3, 2011, www.fpri.org/article/2011/09/911-and-u-s-china-relations/.

5. Robert Lieber, "Oil and Power After the Gulf War," *International Security* 17, no. 1 (1992): 161.

6. George H. W. Bush, "Address Before a Joint Session of the Congress," Public Papers, George H. W. Bush Presidential Library and Museum, September 11, 1990, https://bush41library.tamu.edu/archives/public-papers/2217.

7. "Vietnam Statistics—War Costs: Complete Picture Impossible," CQ Almanac, 1975, https://library.cqpress.com/cqalmanac/document.php?id=cqal75-1213988.

8. Jeffrey Record, "Back to the Weinberger-Powell Doctrine?," Strategic Studies Quarterly (Fall 2007), https://apps.dtic.mil/sti/pdfs/ADA509121.pdf.

9. Eliot Brenner, "Powell: We're Going to Cut It Off . . . Kill It," UPI Archives, January 23, 1991, www.upi.com/Archives/1991/01/23/Powell-Were-going-to-cut-it-off-kill-it/9990332341450; David Petraeus and Andrew Roberts, *Conflict: The Evolution of Warfare from 1945 to Ukraine* (New York: Harper Collins, 2023), 185–202.

10. "Echoes from the Past," History News Network, February 2, 2011, http://hnn.us/articles/631.html.

11. H. H. Asquith, *Letters to Venetia Stanley*, ed. Michael and Eleanor Brock (Oxford, UK: Oxford University Press, 1982), 510.

12. Stephen Walt, "Wikileaks, April Glaspie and Saddam Hussein," *Foreign Policy*, January 9, 2011, https://foreignpolicy.com/2011/01/09 wikileaks-april-glaspie-and-saddam-hussein/; Leslie Gelb, "Foreign Affairs: A Bush Green Light to Iraq," *New York Times*, October 22, 1992, www

.nytimes.com/1992/10/22/opinion/foreign-affairs-a-bush-green-light-to-iraq.html; "War in the Gulf: Bush Statement," *New York Times*, February 16, 1991, www.nytimes.com/1991/02/16/world/war-gulf-bush-statement-excerpts-2-statements-bush-iraq-s-proposal-for-ending.html.

13. George W. Bush, "Address to a Joint Session of Congress and the American People," The White House, September 20, 2001, https://georgewbush-whitehouse.archives.gov/news/releases/2001/09/print/20010920-8.html.

14. Peter Bergen, *The Rise and Fall of Osama bin Laden* (New York: Simon & Schuster, 2021), 67–73.

15. Osama bin Laden's Fatwa 1996, "Declaration of War Against the Americans Occupying the Land of the Two Holy Places," Muni Information System website, August 23, 1996, https://is.muni.cz/el/1423/jaro2010/MVZ203/OBL___AQ__Fatwa_1996.pdf; Bergen, *Rise and Fall*, 117–18, 131–32.

16. Donald Rumsfeld, speech September 10, 2001, broadcast by C-SPAN, posted November 29, 2020, by 10% For The BigGuy, YouTube, www.youtube.com/watch?v=MfMjdKElgqY.

17. Bergen, *Rise and Fall*, 143–46, 148.

18. Bergen, *Rise and Fall*, 158–59.

19. Bergen, *Rise and Fall*, 78–79, 160, 185.

20. George W. Bush, Speech to Joint Session of Congress and the American People, The White House, September 20, 2001, https://georgewbush-whitehouse.archives.gov/news/releases/2001/09/20010920-8.html.

21. Anne Stenerson, *Al-Qaida in Afghanistan* (New York: Cambridge University Press, 2017), 69–95; Bergen, *Rise and Fall*, 86–87.

22. Carter Malkasian, *The American War in Afghanistan: A History* (New York: Oxford University Press, 2023); Bob Woodward, *Bush at War* (New York: Simon and Schuster, 2002), 55–58.

23. Lawrence Wilkerson, "Foreign Policy Mess," interview by Scott MacLeod, *The Cairo Review*, October 19, 2014, www.thecairoreview.com/q-a/foreign-policy-mess/.

24. Peter Krause, "The Last Good Chance: A Reassessment of U.S. Operations at Tora Bora," *Security Studies* 17 (2008): 644–84, http://web.mit.edu/polisci/people/gradstudents/papers/PKrause%20The%20Last%20Good%20Chance.pdf; US Senate, "Tora Bora Revisited: How We Failed to Get Bin Laden and Why It Matters Today," Report to the Senate Foreign Relations Committee, November 30, 2009, 17–19, www.foreign.senate.gov/imo/media/doc/Tora_Bora_Report.pdf; Carlotta Gall, *The Wrong Enemy: America in Afghanistan, 2001–2014* (New York: Houghton Mifflin, 2014), 76; see Benjamin Runkle, "Tora Bora Reconsidered: Lessons from 125 Years of Strategic Manhunts," *Joint Force Quarterly* 70, no. 3 (2013): 45, http://ndupress.ndu.edu/Portals/68/Documents/jfq/jfq-70/JFQ-70_40-46_Runkle.pdf; David

Petraeus and Andrew Roberts, *Conflict: The Evolution of Warfare from 1945 to Ukraine* (New York: Harper Collins, 2023), 243–44, 276.

25. Malkasian, *The American War in Afghanistan*, 58–60.

26. The conventional view before the 9/11 attacks was summed up by US Ambassador to Pakistan Bill Milam and the CIA's section chief in Islamabad, Robert Grenier, who both reported that "the Northern Alliance could not govern Afghanistan and that, secondly, they probably couldn't beat the Taliban anyway." Steve Coll, *Ghost Wars: The Secret History of the CIA, Afghanistan, and Bin Laden, from the Soviet Invasion to September 10, 2001* (New York: Penguin, 2004), 520–21, 571–72. Francesc Vendrell, "What Went Wrong After Bonn," Middle East Institute, May 20, 2011, https://www.mei.edu/publications/what-went-wrong-after-bonn. Among others, veteran Algerian diplomat and peacemaker Lakhdar Brahimi, who chaired the UN mission to Afghanistan, concluded that it had been a mistake to spurn the surrender plans the Taliban had been offering in the north of the country. Reported in an interview with Gall, *The Wrong Enemy*, 36–37. Grenier admitted that because the Taliban was defeated more quickly than expected, he considered them "a spent force." Bruce Geidel, a former CIA official who wrote a strategic review of Afghanistan for the incoming Obama administration, also said that the Americans "considered the Taliban irrelevant once they were defeated." Gall, *The Wrong Enemy*, 163.

27. Malkasian, *The American War in Afghanistan*, 88–89.

28. Anand Gopal, *No Good Men Among the Living: America, the Taliban, and the War Through Afghan Eyes* (New York: Metropolitan Books, 2014), 118–48; Gall, *The Wrong Enemy*, 72–74, 121–24. On the resilience of the Taliban, see also Gilles Dorronsoro, *Revolution Unending: Afghanistan, 1979 to the Present* (New York: Columbia University Press, 2005), 312–56.

29. Jesica Leeder and Alex van Linschoten, "Air Strikes Kill Dozens of Wedding Guests," *Globe and Mail*, November 4, 2008, https://web.archive.org/web/20110203161532/http://www.theglobeandmail.com/news/world/article719745.ece.

30. Malkasian, *The American War in Afghanistan*, 53–217; H. R. McMaster, *Dereliction of Duty: Johnson, McNamara, the Joint Chiefs of Staff, and the Lies That Led to Vietnam* (New York: Harper, 1998); Frederik Logeval, *Embers of War: The Fall of an Empire and the Making of America's Vietnam* (New York: Random House, 2014), 549–699.

31. Tim Weiner, *The Mission: The CIA in the 21st Century* (New York: Mariner Books, 2025), 236.

32. US Central Command rejected repeated requests from field commanders to send US troops to seal off Tora Bora and defeat bin Laden. Among the reasons subsequently given was that they were uncertain that bin Laden was in fact at Tora Bora, but the Senate Foreign Relations Committee report makes it clear that the United States knew he was there. US Senate, "Tora Bora

Revisited," 9, 13–20; Runkle, "Tora Bora Reconsidered," 41; Malkasian, *The American War in Afghanistan*, 78–79.

33. Malkasian, *The American War in Afghanistan*, 79; Colin Powell, "Chaos in Baghdad," *Newsweek*, May 13, 2012, www.newsweek.com/colin-powell-bush-administrations-iraq-war-mistakes-65023.

34. John Dizard, "How Ahmed Chalabi Conned the Neocons," *Salon*, May 4, 2004, www.salon.com/2004/05/04/chalabi_4/; 105th Congress, Public Law 338, Iraq Liberation Act of 1998, October 31, 1998, www.govinfo.gov/content/pkg/PLAW-105publ338/html/PLAW-105publ338.htm.

35. "The Liberation of Iraq: A Progress Report," US Senate Hearing on Iraq Policy, February 5, 1998, www.govinfo.gov/content/pkg/CHRG-106shrg68120/html/CHRG-106shrg68120.htm.

36. Bonnie Powell, "UN Weapons Inspector Hans Blix Faults Bush Administration for Lack of 'Critical Thinking' in Iraq," *UC Berkeley News*, March 18, 2004, https://newsarchive.berkeley.edu/news/media/releases/2004/03/18_blix shtml; Steven Weisman, "Powell Calls His UN Speech a Lasting Blot on His Record," *New York Times*, September 9, 2005, www.nytimes.com/2005/09/09/politics/powell-calls-his-un-speech-a-lasting-blot-on-his-record.html.

37. Petraeus and Roberts, *Conflict*, 283.

38. Petraeus and Roberts, *Conflict*, 295–308.

39. Petraeus and Roberts, *Conflict*, 295–340; David Petraeus and James Amos, *The U.S. Army/Marine Corps Counterinsurgency Field Manual* (Washington, DC: Echo Point Books 2015 [2006]).

40. Petraeus and Roberts, *Conflict*, 330–37.

41. "Afghanistan GDP Per Capita," Macrotrends, 2023, www.macrotrends.net/countries/AFG/afghanistan/gdp-per-capita; Adam Przeworski, Michael E. Alvarez, Jose Antonio Cheibub, and Fernando Limongi, *Democracy and Development: Political Institutions and Well-Being in the World, 1950–1990* (Cambridge, UK: Cambridge University Press, 2000), 78–141.

42. "Iraq GDP Per Capita," Macrotrends, 2023, www.macrotrends.net/countries/IRQ/iraq/gdp-per-capita.

43. Malkasian, *The American War in Afghanistan*. Woodward's books are *Bush at War* (New York: Simon and Schuster, 2002); *Plan of Attack* (New York: Simon and Schuster, 2004); *State of Denial* (New York: Simon and Schuster, 2006); and *The War Within* (New York: Simon and Schuster, 2008). "The president had one question for Negroponte: 'Do you believe democracy is possible in Iraq?' The ambassador gave a diplomat's answer. 'I don't believe it's beyond the wit of man.'" Woodward, *State of Denial*, 308.

44. Malkasian, *The American War in Afghanistan*, 84.

45. George W. Bush, State of the Union Address, The White House, January 20, 2002, https://georgewbush-whitehouse.archives.gov/news/releases/2002/01/20020129-11.html; Ron Suskind, "Faith, Certainty and

the Presidency of George W. Bush," *New York Times Magazine*, October 17, 2004, www.nytimes.com/2004/10/17/magazine/faith-certainty-and-the-presidency-of-george-w-bush.html; Gareth Porter, "Israel Warned the US Not to Invade Iraq After 9/11," Palestinian Initiative for the Promotion of Global Dialogue and Democracy, August 30, 2007, https://miftah.org/Display.cfm?CategoryId=5&DocId=14662&utm.

46. George W. Bush, West Point Commencement Speech, The White House, June 2002, https://georgewbush-whitehouse.archives.gov/news/releases/2002/06/20020601-3.html; Office of the President of the United States, *The National Security Strategy of the United States of America*, September 2002, https://2009-2017.state.gov/documents/organization/63562.pdf. The Bush Doctrine was further elaborated in: Office of the President of the United States, *The National Security Strategy of the United States of America*, March 2006, https://history.defense.gov/Portals/70/Documents/nss/nss2006.pdf; George W. Bush, Speech to Joint Session of Congress, The White House, September 20, 2001, https://georgewbush-whitehouse.archives.gov/news/releases/2001/09/20010920-8.html; and in this overview: The White House, various dates, https://georgewbush-whitehouse.archives.gov/nsc/nssall.html.

47. Steven Weisman, "Rice Admits US Underestimated Hamas Strength," *New York Times*, January 30, 2006, www.nytimes.com/2006/01/30/world/middleeast/rice-admits-us-underestimated-hamas-strength.html. For discussion of Hamas's growing popularity at the expense of Fattah in the late 1990s and early 2000s, see Ian Shapiro, *The Real World of Democratic Theory* (Princeton, NJ: Princeton University Press, 2011), 133–39; Fred Kaplan, *Daydream Believers: How a Few Grand Ideas Wrecked American Power* (New York: Trade Press, 2008), 164–66; Ben Fishman and Mohammad Yaghi, "The Future of a Palestinian Unity Government," Washington Institute for Near East Policy, March 4, 2008, www.washingtoninstitute.org/policy-analysis/future-palestinian-unity-government; Suzanne Goldenberg, "US Plotted Overthrow of Hamas After Election Victory," *The Guardian*, March 4, 2008, www.theguardian.com/world/2008/mar/04/usa.israelandthepalestinians.

48. "Speak softly and carry a big stick" is a West African proverb quoted by Theodore Roosevelt in a letter to Henry Sprague in 1900. "Theodore Roosevelt Quotes," Theodore Roosevelt Center, accessed October 21, 2025, www.theodorerooseveltcenter.org/Learn-About-TR/TR-Quotes?page=130.

Chapter Two: Reviving the Cold War

1. Article 5 could have been triggered in Afghanistan when the Taliban refused to turn over bin Ladin, but the US did not invoke it then. NATO eventually assumed command of the International Security Assistance Force in Afghanistan in August 2003.

2. George Washington, "Farewell Address (1796)," National Constitution Center, October 21, 2025, https://constitutioncenter.org/the-constitution/historic-document-library/detail/george-washington-farewell-address-1796.

3. X (George F. Kennan), "The Sources of Soviet Conduct," *Foreign Affairs*, July 1, 1947, www.foreignaffairs.com/russian-federation/george-kennan-sources-soviet-conduct.

4. David Zabecki, ed., *Germany at War: 400 Years of Military History*, vol. 4 (London: ABC-CLIO, 2014), 570; Graham Allison, "What Happened to the Soviet Superpower's Nuclear Arsenal? Clues for the Nuclear Security Summit" (Harvard Kennedy School Working Paper No. RWP-12-038, August 2012), www.hks.harvard.edu/publications/what-happened-soviet-superpowers-nuclear-arsenal-clues-nuclear-security-summit.

5. Mary Sarotte, *Not One Inch: America, Russia, and the Making of Post–Cold War Stalemate* (New Haven, CT: Yale University Press, 2021), 7, 134.

6. The agreements Yeltsin signed included the Euro-Atlantic Cooperation Council in 1991, the Partnership for Peace, and the NATO Russia Founding Act in 1997. The latter led to the creation of the NATO-Russia Permanent Joint Council, which in 2002 was replaced by the NATO-Russia Council.

7. Joel Hellman, "Winners Take All: The Politics of Partial Reform in Post-Communist Transitions," *World Politics* 50 (1998): 203–34.

8. See Adam Przeworski, *Democracy and the Market* (Cambridge, UK: Cambridge University Press, 1991), 57, 136–87; and Robert Dahl and Ian Shapiro, "Impressions from the Soviet Union," *Dissent*, Summer 1991: 342–45.

9. Sarotte, *Not One Inch*, 56, 90, 110.

10. Sarotte, *Not One Inch*, 137–38.

11. James Goldgeier and Michael McFaul, *Power and Purpose: US Policy Toward Russia After the Cold War* (Washington, DC: Brookings Institution, 2003), 68–72; Robert Powell, "Debt Relief for Poor Countries," International Monetary Fund (IMF), 2000, www.imf.org/external/pubs/ft/fandd/2000/12/powell.htm; "Debt Crisis in Russia: The Road from Default to Sustainability," IMF eLibrary, September 9, 2003, www.elibrary.imf.org/display/book/9781589062078/ch07.xml#ch07tab01; Sarotte, *Not One Inch*, 139.

12. Richard Nixon, "How to Lose the Cold War," Cong. Rec. (daily ed.), 102d Cong., 2d sess., March 5, 1992, 138E4666–E4667, https://www.congress.gov/102/crecb/1992/03/05/GPO-CRECB-1992-pt4-1-3.pdf.

13. Congressional Research Service, "The Marshall Plan: Design, Accomplishments, and Significance," 2018, www.everycrsreport.com/reports/R45079.html; Roger Morris, *Richard Milhous Nixon: The Rise of an American Politician* (New York: Henry Holt, 1990), 365; Andrew Glass, "Marshall Plan Put Forward, June 5, 1947," *Politico*, June 4, 2017, www.politico.com/story/2017/06/04/marshall-plan-put-forward-june-5-1947-239105.

14. Expenditures computed from data in Goldgeier and McFaul, *Power and Purpose*, 114, 945.

15. At a Moscow conference sponsored by the Communist Party of the Soviet Union (CPSU) Central Committee in March 1991, I was approached by an official seeking introductions to anyone in the South African government who might want to buy Soviet weapons, including nuclear weapons. He was well informed enough to know that I had South African connections, but evidently not well informed enough to know that the South African government had decommissioned its nuclear weapons a few years earlier.

16. Winston Churchill, *The Second World War*, vol. 1, *The Gathering Storm* (London: Houghton Mifflin, 1948), epigraph. Kennan believed that the Marshall Plan should supplant the Truman Doctrine, which committed the US to act against threats to democracy anywhere in the world, whether or not a US interest was at stake. See John Gaddis, *George F. Kennan: An American Life* (New York: Penguin, 2011), 269–70.

17. Goldgeier and McFaul, *Power and Purpose*, 80–82, 136–43.

18. Sarotte, *Not One Inch*, 150–52.

19. Goldgeier and McFaul, *Power and Purpose*, 98–102, 111.

20. Chris Miller, *Putinomics: Power and Money in Resurgent Russia* (Chapel Hill: University of North Carolina Press, 2018), 10–14.

21. Madeleine Albright, commencement address at Harvard University, US Department of State, June 6, 1997, https://1997-2001.state.gov/statements/970605.html.

22. Zbigniew Brzezinski, *The Grand Chessboard: American Primacy and Its Geostrategic Imperatives* (New York: Basic Books, 1997), 79–81, 201; Sarotte, *Not One Inch*, 207; Ashton Carter and William Perry, *Preventive Defense: A New Security Strategy for America* (Washington, DC: Brookings Institution, 1999), 32.

23. Sarotte, *Not One Inch*, 207–8; Carter and Perry, *Preventive Defense*, 3, 32; William Perry, *My Journey at the Nuclear Brink* (Stanford, CA: Stanford University Press, 2015), 128–29.

24. Sarotte, *Not One Inch*, 178, 182–96, 234.

25. Jeremy Rosner, "Winning Congressional and Public Support for NATO Enlargement, and the Political Psychology of Collective Defense," in *Open Door: NATO and Euro-Atlantic Security After the Cold War*, ed. Kristina Spohr and Daniel Hamilton (Washington, DC: Transtlantic Leadership Network, 2019), 385–401; Sarotte, *Not One Inch*, 186–87, 189–96, 248–49, 264.

26. Sarotte, *Not One Inch*, 86, 111–14, 169–70, 188–89.

27. Sarotte, *Not One Inch*, 209.

28. Sarotte, *Not One Inch*, 197, 247.

29. The National Security Council estimated the cost of the initial expansion at $2.1 billion to $2.7 billion annually over the thirteen years needed for

the new members' militaries to develop the capabilities required by NATO. The NSC thought the new members would pay between $800 million and $1 billion per year toward those totals, with the balance coming from existing NATO members (and the US share totaling $150 million to $200 million). Those numbers aroused considerable skepticism. The Poles said they would need at least $200 million a year for fifteen years to modernize their military, which they could only cover with credits from the US. See Sarotte, *Not One Inch*, 281–82, 294–95.

30. George Kennan, "A Fateful Error," *New York Times*, February 5, 1997, https://news.google.com/home?hl=en-US&gl=US&ceid=US:en.

31. Sam Nunn and Brent Scowcroft, "NATO: A Debate Recast," *New York Times*, February 4, 1998, www.nytimes.com/1998/02/04/opinion/nato-a-debate-recast.html; Sarotte, *Not One Inch*, 284–86.

32. Sarotte, *Not One Inch*, 177, 276–78, 282–94, 300, 312.

33. "Remarks by President Clinton and Secretary General Solana at NATO Commemorative Ceremony," The White House, April 23, 1999, https://clintonwhitehouse4.archives.gov/WH/New/html/19990423-5920.html; Sarotte, *Not One Inch*, 320.

34. Sarotte, *Not One Inch*, 254, 272, 319.

35. "Russia—Gorbachev Comments on NATO Expansion," April 15, 1990, posted July 21, 2015 by AP, YouTube, 2:15, www.youtube.com/watch?v=3wB9uL2lKaw.

36. Sarotte, *Not One Inch*, 323–24, 328; Elisabeth Braw, "When Putin Loved NATO," *Foreign Policy*, January 10, 2022, https://foreignpolicy.com/2022/01/19/putin russia ukraine nato george robertson/.

37. Braw, "When Putin Loved NATO"; "U.S.-Russia Relations After September 11, 2001," Carnegie Endowment for International Peace, October 24, 2001, https://carnegieendowment.org/2001/10/24/u.s.-russia-relations-after-september-11-2001-pub-840.

38. Sarotte, *Not One Inch*, 303–4; Henry Mance, "John Major Was Warned Against Backing Russia's EU Membership," *Financial Times*, July 23, 2018, www.ft.com/content/77d0991c-8c3b-11e8-b18d-0181731a0340; Vladimir Putin with Nataliya Gevorkyan, Natalya Timakova, and Andrei Kolesnikov, *First Person: An Astonishingly Frank Self-Portrait by Russia's President Vladimir Putin*, trans. Catherine A. Fitzpatrick (New York: Public Affairs, 2000), 169; Simon Saradzhyan, "Alternative History: Would Russia in NATO and the EU Be a Game-Changer in the West's Rivalry with China?," Russia Matters, November 20, 2019, www.russiamatters.org/analysis/alternative-history-would-russia-nato-and-eu-be-game-changer-wests-rivalry-china; Robin Wright, "Ties That Terrorism Transformed," *Los Angeles Times*, March 13, 2002, www.latimes.com/archives/la-xpm-2002-mar-13-mn-32572-story.html.

39. George W. Bush, "Remarks by the President in Address to Faculty and Students of Warsaw University," June 15, 2001, The White House Archive, https://georgewbush-whitehouse.archives.gov/news/releases/2001/06/20010615-1.html.

40. "Anti-War Demo as Part of Worldwide Protests," 2003, posted July 21, 2015 by AP, YouTube, www.youtube.com/watch?v=ESC_CgegvFw; Peter Baker, "Putin's Concessions to U.S. Are Limited. The Bottom Line," *Washington Post*, August 16, 2002, www.washingtonpost.com/archive/politics/2002/08/16/putins-concessions-to-us-are-limited-the-bottom-line/cf78e6cd-0e36-4e12-a355-c73e9331a522/; Aaron Maté, "For Putin, Iraq War Marked a Turning Point in U.S.-Russia Relations," Responsible Statecraft, March 23, 2023, https://responsiblestatecraft.org/2023/03/23/for-putin-iraq-war-marked-a-turning-point-in-us-russia-relations/; Putin et al., *First Person*, 169.

41. "Russia Takes a Negative View of NATO Expansion but Has Always Seen the European Union's Enlargement as a Positive Process," Kremlin press statement, December 10, 2004, www.en.kremlin.ru/events/president/news/32366; Vladimir Putin, interview with French television channel France 3, February 8, 2003, www.en.kremlin.ru/events/president/transcripts/22952; "Speech and the Following Discussion at the Munich Conference on Security Policy," website of the President of Russia, February 10, 2007, www.en.kremlin.ru/events/president/transcripts/24034.

42. William J. Burns, *The Back Channel: A Memoir of American Diplomacy and the Case for Its Renewal* (New York: Penguin Random House, 2020), 233; William J. Burns, memo, "Russia Strategy" (Secret), February 8, 2008, https://ceipfiles.s3.amazonaws.com/pdf/back-channel/2008EmailtoRice1.pdf; "Bush Backs Ukraine and Georgia for NATO Membership," *The Guardian*, April 1, 2008, www.theguardian.com/world/2008/apr/01/nato.georgia; "NATO Decisions on Open Door Policy," North Atlantic Treaty Organization, April 3, 2008, www.nato.int/docu/update/2008/04-april/e0403h.html.

43. "The President's News Conference with President Viktor Yushchenko of Ukraine in Kiev, Ukraine," The American Presidency Project, April 1, 2008, www.presidency.ucsb.edu/documents/the-presidents-news-conference-with-president-viktor-yushchenko-ukraine-kiev-ukraine; Vladimir Putin, "Address to the Federal Assembly," website of the President of Russia, December 12, 2012, www.en.kremlin.ru/events/president/transcripts/messages/17118; "Vladimir Putin Answered Journalists' Questions on Ukraine," website of the President of Russia, March 4, 2014, www.en.kremlin.ru/events/president/news/20796; Vladimir Putin, "Address by the President of the Russian Federation," website of the President of Russia, February 24, 2022, www.en.kremlin.ru/events/president/transcripts/67843. For additional examples of Putin's evolving positions on NATO and Ukraine, see "Accepting

NATO Aspirations to 'Denazifying': 20 Years of Putin's Changing Views on Ukraine," Russia Matters, March 23, 2023, www.russiamatters.org/analysis/accepting-nato-aspirations-denazifying-20-years-putins-changing-views-ukraine.

44. Miller, *Putinomics*, 59–78.

45. Miller, *Putinomics*, 34–37, 41–46.

46. "The more deadly are the weapons monopolized by the international authority, the more obvious will be its capacity to enforce its will, and the less will be the likelihood of resistance to its decrees." Bertrand Russell, *Towards World Government* (London: Thorney House, 1947), 4–5; see Ian Shapiro, *Politics Against Domination* (Cambridge, MA: Harvard University Press, 2016), 106–7.

47. "Speech and the Following Discussion at the Munich Conference on Security Policy."

48. No date for accession to NATO was specified, but the Budapest declaration noted that "intensive engagement" had begun with their governments to accelerate the process. "Bucharest Summit Declaration," press release, NATO, issued April 3, 2008, last updated July 5, 2022, www.nato.int/cps/en/natolive/official_texts_8443.htm.

49. Norway, Latvia, Estonia, Lithuania, Finland, and Poland border Russia or the Russian exclave of Kaliningrad. Miller, *Putinomics*, 137–38.

50. "Medvedev Rejects Putin 'Crusade' Remark over Libya," BBC News, March 21, 2011, www.bbc.com/news/world-europe-12810566; Miller, *Putinomics*, 140–44; Shaun Walker, "Vladimir Putin Offers Ukraine Financial Deal to Stick with Russia," *The Guardian*, December 18, 2013, www.theguardian.com/world/2013/dec/17/ukraine-russia-leaders-talks-kremlin-loan-deal; Adam Tooze, *Crashed: How a Decade of Financial Crises Changed the World* (New York: Viking, 2018), 494–96.

51. Miller, *Putinomics*, 138; Timothy Frye, *Weak Strongman: The Limits of Power in Putin's Russia* (Princeton, NJ: Princeton University Press, 2021), 60–84; Tooze, *Crashed*, 497.

52. Alexander Ward, *The Internationalists: The Fight to Restore American Foreign Policy After Trump* (New York: Penguin, 2024), 232–36, 277. On Putin's perception of the threat that Ukrainian membership in NATO would pose to Russia, see Barry Pozen, "Putin's Preventive War: The 2022 Invasion of Ukraine," *International Security* 49, no. 3 (2025): 7–49; Daniel McLaughlin, "Putin's Move: The Real Story Behind Russia's Syria Strikes," *Politico*, September 30, 2015, www.politico.com/magazine/story/2015/09/putin-russia-syria-strike-real-story-behind-scenes-medvedev-213207/.

53. Sarotte, *Not One Inch*, 323–24; Elizabeth Becker, "U.S. General Was Overruled in Kosovo," *New York Times*, September 10, 1999, www.nytimes.com/1999/09/10/world/us-general-was-overruled-in-kosovo.html.

54. Underscoring the validity of Eisenhower's concern, in 1966 de Gaulle removed France from NATO's integrated military command structure to preserve its freedom of action.

55. Alexandre Debs and Nuno Monteiro, *Nuclear Politics: The Strategic Causes of Proliferation* (Cambridge, UK: Cambridge University Press, 2016).

56. Henry John Temple, 3rd Viscount Palmerston, speech to the House of Commons, March 1, 1848, www.oxfordreference.com/display/10.1093/acref/9780191826719.001.0001/q-oro-ed4-00008130.

Chapter Three: The Demise of Humanitarian Intervention

1. Douglas Jehl, "Officials Told to Avoid Calling Rwanda Killings 'Genocide,'" *New York Times*, June 10, 1994, www.nytimes.com/1994/06/10/world/officials-told-to-avoid-calling-rwanda-killings-genocide.html; "Text of Clinton's Rwanda Speech," CBS News, March 25, 1998, www.cbsnews.com/news/text-of-clintons-rwanda-speech/.

2. Mark Mazower, *Governing the World: History of an Idea* (New York: Penguin Books, 2013), 214–304.

3. William J. Clinton, "Remarks to Kosovo International Security Force Troops in Skopje," American Presidency Project, June 22, 1999, www.presidency.ucsb.edu/documents/remarks-kosovo-international-security-force-troops-skopje; "Civilian Deaths in the NATO Air Campaign," Human Rights Watch, February 2000, www.hrw.org/reports/2000/nato/Natbm200.htm.

4. Albrecht Schnabel and Ramesh Thakur, eds., *Kosovo: The Challenge of Humanitarian Intervention* (Tokyo: UN University, 2000), 7, 30–33; Anthony Sampson, "Mandela Accuses 'Policeman' Britain," *The Guardian*, April 4, 2000, www.theguardian.com/world/2000/apr/05/nelsonmandela.

5. Kofi A. Annan, "We the Peoples: The Role of the United Nations in the 21st Century," United Nations, 2000, https://worldjpn.net/documents/texts/SDGs/20000000.T1E.html; Kofi A. Annan, "Nobel Lecture Delivered by Kofi Annan," United Nations, December 10, 2001, www.un.org/sg/en/content/sg/speeches/2001-12-10/nobel-lecture-delivered-kofi-annan.

6. Independent Commission on Kosovo, *The Kosovo Report* (Oxford, UK: Oxford University Press, 2001), 4.

7. Constitutive Act of the African Union, Article 4 (h), 7, https://au.int/sites/default/files/pages/34873-file-constitutiveact_en.pdf; Patrick Regan, "Third-Party Interventions and the Duration of Intrastate Conflicts," *Journal of Conflict Resolution* 46, no. 1 (2002): 55–73; Noel Anderson Thomas, "Competitive Intervention and Its Consequences for Civil Wars" (PhD diss., Massachusetts Institute of Technology, 2016), https://dspace.mit.edu/handle/1721.1/107541.

8. *The Responsibility to Protect: Report of the International Commission on Intervention and State Sovereignty* (Ottawa: International Development Research

Centre, 2021), 69–78, www.globalr2p.org/resources/the-responsibility-to-protect-report-of-the-international-commission-on-intervention-and-state-sovereignty-2001/.

9. United Nations 2005 World Summit Outcome document, paragraphs 138–39, p. 30, www.un.org/en/development/desa/population/migration/generalassembly/docs/globalcompact/A_RES_60_1.pdf.

10. "Report of the Secretary General on the Sudan," UN Security Council Resolution, September 18, 2004, http://unscr.com/en/resolutions/1564; "Kenya," Global Centre for the Responsibility to Protect, April 2, 2022, www.globalr2p.org/countries/kenya/; "Implementing the Responsibility to Protect," Report of the Secretary General of the United Nations, December 1, 2009, www.un.org/unispal/document/auto-insert-180580/; "Guinea Massacre Crime Against Humanity," *San Diego Union Tribune*, updated August 30, 2016, www.sandiegouniontribune.com/2009/12/21/report-guinea-massacre-crime-against-humanity/; "Trial Resumes in Guinea After Dramatic Jailbreak Raises Concerns," Africa News, updated December 14, 2023, www.africanews.com/2023/11/14/trial-resumes-in-guinea-after-dramatic-jailbreak-raises-concerns/.

11. Thomas L. Friedman, "This Is Just the Start," *New York Times*, March 1, 2011, www.nytimes.com/2011/03/02/opinion/02friedman.html.

12. "Battle for Libya Key Moments," Al Jazeera, April 30, 2017, www.aljazeera.com/news/2017/4/30/battle-for-libya-key-moments-3; UN Security Council Resolution 1970, adopted February 26, 2011, www.nato.int/nato_static_fl2014/assets/pdf/pdf_2011_02/20110927_110226-UNSCR-1970.pdf.

13. US State Department, "Patterns of Global Terrorism," April 1996, www.fas.org/irp/threat/terror 96/overview.html; Ian Shapiro, *Containment: Rebuilding a Strategy Against Global Terror* (Princeton, NJ: Princeton University Press, 2007), 96–97; Andrew Solomon, "Circle of Fire: Libya's Reformers Dream of Rejoining the World," *New Yorker*, May 8, 2006, www.newyorker.com/magazine/2006/05/08/circle-of-fire; Tobias Vanderbruck, "Gaddafi's Legacy of Libyan Oil Deals," Oil-price.net, October 21, 2011, www.oil-price.net/en/articles/gaddafi-legacy-of-libya-oil-deals.php; Alan Kuperman, "A Model Humanitarian Intervention? Reassessing NATO's Libya Campaign," *International Security* 38, no. 1 (2013): 126.

14. Thomas L. Friedman, "The Arab Quarter Century," *New York Times*, April 9, 2013, www.nytimes.com/2013/04/10/opinion/friedman-the-arab-quarter-century.html; "Tunisia: Is Democracy There Being Destroyed?," BBC News, April 20, 2023, www.bbc.com/news/world-europe-65125593; James Petras and Henry Veltmeyer, *Beyond Neoliberalism: A World to Win* (Burlington, VT: Ashgate, 2011), 194–95.

15. "Russia Slams France's 'Crude Violation' of Libya Arms Embargo," France 24, June 30, 2011, www.france24.com/en/20110630-russia-accuses-france-crude-violation-rebel-arms-drop-libya-un-embargo.

16. "Libya Protests: Second City Benghazi Hit by Violence," BBC News Africa, February 16, 2011, www.bbc.co.uk/news/world-africa-12477275; UN Security Council Resolution 1973, March 17, 2011, https://documents.un.org/doc/undoc/gen/n11/268/39/pdf/n1126839.pdf.

17. One widely reported claim that Gaddafi's air force was indiscriminately bombing and strafing civilians in Tripoli and Benghazi was not exposed as false until after the war ended, when the International Crisis Group's Africa Project leader admitted as much. Hugh Roberts, "Who Said Gaddafi Had to Go?," *London Review of Books*, November 2011, 8–18; Kuperman, "A Model Humanitarian Intervention?," 111–12.

18. Chris McGreal, "Allied Strikes Sweep Libya as West Intervenes in Conflict," March 20, 2011, *The Guardian*, www.theguardian.com/world/2011/mar/19/libya-air-strikes-gaddafi-france; Alan Kuperman, reply to Chollet and Fishman, *Foreign Affairs* 94, no. 3 (2015): 158, www.foreignaffairs.com/articles/libya/2015-04-20/who-lost-libya; "African Union Demands End to Military Strikes on Libya, Skips Paris Meeting," *Sudan Tribune*, March 20, 2011, https://web.archive.org/web/20110321212338/http://www.sudantribune.com/NAfrican-Union-demands-end-to%2C38339; Edward Cody, "Arab League Condemns Broad Bombing Campaign in Libya," *Washington Post*, March 20, 2011, www.washingtonpost.com/world/arab-league-condemns-broad-bombing-campaign-in-libya/2011/03/20/AB1pSg1_story.html.

19. Rosa Silverman, "Gaddafi's Air Force 'Destroyed' by Coalition," *Independent UK*, March 23, 2011, www.independent.co.uk/news/world/africa/gaddafi-s-air-force-destroyed-by-coalition-2250427.html; Kuperman, "A Model Humanitarian Intervention?," 116–18; Micah Zenko, "The Big Lie About the Libyan War," *Foreign Policy*, March 22, 2016, https://foreignpolicy.com/2016/03/22/libya-and-the-myth-of-humanitarian-intervention/; Kuperman, reply to Chollet and Fishman, 159.

20. Joseph Lieberman and Marco Rubio, "Victory Is the Answer in Libya," *Wall Street Journal*, June 23, 2011, www.wsj.com/articles/SB10001424052702304070104576399923803151478; Corbett Daly, "Clinton on Qaddafi: 'We Came, We Saw, He Died,'" CBS News, October 20, 2011, www.cbsnews.com/news/clinton-on-qaddafi-we-came-we-saw-he-died/; Kuperman, "A Model Humanitarian Intervention?," 116–23. For an example of the triumphalism, see Robert Pape, "When Duty Calls: A Pragmatic Standard for Humanitarian Intervention," *International Security* 37, no. 1 (Summer 2012): 41–80.

21. Langdon Ogburn, "Libya: State Fragility 10 Years After Intervention," Fund for Peace, November 2, 2011, https://fundforpeace.org/2021/11/02/libya-state-fragility-10-years-after-intervention/; John McCain and Marco Rubio, "The Promise of a Pro-American Libya," *Wall Street Journal*, October 7, 2011, www.wsj.com/articles/SB10001424052970203388804576613290

3623346516; Daveed Gartenstein-Ross, "Successes and Failures of the U.S. and NATO Intervention in Libya," Testimony before the House Committee on Oversight and Government Reform, May 1, 2014, 4–5, www.defend democracy.org/content/uploads/documents/Libya_testimony_final_4_30 _2014.pdf; David Stout, "ISIS Now Controls the Libyan City of Derna and Is Aiming to Expand West," *Time*, November 17, 2014, http://time .com/3593885/isis-libya-iraq-syria-terrorism-derna/. All this is to say nothing of the cascading refugee crisis that would eventually spill into the Mediterranean, spawning humanitarian disasters and vicious anti-immigration politics across Southern Europe. Franziska Brantner, "The Libyan Context of the Migration Crisis," European Council of Foreign Relations, May 22, 2015, www.ecfr.eu/article/commentary_the_libyan_context_of_the_migration _crisis3040. Barack Obama, *A Promised Land* (New York: Crown, 2020), 653–68; Hillary Clinton, *Hard Choices* (New York: Simon and Schuster, 2014), 295–312.

22. Julian Borger, "The Race Is On for Libya's Oil, with Britain and France Both Staking a Claim," *The Guardian*, September 1, 2011, www.theguardian .com/world/2011/sep/01/libya-oil.

23. Robert Booth, "Libya: Coalition Bombing May Be in Breach of UN Resolution's Legal Limits," *The Guardian*, March 28, 2011, www.theguardian .com/world/2011/mar/28/libya-bombing-un-resolution-law; Kuperman, "A Model Humanitarian Intervention?," 107–113; "Government Forces Retreat in Libya's Misrata," Reuters, April 24, 2011, www.reuters.com/article/world /government-forces-retreat-in-libya-s-misrata-idUSJOE73N009/; "Russia Slams France's 'Crude Violation'"; "Libya: Examination of Intervention and Collapse and the UK's Future Policy Options," House of Commons Foreign Affairs Committee, September 14, 2016, https://publications.parliament.uk/pa /cm201617/cmselect/cmfaff/119/119.pdf.

24. Christina Matamoros, "Explained: What We Know About the Gaddafi-Sarkozy Funding Scandal," Euronews, March 20, 2018, www.euronews.com /2018/03/20/sarkozy-in-libya-case-what-does-it-all-mean-; George Wright and Hugh Schofield, "Former French President Sarkozy Given Five-Year Sentence After Libya Case," BBC, September 25, 2025, www.bbc .com/news/articles/cp98kepmj9lo; Richard Brody, "Did Bernard-Henri Lévy Take NATO to War?," *New Yorker*, March 25, 2011, www.newyorker .com/culture/richard-brody/did-bernard-henri-lvy-take-nato-to-war; John Crace, "The Greatest Literary Hoax Ever," *The Guardian*, February 10, 2011, www.theguardian.com/books/2010/feb/10/bernard-henri-levy-hoaxes; Renaud Girard, "La campagne Libyenne de Bernard-Henri Lévy," *Le Figaro*, March 18, 2011, www.lefigaro.fr/international/2011/03/18/01003 -20110318ARTFIG00671-la-campagne-libyenne-de-bernard-henri-levy .php.

25. Philip Gordon, "How Obama Got Pulled into Regime Change in Libya," *New Lines Magazine*, October 11, 2020, https://newlinesmag.com/review/how-obama-got-pulled-into-regime-change-in-libya/; Luke Harding, "Germany Won't Send Forces to Libya, Foreign Minister Declares," *The Guardian*, March 17, 2011, www.theguardian.com/world/2011/mar/17/germany-rules-out-libya-military; Osvaldo Croci and Marco Valigi, "Italy and the International Intervention in Libya," in *Italian Politics: From Berlusconi to Monti*, ed. Anna Bosco and Duncan McDonnell (New York: Bergham Books, 2013), 191–206.

26. These questions were being asked on Capitol Hill by the end of March. See "Libya: Defending US National Security Interests," Hearing Before the House Foreign Affairs Committee, March 31, 2011, www.govinfo.gov/content/pkg/CHRG-112hhrg65492/html/CHRG-112hhrg65492.htm; and Robert Gates, *Duty: Memoirs of a Secretary at War* (New York: Vintage Books, 2015), 510–23.

27. Ryan Lizza, "Leading from Behind," *New Yorker*, April 26, 2011, www.newyorker.com/news/news-desk/leading-from-behind; Gates, *Duty*, 514–16; Anthony Capaccio, "Obama Cites Lack of 'Day After' Plan in Libya as Biggest Mistake," Bloomberg, April 10, 2016, www.bloomberg.com/news/articles/2016-04-10/obama-cites-lack-of-day-after-plan-in-libya-as-biggest-mistake.

28. David Petraeus and James Amos, *The U.S. Army/Marine Corps Counterinsurgency Field Manual* (Washington, DC: Echo Point Books 2015 [2006]).

29. Karl W. Eikenberry, "The Limits of Counterinsurgency Doctrine in Afghanistan," *Foreign Affairs*, September/October 2013, www.foreignaffairs.com/afghanistan/limits-counterinsurgency-doctrine-afghanistan; Matt Malis, Pablo Querubin, and Shanker Satyanath, "Persistent Failure? International Interventions Since World War II," in *The Handbook of Historical Economics*, ed. Alberto Bisin and Giovanni Federico (New York: Academic Press, 2021), 641–73.

30. "Obama Administration Announces $25 Million in Aid to Libyan Rebels," *Democracy Now!*, April 21, 2011, www.democracynow.org/2011/4/21/headlines/obama_administration_announces_25_million_in_aid_to_libyan_rebels; Nick Gass, "Biden: I Was Right About Libya," *Politico*, June 21, 2016, www.politico.com/story/2016/06/joe-biden-libya-wrong-224595; "How Does US Foreign Aid Work and Where Does It Go?," USAFacts.org, updated July 15, 2023, https://usafacts.org/articles/which-countries-receive-the-most-aid-from-the-us/.

31. The quotations from bin Laden are taken from Tim Weiner, *The Mission: The CIA in the 21st Century* (New York: Mariner Books, 2025), 228, 232–33. On Western analysts' misperception of Salafi jihadist understanding

of the opportunities created by the Arab Spring, see Gartenstein-Ross, "Successes and Failures," 2–3; Petras and Veltmeyer, *Beyond Neoliberalism*, 195; Cameron Glenn, "Libya's Islamists: Who They Are—and What They Want," Wilson Center, August 8, 2017, www.wilsoncenter.org/article/libyas-islamists-who-they-are-and-what-they-want.

32. Bob Woodward, *Obama's Wars* (New York: Simon and Schuster, 2011), 16, 34, 76, 266–335.

33. See Marc Lynch's recantation in "Reflections on the Arab Uprisings," *Washington Post*, November 17, 2014, www.washingtonpost.com/blogs/monkey-cage/wp/2014/11/17/reflections-on-the-arab-uprisings/.

34. Chairman Mike Rogers, "Investigative Report on the Terrorist Attacks on U.S. Facilities in Benghazi, Libya, September 11–12, 2012," US House of Representatives Permanent Select Committee on Intelligence, November 21, 2014, https://intelligence.house.gov/sites/intelligence.house.gov/files/documents/benghazi%20report.pdf; Eugene Kiely, "PAC Attack on Clinton's Benghazi Record," FactCheck.org, November 3, 2016, www.factcheck.org/2016/11/pac-attack-on-clintons-benghazi-record/.

35. Kuperman, "A Model Humanitarian Intervention?," 129–30; "Talks Without Hope," *The Economist*, August 26, 2014, www.economist.com/node/21613924/print; Illaria Allegrozzi, "Mali's Peace Deal Ends," Human Rights Watch, January 26, 2024, www.hrw.org/news/2024/01/26/malis-peace-deal-ends.

36. Kuperman, "A Model Humanitarian Intervention?," 134–35; Lynch; "Reflections on the Arab Uprisings."

37. Kenneth Rapoza, "Russia and China Team Up Against NATO Libya Campaign," *Forbes*, June 17, 2011, www.forbes.com/sites/kenrapoza/2011/06/17/russia-and-china-team-up-against-nato-libya-campaign/; "Russia, China, Warn West Not to Intervene in Syria, Following US Threat," *Haaretz*, August 21, 2012, www.haaretz.com/news/middle-east/russia-china-warn-west-not-to-intervene-in-syria-following-u-s-threat-1.459709; Scott Wilson, "Assad Must Go, Obama Says," *Washington Post*, August 18, 2011, www.washingtonpost.com/politics/assad-must-go-obama-says/2011/08/18/gIQAelheOJ_story.html; Daniel Larason, "Ten Years After Obama's Embarrassing 'Red Line' Retreat," Responsible Statecraft, August 28, 2023, https://responsiblestatecraft.org/2023/08/28/what-obamas-red-line-in-syria-taught-us-about-us-credibility/; Aron Lund, "Red Line Redux: How Putin Tore Up Obama's 2013 Syria Deal," The Century Foundation, February 3, 2017, https://tcf.org/content/report/red-line-redux-putin-tore-obamas-2013-syria-deal/.

38. See Catherine Renshaw, "R2P: An Idea Whose Time Never Comes," *The Interpreter* (blog), June 2, 2021, www.lowyinstitute.org/the-interpreter/r2p-idea-whose-time-never-comes.

Chapter Four: Obama's Missteps

1. "Bush's Final Approval Rating: 22 Percent," CBS News, January 16, 2009, www.cbsnews.com/news/bushs-final-approval-rating-22-percent/.

2. Lawrence Summers, "The Great Liberator," *New York Times*, November 19, 2006, www.nytimes.com/2006/11/19/opinion/19summers.html; Ron Suskind, *Confidence Men: Wall Street, Washington, and the Education of a President* (New York: Harper Collins, 2012).

3. Proposition 13—which passed by an almost two-to-one margin in a ballot initiative in California—limited property taxes to 1 percent of assessed value, immediately forcing draconian cuts to state and local spending. Bill Clinton, State of the Union Address, January 23, 1996, https://clintonwhitehouse4.archives.gov/WH/New/other/sotu.html.

4. Michael Graetz and Ian Shapiro, *Death by a Thousand Cuts: The Fight over Taxing Inherited Wealth* (Princeton, NJ: Princeton University Press, 2005), 24–31.

5. George H. W. Bush used the term "voodoo economics" in his failed attempt to defeat Ronald Reagan for the Republican presidential nomination in 1980. See Brian Domitrovic, "George H. W. Bush's Voodoo Rhetoric," *Forbes*, December 2, 2018, www.forbes.com/sites/briandomitrovic/2018/12/02/george-h-w-bushs-voodoo-rhetoric/. On the partisan distribution of safe seats, see Alexander Kustov, Maikol Cerda, Akhil Rajan, Frances Rosenbluth, and Ian Shapiro, "The Rise of Safe Seats and Party Indiscipline in the US Congress" (working paper, Yale Jackson Institute, 2021), https://jackson.yale.edu/wp-content/uploads/2022/08/Kustov-et-al.-2021.pdf; FiveThirtyEight, "What Redistricting Looks Like in Every State," updated July 19, 2022, https://projects.fivethirtyeight.com/redistricting-2022-maps/; Sam Levine, "America Faces Greater Division as Parties Draw Safe Seats for Congressional Districts," *The Guardian*, February 12, 2022, www.theguardian.com/us-news/ng-interactive/2022/feb/12/us-redistricting-house-seats-safe-competitive-districts.

6. Bob Woodward, *The Price of Politics* (New York: Simon and Schuster, 2012), 7–14.

7. Woodward, *Price of Politics*, 16–23.

8. "GOP Leader's Top Goal: Make Obama a One Term President," NBC News, November 4, 2010, www.nbcnews.com/id/wbna40007802; Andy Barr, "The GOP's No Compromise Pledge," *Politico*, October 28, 2010, www.politico.com/story/2010/10/the-gops-no-compromise-pledge-044311.

9. "President Obama Announces Recess Appointment to Key Administration Positions," White House Office of Press Secretary, March 27, 2010, https://obamawhitehouse.archives.gov/the-press-office/president-obama-announces-recess-appointments-key-administration-positions.

10. "The Pledge: Grover Norquist's Hold on the GOP," CBS News, August 26, 2012, www.cbsnews.com/news/the-pledge-grover-norquists-hold-on-the-gop-26-08-2012/.

11. Suskind, *Confidence Men*, 426–38, 720–21.

12. Suskind, *Confidence Men*, 331, 339–405, 455–63; Natasha Tiku, "Citigroup Received More Bailout Money than Any Other Bank," *New York Magazine*, March 16, 2011, https://nymag.com/intelligencer/2011/03/citibank_received_more_bailout.html; "Goldman Sachs Agrees to Pay More Than $5 Billion in Connection with Its Sale of Residential Mortgage Backed Securities," press release, US Department of Justice, Office of Public Affairs, April 11, 2016, www.justice.gov/opa/pr/goldman-sachs-agrees-pay-more-5-billion-connection-its-sale-residential-mortgage-backed.

13. Rahm Emanuel, "Let's Make Sure This Crisis Doesn't Go to Waste," *Washington Post*, March 25, 2020, www.washingtonpost.com/opinions/2020/03/25/lets-make-sure-this-crisis-doesnt-go-waste/; Graetz and Shapiro, *Death by a Thousand Cuts*, 143–53; Ian Shapiro, *Politics Against Domination* (Cambridge, MA: Harvard University Press, 2016), 91–92; Alan Blinder, *After the Music Stopped: The Financial Crisis, the Response, and the Work Ahead* (New York: Penguin, 2013), 312–13.

14. Woodward, *Price of Politics*, 27–28; "A Balanced Plan to Avert the Sequester and Reduce the Deficit," The White House, February 21, 2013, https://obamawhitehouse.archives.gov/blog/2013/02/21/balanced-plan-avert-sequester-and-reduce-deficit.

15. Franklin D. Roosevelt, 1939 Jackson Day speech, quoted in James MacGregor Burns, *Roosevelt: The Lion and the Fox, 1882–1940* (New York: Harcourt Brace, 1956), 543; Conor Clarke, "What Dick Cheney Really Thinks About Deficits," *The Atlantic,* May 28, 2009, www.theatlantic.com/politics/archive/2009/05/what-dick-cheney-really-thinks-about-deficits/18426/.

16. "President Obama: 'They Drove Our Economy into a Ditch,'" August 23, 2012, posted by Barack Obama, YouTube, www.youtube.com/watch?v=QKv-dXHhtMs. For the $4.1 trillion estimate, see Congressional Budget Office Director Philip Swagel's letter to Senator Jeff Merkley, August 4, 2025, www.cbo.gov/system/files/2025-08/61466-DebtService.pdf. For additional evidence of Republican willingness to rely on debt, see Christian Cox, Derek Epp, and Ian Shapiro, "The Political Economy of Fiscal Responsibility," *Public Choice*, published online October 17, 2025, https://doi.org/10.1007/s11127-025-01339-5.

17. Steven A. Holmes, "Fannie Mae Eases Credit to Aid Mortgage Lending," *New York Times,* September 30, 1999, www.nytimes.com/1999/09/30/business/fannie-mae-eases-credit-to-aid-mortgage-lending.html.

18. "Homeownership Rate in the United States," Federal Reserve Bank of Saint Louis, updated April 30, 2024, https://fred.stlouisfed.org/series

/RSAHORUSQ156S. On the real estate bubble, see Robert Shiller, *Irrational Exuberance*, 3rd ed. (Princeton, NJ: Princeton University Press, 2015). On the financial bailout, see Ross Sorkin, *Too Big to Fail* (Penguin, 2010). On the politics of the housing crisis, Gretchen Morgenson and Joshua Rosner, *Reckless Endangerment* (New York: Griffin, 2012).

19. Joshua Rosner, "Housing in the New Millennium: A Home Without Equity Is Just a Rental with Debt," Graham Fisher, June 2001, https://fcic-static.law.stanford.edu/cdn_media/fcic-docs/2001-06-29%20Rosner%20Housing%20in%20the%20New%20Millenium.pdf. The first edition of Shiller's *Irrational Exuberance* was published at the height of the dot-com bubble in 2000, predicting that it would soon burst. Shiller published a second, revised edition in 2005 to address the housing bubble.

20. Woodward, *Price of Politics*, 8; "Examining the Making Home Affordable Program," Hearing before the House Subcommittee on Housing and Community Opportunity, March 19, 2009, www.govinfo.gov/content/pkg/CHRG-111hhrg48869/html/CHRG-111hhrg48869.htm; "Fact Sheet: President Obama's Plan to Help Homeowners and Heal the Housing Market," White House press release, February 1, 2012, https://obamawhitehouse.archives.gov/the-press-office/2012/02/01/fact-sheet-president-obama-s-plan-help-responsible-homeowners-and-heal-h; Debbie Bocian, Wei Li, and Keith Ernst, "Foreclosures by Race and Ethnicity: The Demographics of a Crisis," CRL Report, June 18, 2010, 2, www.mvfairhousing.com/ai2015/2010-06-18_Foreclosures_by_Race_and_Ethnicity.PDF; Maggie Gallagher, "Our Subprime Federal Government," Manhattan Institute, October 20, 2009, https://manhattan.institute/article/our-subprime-federal-government; John Geanakoplos, "Solving the Present Crisis and Managing the Leverage Cycle," Federal Reserve Bureau, New York Economic Policy Review, August 2010, www.newyorkfed.org/medialibrary/media/research/epr/10v16n1/1008gean.pdf; Laura Kusito, "Many Who Lost Homes to Foreclosure in Last Decade Won't Return—NAR," *Wall Street Journal*, April 20, 2015, www.wsj.com/articles/many-who-lost-homes-to-foreclosure-in-last-decade-wont-return-nar-1429548640. Assuming an average household size of 3.1, 9.3 million foreclosures meant that 28.83 million people had to leave their homes. Veera Korhonen, "Average Number of People per Family in the United States from 1960 to 2023," Statista, www.statista.com/statistics/183657/average-size-of-a-family-in-the-us/. This probably understates the number, because most subprime mortgage holders fall below the median income, a population that often has larger-than-average-sized households.

21. Zachary Carter, *The Price of Peace: Money, Democracy, and the Life of John Maynard Keynes* (New York: Random House, 2020), 520–24; Bocian et al., "Foreclosures by Race and Ethnicity"; Rakesh Kochhar and Richard

Fry, "Wealth Inequality Has Widened Along Racial, Ethnic Lines Since End of Great Recession," Pew Research Center, December 12, 2024, www.pewresearch.org/short-reads/2014/12/12/racial-wealth-gaps-great-recession/; Damon Silvers quoted in David Dayen, "A Needless Default," *The American Prospect*, February 9, 2015, https://prospect.org/economy/needless-default/.

22. "A State-by-State Look at the President's Payroll Tax Cuts for Middle-Class Families," US Treasury Office of Tax Policy, November 30, 2011, https://home.treasury.gov/system/files/131/Report-Presidents-Payroll-Tax-Cuts-2011.pdf.

23. The figure of ninety-five hundred families was estimated in "How Many People Pay the Estate Tax," Tax Policy Center Urban Institute and Brookings Institution, updated January 2024, www.taxpolicycenter.org/briefing-book/how-many-people-pay-estate-tax. The cost of the bill estimated by the Joint Committee in Taxation, "Estate Tax Options," Every CRS Report, April 23, 2010, www.everycrsreport.com/reports/R41203.html#_Ref259801109. On Gingrich's advice, see Andy Barr, "The GOP's No Compromise Pledge," *Politico*, October 28, 2010, www.politico.com/story/2010/10/the-gops-no-compromise-pledge-044311; and Chris McGreal, "Barack Obama Gives Way to Republicans over Bush Tax Cuts," *The Guardian*, December 7, 2010, www.theguardian.com/world/2010/dec/06/barack-obama-bush-tax-cuts. On Pelosi's response, see Woodward, *Price of Politics*, 75–76. On the regressivity of the bill, see Avery Fellow, "House Passes $858B Bill Extending Tax Cuts," Courthouse News Service, December 17, 2010, www.courthousenews.com/house-passes-858b-bill-extending-tax-cuts/.

24. "President Obama Remarks on Fiscal Cliff Agreement Passage," C-SPAN, January 1, 2013, www.c-span.org/video/?310151-1/president-obama-remarks-fiscal-cliff-agreement-passage; Ethan Pollack, "The Middle Class Does NOT Extend Up to $400k," Economic Policy Institute, December 21, 2012, www.epi.org/blog/middle-class-income-tax-threshold/; "Obama Willing to Up Threshold for Raising Taxes on Households to $400,000," CBS News, December 18, 2012, www.cbsnews.com/newyork/news/obama-willing-to-up-threshold-for-raising-taxes-on-households-to-400000/. Trump would more than double the threshold in his 2017 law while retaining the indexing so that by 2024 the exemption was $13.61 million ($27.22 million for a married couple), a large additional reduction in progressivity.

25. Eighty-five House Republicans voted for the bill (and 172 Democrats), while 151 (and 16 Democrats) opposed it. Forty Republican senators (and 49 Democrats) voted for the bill, with 3 Republicans (and 5 Democrats) opposed.

26. Bob Woodward, *Maestro: Greenspan's Fed and the American Boom* (New York: Simon and Schuster, 2000); Jeannine Aversa, "Alan Greenspan Enjoys

a Rock Star Renown," *Houston Chronicle*, March 5, 2005, www.chron.com/business/article/alan-greenspan-enjoys-rock-star-renown-1914177.php; Ambrose Evans-Pritchard, "Greenspan Was More a Rock Star than a Feared Fed Sage," *The Telegraph*, September 17, 2007, www.telegraph.co.uk/finance/comment/ambroseevans_pritchard/2815893/Greenspan-was-more-a-rock-star-than-a-feared-Fed-sage.html; James Stock and Mark Watson, "Has the Business Cycle Changed, and Why?," in *NBER Macroeconomics Annual*, ed. Mark Gertler and Ken Rogoff (Cambridge, MA: MIT Press, 2002), 159–218.

27. Alan Greenspan, "Greenspan Admits Flaw to Congress, Predicts More Economic Problems," interview by Judy Woodruff, *PBS News Hour*, October 23, 2008, www.pbs.org/newshour/show/greenspan-admits-flaw-to-congress-predicts-more-economic-problems; "Greenspan Testimony on Sources of Financial Crisis," *Wall Street Journal*, October 23, 2008, www.wsj.com/articles/BL-REB-2187; Ronald Reagan, Inaugural Address 1981, Reagan Presidential Library and Museum, accessed September 23, 2025, www.reaganlibrary.gov/archives/speech/inaugural-address-1981.

28. Stephen Labaton, "Agency's 04 Rule Let Banks Pile Up New Debt," *New York Times*, October 2, 2008, www.nytimes.com/2008/10/03/business/03sec.html.

29. Franklin D. Roosevelt, Address at Madison Square Garden, New York City, October 31, 1936, American Presidency Project, accessed September 23, 2025, www.presidency.ucsb.edu/documents/address-madison-square-garden-new-york-city-1.

30. Adam Tooze, *Crashed: How a Decade of Financial Crises Changed the World* (New York: Penguin Books, 2019), 143–317.

31. Juliana Menasce Horowitz, Ruth Igielnik, and Rakesh Kochhar, "Trends in Income and Wealth Inequality," Pew Research Center, January 9, 2020, www.pewresearch.org/social-trends/2020/01/09/trends-in-income-and wealth-inequality/; Jonathan Cribb, Andrew Hood, Robert Joyce, and Agnes Norris Keiller, "Families Dependent on Fathers' Earnings Alone Have Average Incomes No Higher than 15 Years Ago," Institute for Fiscal Studies, July 10, 2017, https://ifs.org.uk/news/families-dependent-fathers-earnings-alone-have-average-incomes-no-higher-15-years-ago; "Home Equity Lines Have Dried Up Across the US," NBC News Personal Finance, December 27, 2009, www.nbcnews.com/id/wbna34601242.

32. "Crude Oil Prices (1946–2025)," Macrotrends, last updated August 2025, www.macrotrends.net/1369/crude-oil-price-history-chart; Tooze, *Crashed*, 43–51; David Lewin, Thomas Kochan, Joel Cutcher-Gershenfeld et al., "Getting It Right: Empirical Evidence and Policy Implications from Research on Public-Sector Unionism and Collective Bargaining," *SSRN Electronic Journal* (March 2011): 9, fig. 2, www.researchgate.net

/figure/Private-Sector-Defined-Benefit-and-Defined-Contribution-Plan-Coverage-1979-2009_fig2_228236802.

33. Social Security, which paid fewer than 200,000 beneficiaries until 1940, was paying over 35 million by 1980, 45 million by the turn of the century, and 50 million by 2008, at an annual cost of over $600 billion. "Historical Background and Development of Social Security," Social Security Administration, August 2025, www.ssa.gov/history/briefhistory3.html. In 1950, about one in fifty Americans received Social Security; by the turn of the twenty-first century, one in six did. Patricia Martin and David Weaver, "Social Security: A Program and Policy History," *Social Security Bulletin* 66, no. 1 (2005), www.ssa.gov/policy/docs/ssb/v66n1/v66n1p1.html. In 1935, American life expectancy was sixty years. By 1980, it had risen to seventy-three, massively increasing the duration of Social Security payouts. "Annual Life Expectancy at Birth in the United States, 1850–2023, with Projections Until 2100," Statistica, July 30, 2025, www.statista.com/statistics/1040079/life-expectancy-united-states-all-time/.

34. "U.S. Immigrant Population and Share over Time, 1850–Present," Migration Policy Institute, 2023, www.migrationpolicy.org/programs/data-hub/charts/immigrant-population-over-time; "Age Dependency Ratio: Older Dependents to Working-Age Population for the United States," FRED data, Federal Reserve Bank of St. Louis, December 17, 2024, https://fred.stlouisfed.org/series/SPPOPDPNDOLUSA.

35. Michael Schuyler, "A Short History of Government Taxing and Spending in the United States," Tax Foundation, February 19, 2024, https://taxfoundation.org/research/all/federal/short-history-government-taxing-and-spending-united-states/.

36. Emmanuel Saez, "Striking It Richer: The Evolution of Top Incomes in the United States," UC Berkeley, 2024, https://eml.berkeley.edu/~saez/saez-UStopincomes-2022.pdf; Gabriel Zucman, "Global Wealth Inequality," *Annual Review of Economics* 11 (2019): 109–38, http://gabriel-zucman.eu/files/Zucman2019.pdf; Albena Azmanova, *Capitalism on Edge: How Fighting Precarity Can Achieve Radical Change Without Crisis or Utopia* (New York: Columbia University Press, 2020), 105–68.

37. "Number of Jobs, Labor Market Experience, Marital Status, and Health for Those Born 1957–1964," US Bureau of Labor Statistics, August 22, 2023, www.bls.gov/news.release/nlsoy.nr0.htm.

38. Michael Graetz and Ian Shapiro, *The Wolf at the Door: The Menace of Economic Insecurity and How to Fight It* (Cambridge, MA: Harvard University Press, 2020), 10–36, 260–82; Daniel Markovits, *The Meritocracy Trap: How America's Foundational Myth Feeds Inequality, Dismantles the Middle Class, and Devours the Elite* (New York: Penguin, 2019).

39. Carter, *Price of Peace*, 525–27.

40. "Barack Obama at the launch of the Brookings Institute's [*sic*] Hamilton Project," April 5, 2006, posted November 30, 2009, by heckofjob, YouTube, www.youtube.com/watch?v=P-5Y74FrDCc.

41. Suskind, *Confidence Men*, 28–34. Obama quote on p. 31.

42. Editors of *Encyclopedia Britannica*, "Works Progress Administration," *Britannica*, last updated May 8, 2024, www.britannica.com/topic/Works-Progress-administration; editors of History.com, "Civilian Conservation Corps," History.com, updated March 31, 2021, www.history.com/topics/great-depression/civilian-conservation-corps.

43. Tooze, *Crashed*, 289–90.

44. Chris Edwards, "Tax Increases and the Great Depression," Downsizing the Federal Government, November 16, 2022, www.downsizinggovernment.org/tax-increases-and-great-depression.

45. "Congress and the New Deal: Social Security," National Archives, August 2025, www.archives.gov/exhibits/treasures_of_congress/text/page19_text.html.

46. Laura Kalman, *FDR's Gambit: The Court-Packing Fight and the Rise of Legal Liberalism* (Oxford, UK: Oxford University Press, 2022), chap. 3.

Chapter Five: Harvesting Disaster

1. Adam Tooze, *Crashed: How a Decade of Financial Crises Changed the World* (New York: Penguin, 2019), 81–88; "Twenty Years of British Troops in Afghanistan," Imperial War Museum, August 16, 2021, www.iwm.org.uk/history/twenty-years-of-british-troops-in-afghanistan; Billy Perrigo, "'Ultimately, We Have Chosen Defeat.' British Lawmakers Condemn Decision to Follow US Out of Afghanistan After Fall of Kabul," *Time*, August 16, 2021, https://time.com/6090694/afghanistan-taliban-uk/; "Iraq War in Figures," BBC News, December 14, 2021, www.bbc.com/news/world-middle-east-11107739; Matthew Tempest, "George Michael Lampoons 'Poodle' Blair," *The Guardian*, July 1, 2002, www.theguardian.com/politics/2002/jul/01/politicalnews.redbox; UK Government, "The Report of the Iraq Inquiry," July 6, 2016, www.gov.uk/government/publications/the-report-of-the-iraq-inquiry.

2. Tooze, *Crashed*, 94, 288.

3. Björn Bremer, *Austerity from the Left: Social Democratic Parties in the Shadow of the Great Recession* (Oxford, UK: Oxford University Press, 2023), 170–209.

4. Gianmarco Fifi, "From Social Protection to 'Progressive Neoliberalism': Writing the Left," *Review of International Political Economy* (2022), 1436–58; Cornel Ban, "Spain's Embedded Neoliberalism," in *Ruling Ideas: How Global Neoliberalism Goes Local* (online ed., Oxford Academic, 2016), https://doi.org/10.1093/acprof:oso/9780190600389.003.0002; Paul McVeigh, "Embedding Neoliberalism in Spain: From Franquismo to Neoliberalism," in

Internalizing Globalization: International Political Economy Series, ed. Suzanne Soederberg, Georg Menz, and Philip Cerny (London: Palgrave Macmillan, 2005), 90–105; Merijn Oudenampsen, "The Riddle of the Missing Feathers," *European Politics and Society* 22, no. 1 (2020): 38–52; and Stephanie Mudge, *Leftism Reinvented: Western Parties from Socialism to Neoliberalism* (Cambridge, MA: Harvard University Press, 2018), 311–30.

5. Socialist Prime Minister José Sócrates negotiated the €78 billion bailout agreement in May 2011, but he resigned when the parliament rejected it. The center right replaced the Socialists after the subsequent elections. On the changes in inequality, see Carlos Oliveira, "Inequality and Political Cleavages in Portugal," Paris School of Economics, 2024, http://piketty pse.ens.fr/files/Oliveira2024.pdf; Ilyana Kuziemko, Nicolas Longuet-Marx, and Suresh Naidu, "'Compensate the Losers?' Economic Policy and Partisan Realignments in the US" (NBER Working Paper 31794, 2024), www.nber.org/papers/w31794. Portugal is also notable in being less politically fragmented than other countries. The two main parties have accounted for between 64 and 78 percent in every election between 1987 and 2022. Even with the Chega surge in 2024, they still accounted for 56.8 percent. See also Luis Bauluz, Amory Gethin, Clara Martínez-Toledano, and Marc Morgan, "Historical Political Cleavages and Post-Crisis Transformations in Italy, Spain, and Portugal" (World Inequality Lab Working Paper 2021/01, January 2021), https://wid.world/document/historical-political-cleavages-and-post-crisis-transformations-in-italy-spain-portugal-and-ireland-1953-2020-world-inequality-lab-wp-2021-01/. For Krugman's assessment, see "Portugal Branded an 'Economic Miracle,'" *Portugal News*, November 24, 2023, www.theportugalnews.com/news/2023-11-24/portugal-branded-an-economic-miracle/83608.

6. On the effects of the real estate boom, see João Ruy Faustino, "Portugal's Phony Economic Miracle," *Compact*, May 16, 2025, www.compactmag.com/article/portugals-phony-economic-miracle/; and Tamila Nussupbekova, "Portugal's Residential Property Market Analysis 2025," Global Property Guide, June 20, 2025, www.globalpropertyguide.com/europe/portugal/price-history. On the growth of inequality and those at risk of poverty, see Instituto Nacional de Estatística, Statistics Portugal, November 27, 2023, www.ine.pt/xportal/xmain?xpid=INE&xpgid=ine_destaques&DESTAQUESdest_boui=594931817&DESTAQUESmodo=2.

7. Christopher Cox and Ian Shapiro, "Party Realignment and Single-Issue Voters," *PLOS One* 20, no. 3 (2025), https://journals.plos.org/plosone/article?id=10.1371/journal.pone.0319522.

8. Niall McCarthy, "Where Britain's Immigrants Historically Come From," Statista, October 7, 2015, www.statista.com/chart/3860/where-britains-immigrants-historically-come-from/.

9. Sam Knight, "What Have Fourteen Years of Conservative Rule Done to Britain?," *New Yorker*, March 25, 2024, www.newyorker.com/magazine/2024/04/01/what-have-fourteen-years-of-conservative-rule-done-to-britain; Holly Ellyatt, "Osborne's Legacy: What the Austerity Chancellor Leaves Behind," CNBC, July 14, 2016, www.cnbc.com/2016/07/14/osbornes-legacy-what-the-austerity-chancellor-leaves-behind.html.

10. Esther Addley and Ben Quinn, "'We're Coming for Labour': Reform's Small Seat Count Conceals Size of Its Threat," *The Guardian*, July 5, 2024, www.theguardian.com/politics/article/2024/jul/05/reform-few-seats-conceal-size-threat; Toby Helm and Michael Savage, "Archbishop of Canterbury Urges Starmer to Ditch 'Cruel' Two-Child Benefit Cap," *The Guardian*, May 18, 2024, www.theguardian.com/society/article/2024/may/18/archbishop-canterbury-urges-starmer-to-ditch-cruel-two-child-benefit-cap; Sam Knight, "Keir Starmer's Bafflingly Bad Start as the UK's Prime Minister." *New Yorker*, October 12, 2024, www.newyorker.com/news/the-lede/keir-starmers-bafflingly-bad-start-as-the-uk-prime-minister; Pippa Crerar and Peter Walker, "Keir Starmer Confirms U-Turn on Winter Fuel Payment Cuts," *The Guardian*, May 21, 2025, www.theguardian.com/society/2025/may/21/keir-starmer-confirms-u-turn-on-winter-fuel-payment-cuts.

11. "United Kingdom—Parliament Voting Intention," *Politico*, December 2024, www.politico.eu/europe-poll-of-polls/united-kingdom/; Faye Brown, "As Starmer's Approval Rating Plummets, Farage's Is on the Rise: Can Labour Turn Things Around?," Sky News, November 23, 2024, news.sky.com/story/as-starmers-approval-rating-plummets-farages-is-on-the-rise-can-labour-turn-things-around-13257768; Andy Beckett, "Have Those Who Say Starmer Is Failing Forgotten the Madness of the Tory Years Already?," *The Guardian*, December 16, 2024, www.theguardian.com/commentisfree/2024/dec/16/keir-starmer-failing-madness-tory-years; Patrick Maguire and Gabriel Pogrund, *Get In: The Inside Story of Labour Under Starmer* (London: Bodley Head, 2025), 368–438; Bremer, *Austerity from the Left*, 128–69.

12. Tooze, *Crashed*, 97, 187, 288–89, 356, 416–17.

13. Mark Blyth, *Austerity: The History of a Dangerous Idea* (Oxford, UK: Oxford University Press, 2015), 51–103.

14. Two smaller French ETUC members abstained, but the only one that opposed it was the Force Ouvrière. There was more opposition among non-ETUC members, such as teachers' unions and some agricultural unions, a harbinger of things to come.

15. "EU Constitution Roadmap," Deutsche Welle, October 25, 2006, www.dw.com/en/germany-aims-to-revive-european-constitution/a-2184080.

16. Gaëtane Ricard-Nihoul, "The French 'No' Vote on 29 May, 2005: Understanding and Action," *Notre Europe*, Studies and Research No. 44 (January 2024), https://institutdelors.eu/content/uploads/2025/04/etud44-en

-3.pdf; Madeleine O. Hosli, Caterina Zamparini, and Luiza Martins Santos, "European Union Voting and the Dutch 'Double No': The 2005 and 2016 Referendums," *European Integration—Realities and Perspectives: Proceedings* (2024), www.researchgate.net/publication/383665967_European_Union_Voting_and_the_Dutch_'Double_No'_The_2005_and_2016_Referendums.

17. Tony Judt's prescient warning: "If 'Europe' stands for the winners, who shall speak for the losers—the 'south,' the poor, the linguistically, educationally, or culturally disadvantaged, underprivileged, or despised Europeans who don't live in golden triangles along vanished frontiers? The risk is that what remains to *these* Europeans is 'the nation,' or, more precisely, nationalism; not the national separatism of Catalans or the regional self-advancement of Lombards but the preservation of the nineteenth-century state as a bulwark against change." Tony Judt, "Europe: The Grand Illusion," *New York Review of Books*, July 11, 1996, www.nybooks.com/articles/1996/07/11/europe-the-grand-illusion/. The term "democratic deficit" was first used in relation to the EU by the Young European Federalists in their 1977 manifesto. "The First Use of the Term 'Democratic Deficit,'" Federal Union, October 10, 1977, https://federalunion.org.uk/the-first-use-of-the-term-democratic-deficit/.

18. Philippe Marlière, "Has François Hollande Gone from Being Mr Normal to Mr Neoliberal?," *The Guardian*, August 19, 2012, www.theguardian.com/commentisfree/2012/aug/19/francois-hollande-president-france-neoliberal.

19. On Hollande's praise for Germany's neoliberal reforms, see Philippe Le Corre, "François Hollande's Legacy: Strong Abroad, Weak at Home," Brookings Institution, April 21, 2017, www.brookings.edu/articles/francois-hollandes-legacy-strong-abroad-weak-at-home/; Quentin Peel, "Hollande Praises Germany's 'Courageous' Reformers," *Financial Times*, May 22, 2013, www.ft.com/content/5c1bc6e6-c301-11e2-9bcb-00144feab7de. On the repetition of these patterns elsewhere, see Christian Salas, Frances Rosenbluth, and Ian Shapiro, "Political Parties and the New Politics of Insecurity," in *Who Gets What: The New Politics of Insecurity*, ed. Frances Rosenbluth and Margaret Weir (Cambridge, UK: Cambridge University Press, 2000), 247–58.

20. Maikol Cerda, Alexander Kustov, Frances Rosenbluth, and Ian Shapiro, "Party Institutions and Social Welfare," paper presented at the virtual annual meeting of the American Political Science Association, August 2020, https://jackson.yale.edu/wp-content/uploads/2022/08/Cerda-et-al.-2020.pdf.

21. "Germany—National Parliament Voting Intention," *Politico*, October 2025, www.politico.eu/europe-poll-of-polls/germany/.

22. Tucker Carlson, *Ship of Fools: How a Selfish Ruling Class Is Bringing America to the Brink of Revolution* (New York: Free Press, 2018), 3.

23. Bruno Amable and Stefano Palombarini, *The Last Neoliberal: Macron and the Origins of France's Political Crisis* (New York: Verso, 2021), 105–9.

24. Marine Le Pen, speech in Tours, January 16, 2011, and press release, December 17, 2012, quoted in Amable and Palombarini, *The Last Neoliberal*, 108–9. The second quotation is taken from François Ruffin, *Pauvres actionnaires!: 40 ans de discours économiques du Front national passés au cribble* (Fakir, 2014), 87–90; Cécile Alduy, "Nouveau discours, nouveaux succès," *Pouvoirs: Revue française d'études constitutionnelles et politiques*, no. 4 (2016): 25, https://shs.cairn.info/revue-pouvoirs-2016-2-page-17?lang=fr.

25. Amable and Palombarini, *The Last Neoliberal*, 108–10.

26. In the legislative elections, a record 51.3 percent of voters did not vote in the first round, a number that rose to over 57.3 percent in the second round. Abel Mestre, "French Legislative Elections: Sharp Decline in Voter Turnout Highlights a Worrying Trend," *Le Monde*, June 19, 2022, www.lemonde.fr/en/politics/article/2022/06/19/french-legislative-elections-sharp-decline-in-voter-turnout-highlights-a-worrying-trend_5987291_5.html. In the first round of the presidential election, Macron won 43 percent of voters who identified as sympathetic to the Socialists and 20 percent of those who identified with the Greens. In the National Assembly elections, those numbers were 27 percent and 10 percent, respectively. Amable and Palombarini, *The Last Neoliberal*, 161.

27. "Emmanuel Macron: What Are the French President's Policies?," BBC News, May 10, 2017, www.bbc.com/news/world-europe-39845905; Seán Clarke and Josh Holder, "French Presidential Election 2017: First Round Results in Charts and Maps," *The Guardian*, April 23, 2017, www.theguardian.com/world/ng-interactive/2017/apr/23/french-presidential-election-results-2017-latest.

28. Matthew Goodwin and Oliver Heath, "Brexit Vote Explained: Poverty, Low Skills and Lack of Opportunities," Joseph Rowntree Foundation, August 31, 2016, www.jrf.org.uk/public-attitudes/brexit-vote-explained-poverty-low-skills-and-lack-of-opportunities.

29. Angelique Chrisafis, "French PM Warns of More Cuts to Tackle the Country's Debt 'Volcano,'" *The Guardian*, July 4, 2017, www.theguardian.com/world/2017/jul/04/french-pm-edouard-philippe-warns-cuts-reduce-debt-volcano-public-spending; Tristan Perrier, "Macron's 2017–2022 Economic Policies: Predominantly Supply-Side, Before Covid Shifted the Priority to Fiscal Support," Amundi Research Center, April 5, 2022, https://research-center.amundi.com/files/nuxeo/dl/6cae5ed1-e57d-46e4-adbf-a41a52887415?inline=.

30. Perrier, "Macron's 2017–2022 Economic Policies."

31. Daniel Boffey, "Majority of Europeans 'Expect End of EU Within 20 Years,'" *The Guardian*, May 15, 2019, www.theguardian.com/world/2019/may/15/majority-of-europeans-expect-end-of-eu-within-20-years.

32. Philippe Askenazy, "The Transformations of the French Labor Market, 2000–2021," *IZA World of Labor*, November 2022, https://wol.iza

.org/articles/the-changing-of-the-french-labor-market/long; Adam Nossiter, "France's Macron's Unwanted New Title: 'President of the Rich,'" *New York Times*, November 1, 2017, www.nytimes.com/2017/11/01/world/europe/france-emmanuel-macron.html; Mark Rice-Oxley and Patrick Butler, "Cash, Credits and Crisis: Life in the New European 'Precariat,'" *The Guardian*, May 15, 2019, www.theguardian.com/world/2019/may/15/cash-credits-and-crisis-life-in-the-new-european-precariat; Liz Alderman, "Macron, with Popularity Slumping, Tries Tax Cuts for France's Working Class," *New York Times*, October 4, 2018, www.nytimes.com/2018/10/04/business/economy/mcaron-popularity-tax-cuts-working-class.html.

33. David Revault d'Allonnes, "EXCLUSIF. Macron au JDD: 'Je ne changerai pas de politique,'" *Le Journal du Dimanche*, October 29, 2018, www.lejdd.fr/Politique/exclusif-macron-au-jdd-je-ne-changerai-pas-de-politique-3767252.

34. Kim Willsher, "Macron Bows to Protesters' Demands and Says: I Know I Have Hurt Some of You," *The Guardian*, December 10, 2018, www.theguardian.com/world/2018/dec/10/macron-pledges-to-raise-french-minimum-wage-gilet-jaunes-protests; Benjamin Dodman, "'All Smoke and Mirrors': Yellow Vest Protesters Reject Macron's 'Crumbs,'" France 24, December 11, 2018, www.france24.com/en/20181211-yellow-vest-protesters-react-macron-concessions-address-france-crumbs.

35. Giorgio Leali, "France Plans Eye-Watering €40B in Budget Cuts for 2025," *Politico*, October 2, 2024, www.politico.eu/article/france-eye-watering-40-billion-euro-budget-cut-2025-eu-commission-debt-michel-barnier/.

36. "Economic Forecast for France," European Commission—Economy and Finance, May 19, 2025, https://economy-finance.ec.europa.eu/economic-surveillance-eu-economies/france/economic-forecast-france_en; Blyth, *Austerity*, 170–76, 212–16.

37. "France—National Parliament Voting Intention," *Politico*, October 13, 2025, www.politico.eu/europe-poll-of-polls/france/; Elizabeth Pineau and Michel Rose, "French PM to Suspend Macron's Flagship Pension Reform," Reuters, October 14, 2025, www.reuters.com/world/europe/french-pm-lecornu-deliver-key-speech-his-fate-hangs-balance-2025-10-14/.

38. Aaron Blake, "78 Republican Politicians, Donors and Officials Who Are Supporting Hillary Clinton," *Washington Post*, November 7, 2016, www.washingtonpost.com/news/the-fix/wp/2016/06/30/heres-the-growing-list-of-big-name-republicans-supporting-hillary-clinton/.

39. "The Federal Budget in 2016: An Infographic," Congressional Budget Office, February 8, 2017, https://www.cbo.gov/publication/52408.

40. Gabriella Cruz-Martínez, "Earned Income Tax Credit (EITC) 2025: How Much Will You Get?," Kiplinger, February 28, 2025, www.kiplinger

.com/taxes/earned-income-tax-credit; "What Is the Earned Income Tax Credit?," Tax Policy Center, March 6, 2025, https://taxpolicycenter.org/briefing-book/what-earned-income-tax-credit; "States and Local Governments with Earned Income Tax Credit," Internal Revenue Service, March 6, 2025, www.irs.gov/credits-deductions/individuals/earned-income-tax-credit/states-and-local-governments-with-earned-income-tax-credit; Conor F. Boyle, Margot L. Crandall-Hollick, and Brendan McDermott, "The Earned Income Tax Credit: How It Works and Who Receives It," Congressional Research Service Report R43805, November 14, 2023, www.congress.gov/crs-product/R43805.

41. Dan Fuller and Doris Geide-Stevenson, "Consensus Among Economists: An Update," *Journal of Economic Education* 45, no. 2 (2014): 131–46, https://doi.org/10.1080/00220485.2014.889963; Doris Geide-Stevenson and Álvaro La Parra-Pérez, "Consensus Among Economists 2020: A Sharpening of the Picture," *Journal of Economic Education* 55, no. 4 (2024): 461–78, https://doi.org/10.1080/00220485.2024.2386328.

42. Rod Hick and Ive Marx, "Poor Workers in Rich Democracies: On the Nature of In-Work Poverty and Its Relationship to Labour Market Policies" (University of Antwerp Working Paper No. 22/02, March 2022), https://medialibrary.uantwerpen.be/files/57001/fe124f03-01a4-4e4a-9dc4-aadd11f4e756.pdf; Gabrielle Paluch, "Why Wasn't a Tax Cut with Rare Bipartisan Support Part of Tax Overhaul Talks?," Center for Public Integrity, April 17, 2019, https://publicintegrity.org/inequality-poverty-opportunity/taxes/trumps-tax-cuts/even-republicans-like-this-tax-cut-for-the-working-poor-why-wasnt-it-expanded-by-trumps-tax-law/.

43. Michael Smolyansky, Gustavo Suarez, and Alexandra Tabova, "US Corporations' Repatriation of Offshore Profits: Evidence from 2018," FEDS Notes, Board of Governors of the Federal Reserve System, August 6, 2019, www.federalreserve.gov/econres/notes/feds-notes/us-corporations-repatriation-of-offshore-profits-20190806.html; Patrick Kennedy, Christine Dobridge, Paul Landefeld, and Jacob Mortenson, "The Efficiency-Equity Tradeoff of the Corporate Income Tax: Evidence from the Tax Cuts and Jobs Act" (working paper, 2024), https://patrick-kennedy.github.io/files/TCJA_KDLM_2024.pdf.

44. For one such proposal, see Benjamin Austin, Edward Glaeser, and Lawrence Summers, "Jobs for the Heartland: Place-Based Policies in Twenty-First Century America" (Brookings Papers on Economic Activity, Spring 2018), 151–232, www.brookings.edu/wp-content/uploads/2018/03/AustinEtAl_Text.pdf.

45. "Peru's Works for Taxes Scheme: An Innovative Solution to Accelerate Private Provision of Infrastructure Investment," Fresh Ideas About Business in Emerging Markets, June 2018, https://openknowledge.worldbank.org/server/api/core/bitstreams/55282690-f795-50e2-87a2-0204d430d88b/content; Jaan

Elias, Nicolás Jiménez, Greg MacDonald, and Ian Shapiro, "Colombia: Works for Taxes," Yale School of Management, 2022, https://sk.sagepub.com/cases/colombia-works-for-taxes.

46. Edward Alden, *Failure to Adjust: How Americans Got Left Behind in the Global Economy* (New York: Rowman and Littlefield, 2016); "Annual Statistical Report on the Social Security Disability Insurance Program, 2021," Social Security Administration, 2022, www.ssa.gov/policy/docs/statcomps/di_asr/2021/sect01.html.

47. Michael J. Graetz and Ian Shapiro, *The Wolf at the Door: The Menace of Economic Insecurity and How to Fight It* (Cambridge, MA: Harvard University Press, 2020), 202–10.

48. For advice to avoid scaling up the war from senators as different as liberal Democrat Mike Mansfield and conservative Republican Richard Russell Jr., see Michael Beschloss, ed., *Taking Charge: The Johnson White House Tapes, 1963–1964* (New York: Simon and Schuster, 1998), 33, 363–71, 377, 398, 401–3; and Michael Beschloss, *Reaching for Glory: Lyndon Johnson's Secret White House Tapes, 1964–1965* (New York: Simon and Schuster, 2002), 136–37, 185–86, 344–48. The most persistent dissonant voice within the administration was Undersecretary of State George Ball. See Beschloss, *Reaching for Glory*, 381.

Chapter Six: Taking Stock and Looking Forward

1. Alejandro Werner, "Can Mexico's New President Sustain AMLOnomics?," Peterson Institute for International Economics, January 2024, www.piie.com/blogs/realtime-economics/2024/can-mexicos-new-president-sustain-amlonomics.

2. Timothy W. Ryback, *Takeover: Hitler's Final Rise to Power* (New York: Knopf, 2024); Peter Fritzsche, *Hitler's First Hundred Days: When Germans Embraced the Third Reich* (New York: Basic Books, 2020); Sefton Delmer, *Weimar Germany: Democracy on Trial* (New York: American Heritage Press, 1972), 97; Jeff Wallenfeldt, "British Union of Fascists," *Encyclopedia Britannica*, www.britannica.com/topic/British-Union-of-Fascists.

3. Ian Shapiro, *Containment: Rebuilding a Strategy Against Global Terror* (Princeton, NJ: Princeton University Press, 2007).

4. Peter Swenson, *Fair Shares: Unions, Pay, and Politics in Sweden and West Germany* (Ithaca, NY: Cornell University Press, 1989); *Capitalists Against Markets: The Making of Labor Markets and Welfare States in the United States and Sweden* (New York: Oxford University Press, 2002); Ralph Miliband, *The State in Capitalist Society* (London: Merlin Press 2009 [1969]).

5. Meeting with Zagladin at a conference on the future of the USSR sponsored by the CPSU Central Committee in Moscow, March 1991.

6. Viktor Valgarðsson, Will Jennings, Gerry Stoker, et al., "A Crisis of Political Trust? Global Trends in Institutional Trust from 1958 to 2019," *British Journal of Political Science* 55 (2025), https://doi.org/10.1017/S0007123424000498.

7. See Christian Cox, Derek Epp, and Ian Shapiro, "The Political Economy of Fiscal Responsibility," *Public Choice*, published online October 17, 2025, https://doi.org/10.1007/s11127-025-01339-5.

8. Björn Bremer, *Austerity from the Left: Social Democratic Parties in the Shadow of the Great Recession* (New York: Oxford University Press, 2023); Richard Rubin, "Senate Pencils in $5 Trillion for Tax Relief, Leaving Blank Space for Spending Cuts," *Wall Street Journal*, April 2, 2025, www.wsj.com/politics/policy/senate-gop-budget-plan-vote-6668bd41.

9. Jake Sullivan, "The New Old Democrats," *Democracy: A Journal of Ideas*, June 20, 2018, https://democracyjournal.org/arguments/the-new-old-democrats/.

10. Jake Sullivan, "The New Old Democrats"; Benjamin Austin, Edward Glaeser, and Lawrence Summers, "Jobs for the Heartland: Place-Based Policies in Twenty-First Century America," *Brookings Papers on Economic Activity* (Spring 2018): 151–232, www.brookings.edu/wp-content/uploads/2018/03/AustinEtAl_Text.pdf.

11. Joseph Gagnon and Asher Rose, "Why Did Inflation Rise and Fall So Rapidly?" (Peterson Institute for International Economics Working Paper No. 25-1, January 2025), www.piie.com/sites/default/files/2025-01/wp25-1.pdf; Gene Sperling, "Tragedy of a One-Sided Biden Critique," *Democracy Journal*, March 7, 2025, https://democracyjournal.org/arguments/tragedy-of-a-one-sided-biden-critique/; Mary Amiti, Oleg Itskhoki, and David Weinstein, "What Drives US Import Price Inflation?," (National Bureau of Economic Research Working Paper No. 32133, February 2024), www.nber.org/papers/w32133.

12. John Lowy, "Obama Signs 5-Year Infrastructure Bill," Associated Press, December 4, 2015, https://apnews.com/united-states-congress-travel-united-states-government-f1b2c8dee7ea45b2a91b2d306b180429.

13. "Fact Sheet: How the Inflation Reduction Act's Tax Incentives Are Ensuring All Americans Benefit from the Growth of the Clean Energy Economy," US Department of the Treasury, October 20, 2023, https://home.treasury.gov/news/press-releases/jy1830; "America's Chip Resurgence: Over $630 Billion in Semiconductor Supply-Chain Investments," Semiconductor Industry Association, last updated July 28, 2025, www.semiconductors.org/chip-supply-chain-investments/; "Biden-Harris Administration Announces Preliminary Terms with Samsung," press release, US Department of Commerce, April 2024, www.commerce.gov/news/press-releases/2024/04/biden-harris-administration-announces-preliminary-terms-samsung; "Fact Sheet: President Biden Announces Up to $8.5 Billion Preliminary Agreement

with Intel," White House, March 20, 2024, https://bidenwhitehouse.archives.gov/briefing-room/statements-releases/2024/03/20/fact-sheet-president-biden-announces-up-to-8-5-billion-preliminary-agreement-with-intel-under-the-chips-science-act/; "Biden-Harris Administration Announces Preliminary Terms with GlobalFoundries," National Institute of Standards and Technology, February–April 2024, www.nist.gov/news-events/news/2024/02/biden-harris-administration-announces-preliminary-terms-globalfoundries; "Biden-Harris administration Announces Preliminary Terms with Micron to Onshore Leading Edge Memory Chip Production in the US," National Institute of Standards and Technology, April 2024, www.nist.gov/news-events/news/2024/04/biden-harris-administration-announces-preliminary-terms-micron-onshore; "Biden-Harris Administration Announces Preliminary Terms with TSMC," press release, US Department of Commerce, April 2024, www.commerce.gov/news/press-releases/2024/04/biden-harris-administration-announces-preliminary-terms-tsmc-expanded; "Biden-Harris Administration Announces Preliminary Terms with Texas Instruments," press release, US Department of Commerce, August 2024, www.commerce.gov/news/press-releases/2024/08/biden-harris-administration-announces-preliminary-terms-texas; "Department of Labor Awards $65 Million to Help States Expand Access to Registered Apprenticeships in High-Growth, High-Demand Industries," news release, US Department of Labor, July 19, 2023, www.dol.gov/newsroom/releases/eta/eta20230719; "Biden-Harris Administration Announces Nearly $200m Available in Grants to Expand Apprenticeships," news release, US Department of Labor, February 21, 2024, www.dol.gov/newsroom/releases/eta/eta20240221, "US Department of Labor Announces Apprenticeship Building America Program," news release, US Department of Labor, February 23, 2022, www.dol.gov/newsroom/releases/eta/eta20220223; "Scaling and Expanding the Use of Registered Apprenticeships in Industries and the Federal Government," *Federal Register* 89, no. 48 (March 11, 2024), www.federalregister.gov/documents/2024/03/11/2024-05220/scaling-and-expanding-the-use-of-registered-apprenticeships-in-industries-and-the-federal-government; "FY 2024 Budget in Brief," US Department of Labor, www.dol.gov/sites/dolgov/files/ETA/budget/pdfs/FY2024BIB_ETA.pdf.

14. "President Biden Says It Was 'Stupid' Not to Put Name on COVID Checks like Trump," *USA Today*, December 10, 2024, www.usatoday.com/story/news/politics/elections/2024/12/10/biden-stupid-leave-name-off-covid-checks/76892475007/; "Fact Sheet: The Biden-Harris Administration Record," The American Presidency Project, January 15, 2025, www.presidency.ucsb.edu/documents/fact-sheet-the-biden-harris-administration-record; Robert Brooks and Ben Harris, "The U.S. Recovery from COVID-19 in International Comparison," Brookings Institution, October 17, 2024,

www.brookings.edu/articles/the-us-recovery-from-covid-19-in-international-comparison/.

15. "Fact Sheet: The Biden-Harris Administration Record"; John Burn-Murdoch, "Democrats Join 2024's Graveyard of Incumbents," *Financial Times*, November 7, 2024, www.ft.com/content/e8ac09ea-c300-4249-af7d-109003afb893.

16. Daniel Kahneman and Amos Tversky, "Prospect Theory: An Analysis of Decision Under Risk," *Econometrica* 47, no. 2 (1979): 263–92.

17. "Kamala Harris Speech Transcript," *New York Times*, August 23, 2024, www.nytimes.com/2024/08/23/us/politics/kamala-harris-speech-transcript.html; Alex Gangitano, "Voters' Sour Moods Stand to Test Harris 'Joy' Campaign," *The Hill*, https://thehill.com/homenews/4824496-harris-campaign-joy-sour-moods/.

18. Jeff Cox, "Charting the Biden Economy: Deeply Unpopular Despite Growth and Jobs," CNBC, January 19, 2025, www.cnbc.com/2025/01/19/charting-the-biden-economy-deeply-unpopular-despite-growth-and-jobs.html; Howard Schneider, "Despite Sharp Decline, Inflation Remains a Sore Point for Harris," Reuters, November 4, 2024, www.reuters.com/world/us/despite-sharp-decline-inflation-remains-sore-point-harris-2024-11-04/; "Report on the Economic Well-Being of US Households," US Federal Reserve, May 28, 2025, www.federalreserve.gov/consumerscommunities/sheddataviz/worseoff.html.

19. "Survey of Household Economics and Decisionmaking: Interactive Charts," US Federal Reserve, May 28, 2025, www.federalreserve.gov/consumerscommunities/sheddataviz.htm; Wolf Richter, "Credit Card Delinquency Rates, Balances, Burden, and Available Credit in Q3 2024," *Wolf Street*, November 19, 2024, https://wolfstreet.com/2024/11/19/credit-card-delinquency-rates-balances-burden-and-available-credit-in-q3-2024/; HighYieldLarry, "Serious delinquencies on US auto loans are skyrocketing," Reddit, 2024, www.reddit.com/r/FluentInFinance/comments/1g4eas7/serious_delinquencies_on_us_auto_loans_are/; John Burn-Murdoch, "Inequality Hasn't Risen. Here's Why It Feels like It Has," *Financial Times*, January 3, 2025, www.ft.com/content/b325af8f-1864-448e-9b3e-bd1a18333a08; Daniel Markovits, *The Meritocracy Trap: How America's Foundational Myth Feeds Inequality, Dismantles the Middle Class, and Devours the Elite* (New York: Penguin, 2020); Barbara Field, "The Sandwich Generation," Senior Living, January 31, 2025, www.seniorliving.org/caregiving/sandwich-generation/.

20. Drew Goins, "Harris's Agenda Is Way More Popular than Trump's (If That Matters)," *Washington Post*, October 22, 2024, www.washingtonpost.com/opinions/2024/10/22/trump-harris-agenda-comparison-poll-venezuelan-gangs/; "The Election and Gen Z's Housing Problem," CNET, October 21, 2024, www.cnet.com/personal-finance/the-election-and-gen-zs-housing-problem/.

21. "Kamala Harris Speech Transcript."

22. Sahil Chinoy, Nathan Nunn, Sandra Sequeira, and Stefanie Stantcheva, "Zero-Sum Thinking and the Roots of Political Divides" (Harvard University Working Paper, May 15, 2024), https://scholar.harvard.edu/files/stantcheva/files/zero_sum_political_divides.pdf#page=29; Augustin Bergeron, Jean-Paul Carvalho, Joseph Henrich, Nathan Nunn, and Jonathan L. Weigel, "Zero-Sum Environments, the Evolution of Effort-Suppressing Beliefs, and Economic Development" (NBER Working Paper No. 31663, revised August 2025), www.nber.org/papers/w31663; Patricia Andrews Fearon, Friedrich M. Götz, Gregory Serapio-García, and David Good, "Zero-Sum Mindset and Its Discontents" (Blavatnik School of Government, Social Macroeconomics Working Paper Series SM-WP-2021-001, February 2021), www.bsg.ox.ac.uk/sites/default/files/2021-02/SM-WP-2021-001%20Zero-sum%20mindset%20and%20its%20discontents.pdf; John Burn-Murdoch, "Are We Destined for a Zero-Sum Future?," *Financial Times*, September 22, 2023, www.ft.com/content/980cbbe2-0f5d-4330-872d-c7a9d6a97bf6.

23. "Young Voters Shifted Toward Trump but Still Favored Harris Overall," Tufts Now, November 12, 2024, https://now.tufts.edu/2024/11/12/young-voters-shifted-toward-trump-still-favored-harris-overall; "First-Time Home Buyers Shrink to Historic Low of 24% as Buyer Age Hits Record High," National Association of Realtors, www.nar.realtor/newsroom/first-time-home-buyers-shrink-to-historic-low-of-24-as-buyer-age-hits-record-high. The declining affordability of home ownership in the US replicates a widespread pattern across the older democracies, contributing to political alienation of young voters. See Katrina Scalise, "Generation Locked-Out: Why Young People Around the World Can't Buy Homes Anymore," Worldcrunch, June 11, 2025, https://worldcrunch.com/business-finance/young-people-home owners/; Benedict Vigers, "Younger Men Among the Loneliest in the West," Gallup, May 20, 2025, https://news.gallup.com/poll/690788/younger-men-among-loneliest-west.aspx; "Kamala Harris Speech Transcript."

24. Burn-Murdoch, "Are We Destined for a Zero-Sum Future?"

25. Daniel Boffey, "Majority of Europeans 'Expect End of EU Within 20 Years,'" *The Guardian*, May 15, 2019, www.theguardian.com/world/2019/may/15/majority-of-europeans-expect-end-of-eu-within-20-years. The *Guardian* report relies on data from a study by Susi Dennison, Mark Leonard, and Adam Lury, "What Europeans Really Feel: The Battle for the Political System," European Council on Foreign Relations, May 16, 2019, which we draw on with permission from the ECFR in Figure 6.1. https://ecfr.eu/publication/what_europeans_really_feel_the_battle_for_the_political_system_eu_election/#methodology.

26. Zack Beauchamp, "The European Country Where 'Replacement Theory' Reigns Supreme," *Vox*, May 19, 2022, www.vox.com/2022/5/19/23123050

/hungary-cpac-2022-replacement-theory; Carlo Martussceli, "The Populist Right Want You to Make More Babies," *Politico*, September 11, 2023, www.politico.eu/article/eu-populist-right-want-you-make-more-babies-viktor-orban/; Hannah Demissie and Katherine Faulders, "Trump Administration Looking at $5,000 'Baby Bonus,' to Incentivize Public to Have More Children," ABC News, April 23, 2025, https://abcnews.go.com/Politics/trump-administration-5000-baby-bonus-incentivize-public-children/story?id=121094707.

27. The foundational paper on the world demographic transition was Warren Thompson, "Population," *American Journal of Sociology* 34, no. 6 (1929): 957–1212, www.journals.uchicago.edu/doi/epdf/10.1086/214874.

28. "China's Demographics at a Turning Point," Populyst, November 4, 2015, https://populyst.net/2015/11/chinas-demographics-at-a-turning-point/.

29. Maria de la Baume, "Orbán, Le Pen, Salvini Join Forces to Blast EU Integration," *Politico*, July 2, 2021, www.politico.eu/article/viktor-orban-marine-le-pen-matteo-salvini-eu-integration-european-superstate-radical-forces/.

30. Martuscelli, "The Populist Right Want You to Make More Babies"; "Fertility Rate, Total for Ireland," Federal Reserve Bank of St. Louis, updated April 16, 2025, https://fred.stlouisfed.org/series/SPDYNTFRTINIRL.

31. Roger Cohen, "Macron, Risking Backlash, Pushes Through Law Raising Retirement Age," *New York Times*, March 16, 2023, www.nytimes.com/2023/03/16/world/europe/macron-france-pension.html; Kathleen Romig, "Raising Social Security's Retirement Age Would Cut Benefits for All New Retirees," Center on Budget and Policy Priorities, April 25, 2023, www.cbpp.org/research/social-security/raising-social-securitys-retirement-age-would-cut-benefits-for-all-new; Anthony Trollope, *The Fixed Period* (Oxford, UK: Oxford University Press, 1993 [1882]).

32. Regin Poulsen, "How the Danish Left Adopted a Far-Right Immigration Policy," *Foreign Policy*, July 12, 2021, https://foreignpolicy.com/2021/07/12/denmark-refugees-frederiksen-danish-left-adopted-a-far-right-immigration-policy/; David Leonhart, "In an Age of Right-Wing Populism, Why Are Denmark's Liberals Winning?," *New York Times*, February 24, 2025, www.nytimes.com/2025/02/24/magazine/denmark-immigration-policy-progressives.html; on Denmark's adjustment assistance, see Edward Alden, *Failure to Adjust: How Americans Got Left Behind in the Global Economy* (New York: Council on Foreign Relations, 2017), 114.

33. "Denmark," Pensions Systems in Europe, EcoAustria, September 2024, https://ecoaustria.ac.at/wp-content/uploads/2024/09/Country-Report_Denmark.pdf.

34. J. C. Kofner, "AfD Tax Plans: Studies Confirm Financial Viability," MIWI, February 5, 2025, https://miwi-institut.de/archives/3390; Leigh Thomas,

"French Far-Right's Finance Point Man Vows Fiscal Restraint, Pro-Business Stance," Reuters, June 24, 2024, www.reuters.com/world/europe/french-far-rights-finance-point-man-vows-fiscal-restraint-pro-business-stance-2024-06-24/; "L'union fait la France: Un project, une méthode," Rassemblement National, July 7, 2024, https://rassemblementnational.fr/documents/202406-programme.pdf; Liz Alderman, "Macron's Rivals Say They'll Fix the Economy, but Economists Are Skeptical," *New York Times*, July 2, 2024, www.nytimes.com/2024/07/02/business/france-economy-macron-national-rally.html; Carl Emmerson, Robert Joyce, and Helen Miller, "Reform UK Manifesto: A Reaction," Institute for Fiscal Studies, June 17, 2024, https://ifs.org.uk/articles/reform-uk-manifesto-reaction.

35. Poll, "In hindsight, do you think Britain was right or wrong to leave the European Union?," Statista, June 2025, www.statista.com/statistics/987347/brexit-opinion-poll/. For the $4.1 trillion CBO estimate, see CBO Director Philip Swagel's letter to Senator Jeff Merkley, Congressional Budget Office, August 4, 2025, www.cbo.gov/system/files/2025-08/61466-DebtService.pdf.

36. Kweilin Ellingrud, Saurabh Sanghvi, Gurneet Singh Dandona, et al., "Generative AI and the Future of Work in America," McKinsey Global Institute, July 26, 2023, www.mckinsey.com/mgi/our-research/generative-ai-and-the-future-of-work-in-america; "Future of Jobs Report 2025," World Economic Forum, January 2025, https://reports.weforum.org/docs/WEF_Future_of_Jobs_Report_2025.pdf; David Autor and Gordon Hansen, "We Warned About the First China Shock. The Next One Will Be Worse," *New York Times*, July 14, 2024, www.nytimes.com/2025/07/14/opinion/china-shock-economy-manufacturing.html; David Autor, "The Labor Market Impact of Technological Change: From Unbridled Enthusiasm to Qualified Optimism to Vast Uncertainty" (NBER Working Paper No. 30074, July 2022), www.nber.org/system/files/working_papers/w30074/w30074.pdf; David Autor, "How AI Could Help Rebuild the Middle Class," Noema, February 12, 2024, www.noemamag.com/how-ai-could-help-rebuild-the-middle-class/.

37. In addition to § 232 of the Trade Expansion Act of 1962, Trump invoked § 301 of the Trade Act of 1974 and, most controversially (since it doesn't mention tariffs), §§ 1701 and 1702 of the International Emergency Economic Powers Act of 1977. Unsurprisingly, this last was the first to run into legal trouble when in August 2025 the US Court of Appeals for the Federal Circuit upheld a finding by the Court of International Trade in *V.O.S. Selections, Inc. et al. v. Donald J. Trump* that the law does not authorize most of his tariffs. Whether the Supreme Court would sustain these rulings remained to be seen at the time of writing.

38. Frances Mao, "Can Europe Still Count on the US Coming to Its Defence?," BBC News, February 25, 2025, www.bbc.com/news/articles

/c0l1w1w41xzo; Alexandr Burilkov, "Defending Europe Without the US: First Estimates of What Is Needed," Bruegel, February 21, 2025, www.bruegel.org/analysis/defending-europe-without-us-first-estimates-what-needed; Juan Majino-Lopez and Gutram Wolff, "European Defense Industrial Strategy for a Hostile World," Bruegel, November 20, 2024, www.bruegel.org/policy-brief/european-defence-industrial-strategy-hostile-world; Lara Jakes, "Goal to Spend More on Militaries Splits NATO Allies," *New York Times*, June 5, 2025, www.nytimes.com/2025/06/05/world/europe/nato-defense-ministers-spending.html.

39. Dana Vorisek, ed., *Global Economic Prospects*, A World Bank Group Flagship Report, June 2025, 44, https://thedocs.worldbank.org/en/doc/8bf0b62ec6bcb886d97295ad930059e9-0050012025/original/GEP-June-2025.pdf.

40. Ilyana Kuziemko, Nicolas Longuet-Marx, and Suresh Naidu, "'Compensate the Losers?' Economic Policy and Partisan Realignment in the US" (Princeton University, Griswold Center for Economic Policy Studies, Working Paper No. 321, March 2024), https://gceps.princeton.edu/wp-content/uploads/2024/03/wp321_Kuziemko_CompensateLosers.pdf.

41. Peter Bofinger, "Germany Ditches Debt Brake: A Fiscal Revolution Begins," Social Europe, March 21, 2025, www.socialeurope.eu/germany-ditches-debt-brake-a-fiscal-revolution-begins; "Defense Expenditures and NATO's 5 Percent Commitment," North Atlantic Treaty Organization, June 27, 2025, www.nato.int/cps/en/natohq/topics_49198.htm; Corey Runkel, "Eurozone: Pandemic Emergency Purchase Program," *Journal of Financial Crises* 4, no. 2 (2022), https://elischolar.library.yale.edu/cgi/viewcontent.cgi?article=1362&context=journal-of-financial-crises.

42. Poll of Polls for the United Kingdom, updated daily, *Politico*, June 15, 2025, www.politico.eu/europe-poll-of-polls/united-kingdom/; "Which Countries Would Benefit Most from an American Brain Drain?," *The Economist*, April 11, 2025, www.economist.com/graphic-detail/2025/04/11/which-countries-would-benefit-most-from-an-american-brain-drain; David Miliken and Elizabeth Piper, "UK's Reeves Sets Out £2 Trillion of Spending to Revive Government," Reuters, June 11, 2025, www.reuters.com/business/finance/uks-reeves-make-27-trillion-bet-britains-renewal-2025-06-10/.

43. Sam Freedman, "Everything You Need to Know About the Spending Review," *Comment Is Freed*, June 12, 2025, https://samf.substack.com/p/everything-you-need-to-know-about.

44. Harry Hopkins, quoted in James MacGregor Burns, *The Definitive FDR*, vol. 1, *Roosevelt: The Lion and the Fox, 1882–1940* (New York: Mariner Books, 2002 [1956]), 298–99.

45. Freedman, "Everything You Need to Know"; Sarah Neville, "The Future of the NHS," *Financial Times*, July 2, 2025, www.ft.com/content

/4a002865-508b-4fa5-9a71-0747a49c2317?utm_source=substack&utm_medium=email; Sally Gainsbury, "Down Payment or Making Ends Meet: NHS Financial Pressures in the Run-Up to the Spending Review," Nuffield Trust, June 5, 2025, www.nuffieldtrust.org.uk/resource/down-payment-or-making-ends-meet-nhs-financial-pressures-in-the-run-up-to-the-spending-review.

46. Claudia Finotelli and Sebastian Rinken, "A Pragmatic Bet: The Evolution of Spain's Immigration System," Migration Policy Institute County Profile, April 18, 2023, www.migrationpolicy.org/article/spain-immigration-system-evolution; Pedro Sánchez in a speech to Spain's Parliament, October 2024, as reported in Ashifa Kassam, "How Spain's Radically Different Approach to Immigration Helped Its Economy Soar," *The Guardian*, February 18, 2025, www.theguardian.com/world/2025/feb/18/how-spains-radically-different-approach-to-migration-helped-its-economy-soar.

47. Juliette Cohen, "Spain, A Growth Rate Significantly Higher than the European Average," CPRAM, December 10, 2024, https://cpram.com/fra/en/individual/publications/experts/article/spain-a-growth-rate-significantly-higher-than-the-european-average; "Which Economy Did Best in 2024?," *The Economist*, December 10, 2024, www.economist.com/finance-and-economics/2024/12/10/which-economy-did-best-in-2024; "Spain and Portugal Will Continue to Shine This Year," Oxford Economics Research Briefing, February 3, 2025, www.oxfordeconomics.com/resource/spain-and-portugal-will-continue-to-shine-this-year/; Alfonso Torices, "Spain Achieves Lowest Poverty Rate in a Decade," *Todo Alicante*, February 13, 2025, www.todoalicante.es/english/spain-achieves-lowest-poverty-20250213120227-nt.html?ref=https%3A%2F%2Fwww.google.com%2F.

48. Denis MacShane, "As Spain's Economy Soars Thanks to Immigration, Its Politics Stagnates," *Tomorrow's Europe Today*, June 13, 2025, https://denismacshane.substack.com/p/as-spains-economy-soars-thanks-to.

49. Dijsselbloem, quoted in Merijn Oudenampsen, "The Riddle of the Missing Feathers: Rise and Decline of the Dutch Third Way," *European Politics and Society* 22, no. 1 (2021), www.tandfonline.com/doi/full/10.1080/23745118.2020.1739198#abstract.

50. Alexis de Tocqueville, *Democracy in America*, ed. P. J. Mayer (New York: Perennial Classics, 1969 [1835, 1840]), 525–28. For his "I told you so," see the preface to the 1848 edition, xiii-xiv. By the late 1850s, Tocqueville had revised his sanguine judgment of Americans. See Aurelian Craitu and Jeremy Jennings, "The Third 'Democracy:' Tocqueville's Views of America After 1840," *American Political Science Review* 98, no. 3 (2004): 391–404.

51. Nancy Cook, "Trump's Economic Agenda Is Losing Support but Democrats See Few Gains," Bloomberg, August 1, 2025, www.bloomberg.com/news/articles/2025-08-01/trump-polls-on-economic-agenda-show-voter-approval-declining; "How Trump's Poll Numbers on Immigration Have Shifted as He Has

Enacted His Agenda," NBC News, July 30, 2025, www.nbcnews.com/politics/trump-administration/trumps-poll-numbers-immigration-shifted-enacted-agenda-rcna220826; Aaron Zitner, "Democrats Get Lowest Rating from Voters in 35 Years, WSJ Poll Finds," *Wall Street Journal*, July 25, 2025, www.wsj.com/politics/elections/democratic-party-poll-voter-confidence-july-2025-9db38021.

52. FDR quoted in Burns, *The Lion and the Fox*, 160.

53. Franklin Roosevelt, State of the Union Message to Congress, January 11, 1944, Franklin D. Roosevelt Library and Museum, www.fdrlibrary.org/address-text.

Index

Credit: Mara Lavitt

Ian Shapiro is the Sterling Professor of Political Science and Global Affairs at Yale University. He is a fellow of the American Academy of Arts and Sciences, the American Philosophical Society, and the Council on Foreign Relations. He is author, most recently, of *Responsible Parties: Saving Democracy from Itself*, with Frances Rosenbluth (2018), *The Wolf at the Door: The Menace of Economic Insecurity and How to Fight It*, with Michael Graetz (2020), and *Uncommon Sense* (2024). He lives in New Haven, Connecticut.